It's Greek to Me

A young American family lives with rural Greeks before there was an EU and discovers a powerful, ancient way of life

Andrea Granahan

Published by Joy Woods Press, Bodega, CA 94922, U.S.A.

Printed on acid-free paper.

Some names have been changed to protect the guilty as well as the innocent!

Joy Woods Press
POB 25
Bodega, CA 94922
2015

MeanderingWithAndrwa.com
Andrea.Granahan@yahoo.com

First Edition

This book is dedicated to my late husband, my Greek "family" even though most of them are now departed, and to my children, Heather, David and Devin, with apologies to Devin because he hadn't been born then.

Table of Contents

Prologue

Why Greece? That's what people kept asking us.

When my husband, David, and I first got together I had two children from my former marriage. They were very young, two and four. He was in an Ivy League university finishing up his MFA in sculpture. He was the star of the art department. He had won a Fulbright to study in Italy for a year, but it would not cover me and the children, so he turned it down. He didn't tell me, but his professors did and made it clear they considered me and the children an impediment to my husband's career and the art world.

I asked David about the refused year in Italy.

"It doesn't matter," he said. "We'll go together some day."

I was determined that he never have regrets over the Fulbright so started learning about Italy. Right away we realized it was way too expensive for us.

"We'll go somewhere else," David said cheerfully.

Not having a television or money for babysitters while he was in school, we often entertained ourselves by reading aloud to each other in the evenings when the kids were in bed, or pored over art books together. One day someone lent us Henry Miller's *Colossus of Maroussi*. We laughed together at parts. When we finished the book we looked at each other.

"I think we've found our place," David said. "I want to go where people laugh a lot."

I liked that thought.

Over the next two years we worked at various jobs, scrimped and saved. Then David and I met some gallery owners in Georgetown. They promised him a one man show when we returned from Greece.

At that time freighter travel was not the "luxury" it has become now. It was a cheap way to get someplace with no limits on luggage. We were not going to visit Greece, we were going to move there. Not only were we taking basics like clothes and some household items, we had to bring all of David's tools and what I would need to educate the children. We finally had saved enough for our tickets plus $900. We decided to go.

"What happens if the money runs out before a year," asked my in-laws.

"Then we'll come home early," we breezily replied.

My mother was mystified, "Isn't it all ruins there? Why do you have to go?"

Eventually we spent two years in Greece. They were pivotal years in our lives. We lived like our peasant friends, most of whom were at least one generation older than us. We knew some of the younger town Greeks, but our hearts belonged to these older, wiser people who had so much to teach us. I have tried to understand just why it was so important to us, and as I wrote about it, it became clear to me. I hope you, too, will understand what Greece had to offer so many years ago and I hope the country will rediscover in itself once again.

This is a story of a Greece that no longer exists, alas. The European Union has eaten up that ancient way of life for good or ill. I hope this helps some of younger Greeks and those who have never known the old country since so many more Greeks live outside of Greece, scattered throughout the world, than actually live in Greece itself, understand something about their marvelous roots and a way of life that successfully endured and kept Greeks alive and happy for literally thousands of years.

Chapter 1

A Brave Old World

The lurch I felt in my stomach as I stood on the deck of the small Greek freighter was not due to seasickness. I was watching the Statue of Liberty get smaller and smaller in the distance.

"Oh, my God. This is real. We are really doing this. We're leaving home."

The finality of it suddenly hit me after all the months of planning. It was the same feeling I had when I got married or went into labor the first time. There was no turning back.

We were headed towards not just the "Old World", but the oldest world for Western civilization, Greece. My husband, David, and I, and our two children were now emigrants, heading to an unknown country, an unknown culture.

David's Swedish grandparents came to mind because they had entered America through Ellis Island, and had seen the Statue of Liberty towering over them offering them hope.

First, Grandpa Eric had come from Sweden and watched the immigration official change his name from Badman to Wadman because "Oh, your name means something very bad."

A few years later Grandma Jenny had come at age sixteen clutching the address of an aunt in Minnesota, a few dollars and a change of clothes in a basket. I wondered how they would feel about us voluntarily leaving behind what they had worked so hard to reach.

I swallowed my misgivings. We had planned and saved for this for over two years. This was no time for second thoughts. I threw a farewell kiss to the statue then rejoined the family down below so David could also have his final look before the beloved icon of freedom faded completely from sight.

Earlier that morning the Brooklyn dock had been a hive of activity. Cranes lifted cargo nets filled with bundles of rags. The men on the dock shouted to one of the men who rode up with a net as it swung over the small ship that was going to be our home for the next few weeks.

We had presented our tickets and passports to a very busy shipping agent who had impatiently pointed to where our trunks should be put for loading, then waved us on board.

David and I looked at each other in relief then carried the children on board straight to our cabins. My brother and a friend of his who had driven us to the port followed with our luggage.

We were anxious to get the children, four and six, out of sight, because they had caught chicken pox about ten days before we were to leave. Their fevers were gone and they were feeling fine and energetic, but one or two spots were still healing and I was afraid that would be enough for the shipping company to refuse us passage on the tramp freighter.

"Okay, kids, this is your room on the ship. Daddy and I will sleep right next door. Here's some story books. Don't open the door to anybody until we come right back from upstairs. We have to make sure our stuff gets put on the boat."

They were delighted with their cozy little bunks. The separate stateroom had become available when two women scheduled to make the trip with us had canceled because of a sudden coup by a group of Greek colonels. The news had just hit the papers that week. Since there seemed to be no reports of violence we had gone ahead with our plans despite the concerns of friends and family.

"We'll come right back if we have to," I had promised.

On deck all was confusion as the last of the cargo was loaded.

"Rags?" I asked a dock worker as I pointed to the laden net.

"For de paper factories," he explained in a thick Brooklyn accent. "You goin on dis here Greek ship?"

"Yes."

"Well be glad you ain't on dat one over dere," he pointed to a Yugoslav vessel. "You know what dem commies eat for breakfast?"

"What?" my brother asked curiously.

"Soup!" the man spat out with disgust.

David and I looked at each other suppressing our grins. Soup for breakfast, a communist plot if we ever heard one.

We saw with relief that our trunks were being carried on board. They held not just all our household goods, but David's precious sculpting tools. He had been promised a one-man show at a Washington D.C. gallery on our return. We hoped he'd be able to complete it in the year we planned on living in Greece. They also held homeschooling materials I had collected to educate the children.

In very short time we said our good-byes to everyone and were down below with the children again.

"Look, Mommy, the windows are round," little Dave pointed out.

"Those are called portholes," I replied. "Lots of things on a ship have different names than on land. Like the walls are bulkheads."

"And the potties are called heads," David added.

That sent the children into peals of laughter. They didn't believe him. He liked to tease them.

"What are the feet?"

"I don't know if a ship has feet, but it has a poop deck," David grinned.

That caused another gleeful outburst. We cautioned the children to stay put until we were well out to sea and went back on deck. The last of the dock workers had just finished securing a bunch of tractors to the open deck, lashing them tightly with cables. Papers were signed and the harassed agent left to see to another vessel. The pilot boarded and we hurried below to be with the kids as we left the harbor.

After I bade farewell to the grand old lady with the torch, I returned to the cabin. Heather and little Dave wanted more Greek mythology stories. I had been feeding the tales to them as a series of cliff-hangers. Well, maybe the land we were headed to wasn't so unknown. But no matter how ancient Greece had affected our culture, I wondered how modern Greece would affect us.

David returned and told us that lunch would be served in the dining saloon in an hour. We were out in the open waters now and the little freighter was rolling.

"Mommy, I don't feel good," Heather announced.

I felt her forehead worried there was a return of the chicken pox but David began chuckling.

"Seasick," he pronounced. That surprised me. It was usually little Dave that was subject to motion sickness, not Heather. Just then Dave began retching and I dashed with him for the head.

"They'll get over it in a day or so," David assured me.

At lunch time I discovered the same malady had hit at least half of the other eight passengers on board.

Life on board the ship became tougher a few days later when we ran into storms on the Atlantic. We got caught on the outer verges of an early hurricane. Just keeping our balance became a problem. The kids got over their initial adjustment to the sea and began making friends among the crew. The Greek men, missing their own children so much, couldn't get enough of the kids and I had to remonstrate with them, using a Greek dictionary when they started feeding them so many sweets they got sick again.

"Please. Bad stomachs with candy," I pleaded in broken Greek much to the cook's amusement.

I used the small ship library as a classroom despite the violent seas and the children and I held daily lessons. Some of the other passengers were amused and offered to pitch in.

Our passengers were a motley lot. One older woman, Louise, was retiring to Greece on her Social Security income because she could no longer afford to live in her native New York City, one couple were making a trip so his Greek family, whom he had never met, could meet him and his bride. He proudly told us his family were Lesbians because they were from the island of Lesbos. Two single men, Gordon and Ben shared a cabin, one on his way to an Israeli kibbutz, the other, a very shy fellow named Gordon was on a personal adventure. We thought of them as "the Single Guys". Gordon took on teaching the kids about clocks and time.

The captain kept promising us that the seas would flatten out but each day they grew worse. Since the ship was so small, just a little over 300 feet long, we had free run of it and spent a lot of time on the bridge, and in the navigation or radio room. The officers even let us take a turn at the wheel the first couple days until the seas grew too rough. One day when we were well into the storms we received a distress call from a Russian submarine.

"We cannot go," Captain Dimitrios told us. "It is too dangerous. Today we do nothing but move in a circle until the seas subside. A larger vessel will go, although it is farther away."

On the bridge which was about six stories above the sea, we plowed into a wave so huge it washed over us obliterating everything. In our cabin the porthole would frame sky one moment and be underwater the next. Because the crew seemed so competent, I never felt fear so much as discomfort. What I disliked most was when we crested a wave and ship's propellers came out of the water sending a sickening shudder throughout the entire vessel until it finally bit into water again.

In the dining saloon the crew pulled up the wooden rails around the tables intended to keep dishes from sliding off, and wet the tablecloths to provide better grip. The plates were thrown off anyway and those of us who could eat did so gripping our dishes. The cook didn't even try to serve soup. In my mind's eye I pictured Yugoslav communists going breakfastless in the storm.

The sensation of pitching and rolling did not bother me so much, but the sudden descents from the peaks of the swells gave the sensation of an elevator suddenly dropping and after a few days of it I had an incessant headache.

Captain Dimitrios admitted he shared the problem and doctored himself with continual glasses of Metaxa brandy. I began to wonder about his abilities, but the crew assured me they'd rather have him drunk as a captain than any other they had sailed under sober. Since none of them seemed afraid, I felt safe and just tried to keep us all as comfortable as possible.

In the middle of all this, Greek Easter arrived. Storms or no storms, the Greeks had to celebrate. In his indefatigable optimism our captain had ordered the carpenters to build picnic tables for a celebration on deck, but by the time the day actually arrived no one, not even the most experienced crewman was permitted to go on deck because it was continually awash with frighteningly vicious waves that smashed the tables and washed them away.

So the dining saloon became the setting for the revelry. It was our first exposure to Greeks partying and all of us passengers were startled. The party began at midnight when the crew set off flares. Even though we had to all hang on to the plates the cook had managed to provide a magnificent feast. He had roasted whole legs of lamb with rosemary, made a lovely egg and lemon soup which was served in mugs so it was less likely to spill, spicy macaroni and cheese with egg custard called *pastitsio*, *mousaka* made from eggplants and spiced meats, and salads of all kinds We wondered how he had been able to cook it all on the violently tossing ship. The traditional breads with bright red eggs embedded in them decorated all the tables and for the children he had concocted baskets made of bread filled with the eggs and decorated with rock sugar and nuts.

Despite the pitching deck, dancing began and much to my horror the Greeks began breaking glasses at the dancers' feet. The teenage cabin boy laughed as he chased the sliding glass shards that shifted from one side of the ship to the other with his broom dodging the leaping dancers.

I was afraid that someone would get injured but no one did and David remarked that he was sure that they couldn't pull off that feat if they were sober. The crew began singing at the top of their lungs. Captain Dimitrios who had been steadily emptying a new bottle of Metaxa asked me to put the kids in the cabin in case it got too dangerous. I was on my way to do just that when the captain, not willing to part with his Metaxa glass grabbed an orange to toss at the dancers feet and instead got Heather squarely on the nose.

Early the next morning a few of us passengers gathered on the bridge joking that we'd take turns at the helm while the crew slept off their hangovers. But instead we found Costas, a young officer, firmly in charge, bright-eyed and full of glee over having watched his superiors dance their way through the broken glass the night before. Before long the captain showed up, still clutching his Metaxa. The party resumed at noon when the cook had duplicated the feast of the night before, and celebrations continued until daybreak the following day.

After almost two weeks, one day the captain told us we would reach Gibraltar at midnight that night. We all took long naps despite tossing seas. We were determined to be awake for the sight of land again. The storms had doubled our time at sea. We had gone back to bed after dinner, making Yiannis the purser promise to wake us for Gibraltar.

"Is no problem. You will wake," he assured us.

About an hour from Gibraltar we were jolted out of bed by an eardrum-shattering blast. Startled passengers gathered in the hall in their pajamas. The noise turned out to be our foghorn. Then we all noticed for the first time in two weeks the seas were calm.

There was no possibility of any of us getting sleep with that incredible racket going off every few seconds, so we all dressed and gathered on the bridge.

Heather and little Dave thought this all very exciting and kept their hands over their ears. Yiannis produced a fresh pot of coffee and looked very happy. In fact, all the crewmen were smiling and laughing.

"Soon home," Captain Dimitrios explained.

After about an hour we passed the strait and the fog was suddenly gone. A light ship, looking like a glorious birthday cake for Methuselah, lit up the water with its reflection. We could see the lights of a city that the navigator told us was Tangiers.

Then the captain carried on a long conversation via signal lamps with the shore. He began laughing. The name of our ship was the Turkos, so christened during one of the periods when Greece and Turkey made an attempt to patch up their differences.

"They are not believing that a Greek ship is named Turkos. Every time at Gibraltar we do this and they must check the registry," the captain chuckled.

At last, formalities over, we sailed into the smooth waters of the Mediterranean. As the lights of the shore fell behind us most of the sleepy passengers went back to enjoy some quiet sleep.

"Honey, this will be our first dawn on the Mediterranean. Why don't we stay awake for it?"

David liked the idea and so did the Single Guys and the couple heading to Lesbos. We tucked the children safely back in bed, and finding some deck chairs prepared to enjoy the first time we had been able to go outside on the ship since the day we had boarded it.

Heather had become fascinated by the multiplicity of Greek gods and while we had been battling storms she had decided she should send Posiedon a letter – perhaps in hopes he'd calm his seas. She worked hard to prepare it. We told her she'd have to wait until we could go outside to throw it overboard. As we sat outside that night the Single Guys came up with a scheme to write a letter of reply.

Wrapped in blankets, snuggled into our chairs we shared cups of hot coffee, periodically refreshed by the bridge crew who enjoyed our company. Under the brilliant stars we talked about our hopes, our dreams, physics, metaphysics. We told jokes, exchanged family stories and whenever one of the crew joined us we tried to learn some more Greek words.

"Important word is '*then perazi*'," Costas told us.

"What does that mean?"

"Means, it is no matter. Not worry."

As the sky lightened we marveled at the sight of our own wake which we could see all the way to the horizon.

"Feel the air," David remarked. "It's soft."

"You're right. I never noticed such a thing before. It's like soft water the first time you feel it when you are used to hard water. It's like silk," I said.

Just as we noted that, the surface of the sea was broken by dolphins leaping up to greet the dawn. These were the classical black and white type and they accompanied the ship for several minutes. David and I looked at each other in silent rapture.

We were not the only witnesses to the dolphins, on the deck below us we suddenly heard the cook, who did not know we were above and thought he was alone, as he broke into song. Our Greek was limited to the few words we had picked up on board and some I had tried to learn from books before we left but we could tell it was a love song to the city of Athens.

I tried to imagine the dock worker singing a love song to Brooklyn. The picture was beyond me. We really had entered a new world.

As we sailed past the coast of Spain we began seeing structures.

"What's that?" asked Gordon once.

"It's a castle in Spain," I answered, and got ridiculed for being a romantic until we got close enough to see it was indeed a castle.

Being able to get on deck was liberating. The Single Guys got the idea to build a kite, a box kite, to sail off the rear of the ship. They christened it the Ramona, and us women and the children wrote poems on it to sail in the sky.

The moment of the great launching arrived and the Ramona sank like a stone, sending the crew into gales of laughter. They teased us the rest of the trip. Despite calm seas we would not let the children run on deck. "The minute we are on land you can run as fast as you want," we promised them repeatedly. Heather did cast a bottle overboard with her letter.

I was in the library with the children for their lessons. We heard whistling then suddenly a wet plastic bag came hurtling through the open porthole. The startled children ran to it. Inside was a letter from Poseidon to Heather. She still believed in Santa Claus at six, so after a rough three weeks at sea, she had no trouble believing in Poseidon and clutched the letter with great pride.

We reached the coast of the Peloponesus in Greece. A small white structure was drowning in wildflowers that we could smell from the ship.

"I wonder what that building is," said one of the passengers.

"It's a hermitage," I answered with certainty. Again I was laughed at, and just then a monk came out of the door and waved to our ship.

No one called me a foolish romantic after that – they just sought my opinion.

Our night in quarantine outside Pireaus we stood on the deck sharing a bottle of champagne with our fellow passengers, gazing in awe at the Acropolis lit up in the distance.

The next morning as we eased up to a dock one of the crewman, a handsome young man, looked across the narrowing gap between the ship and shore, reaching his hand as far as he could towards a beautiful young woman reaching out to him from the dock. "My betrothed," he told us proudly and as the gap closed the lovers finally locked hands.

The gangway was lowered.

"Okay, kids, you can run now," David told the children. They jumped to the dock, tried to run and fell flat. As soon as we touched the dock we realized why and had to struggle for balance as well. All those days of struggling for balance on the ship had ruined our "land legs." Greece had literally knocked us off our feet.

Chapter 2

Vourvoura

The crowded bus jolted its way from pothole to pothole. In some places the mountain road vanished altogether, the gravel disappearing into surrounding dust, so the driver had to make his way between rocks by memory. The front of the vehicle was plastered with saints' pictures and dripped with holy medallions. Little vases filled with fresh flowers and aromatic herbs were clamped to the dashboard. The driver sang at the top of his lungs and from time to time some of the passengers joined in. A large decal obscured much of the windshield. It said, "The Holy Mother Rides With Us." We hoped so. The driver was treating the precipitous road with reckless contempt.

David and I and the children were the center of attention. We anxiously thumbed our Greek-English dictionary. The people fired questions at us from all directions.

"How old are you?" we deciphered. We thought they meant the children and replied, "Four and six." But, no, it was our ages they wanted. "How much money do you have?" was another question. We repeated it haltingly to make sure we understood, then pretended we hadn't; we didn't have very much at all. We had come with just nine hundred dollars and hoped it, with whatever we could earn, would last a year.

How old were our parents? What were their names? How many brothers and sisters did we have? How old were they? The questions went on and on. Not only were our new neighbors curious, but their curiosity was entirely of a personal nature. No one asked if we liked the country, how our trip had been, or any of the typical questions Americans might ask in a similar situation.

We squeezed in a few queries of our own for all the good it did us. How long would it be before we reached the village? The answer was a vague "little while." How many people lived in the village of Vourvoura? "Oh, some."

Time passed and nothing but rocky cliffs and sand colored slopes rolled by us. There was an occasional scrubby little plant. The old man next to me pointed to the hills and said, "Turkos," then struck a match indicating the area had been burned by the Turks. His gray mustache bristled in anger.

"How many years ago?" we asked with the help of the dictionary.

"One hundred and more," he replied. Then again he said "Turkos," and spat with disgust. The people nearby nodded in agreement.

I had thought from the passion of their response that it must have happened in recent years. I was to learn that one hundred years in Greece *was* recent.

The passengers were dressed in heavy cotton clothing, black, brown and navy blue predominating. The men's loose shirts and pants, and women's long skirts had been patched and repatched so many times they looked more like collages than garments. Everyone carried bundles: bulky paper wrapped parcels or lumpy plastic woven bags striped in rainbow colors. These latter had also been patched but in brilliant colors the people didn't allow themselves to wear. I wondered if that were out of choice or if brighter colored cloth cost more. The bus was pungent with the smells emanating from all the bundles, especially the live ones; a number of people carried chickens. The smells combined with the interesting odors from the people themselves, especially a sour odor we would come to recognize as feta cheese. The smells were intensified by the closeness of the atmosphere. No one would open a window.

These mountaineers stood in sharp contrast to the fashionable Athenians we had seen during our week in the city. The people there had been short with olive skin and bright, dark eyes. They favored flashy colors, short skirts and polyesters.

The mountain people were taller, fairer. The women had brown or red hair, many of the men were blond and most of the people were blue-eyed. One thing they had in common with the Athenians though was their unwillingness to discuss their own government. I remembered when we first got off the ship in Piraeus and all of us passengers from the small freighter decided to go to a dockside cafe and share a beer together as we waited for our things to be unloaded. The night before we had all marveled to see the Acropolis in the distance from the deck of the ship that had delivered us to Greece. When we disembarked I was startled to see tanks in the street next to the cafe. I asked the portly cafe owner about the tank next to his cafe when he came to take our orders and he looked at me blankly and said, "What tank?"

David kicked me under the table and promptly shut me up. I was too happy, rejoicing in my first outdoor cafe to care just then. But we ran into the same blank look each time we tried to inquire about the political situation to determine if we should go on to the mountains. It was frustrating, but we took the silence as a positive response and proceeded with our plans. At the bus station where we had boarded this vehicle, everyone had been equally mute about the government.

A cheerful looking lady with a chicken on her lap across the aisle from me on the bus passed down some foil wrapped chocolates and spicy hard candies for the children. Four year old little Dave was subject to motion sickness and looked queasy from the bumpy bus ride. I asked him to save the candy but the woman insistently gestured for him to eat it. I pantomimed vomiting and the whole bus load of people burst into laughter. The old man beside me handed my son a brown paper bag.

Suddenly the bus made a heroic leap for the crest of a hill and as we plunged down the other side we entered a new world. We had come to a rich, fertile valley alive with waterfalls, flowers and trees. Our fellow travelers gestured proudly.

"*Prasino ekei,*" they said, and we translated, "green here."

As we wound our way deeper into the beautiful valley we saw the village. A couple of hundred whitewashed stone houses with red tiled roofs spilled down a slope to the river at the bottom of the valley. The steep hill and the clustered houses looked like a glacier in the midst of greenery. Somewhere in the village was Yorgo's house. Yorgo, our Greek friend in the States, had told us about this village and offered us the free use of his old family home for as long as we wished.

The driver leaned on his horn for the last mile of the trip.

"Vourvoura," he announced smiling as we pulled to a sudden stop at a small square beside a large church.

The entire village was there to greet us. We were swept off the bus by the enthusiastic crowd. The children and the luggage were lifted high and people grabbed David and me by our arms and propelled us along. The noisy procession marched up the street to a tall arched gate with heavy wooden doors and huge iron hinges. I had been expecting a small stone house.

"Yorgo's house," someone said as we gasped at the castle-like entrance.

16

The crowd hushed as a man stepped forward and enthusiastically threw open the massive doors. Inside a tiny ancient-looking lady with a face as wrinkled as a raisin, completely shrouded in black from her head to her feet, leaned on a crooked cane and held aloft a tin candle lantern, the first I had ever seen outside a museum. She smiled toothlessly.

"*Kalos oriste*," she croaked. Welcome.

The crowd surged forward and pushed us into a courtyard and up a flight of steps into the house while they all talked to each other loudly and laughed. The courtyard was fragrant with flowers and basil which was growing everywhere.

The people brought us to a large room, deposited our luggage in a corner and fetched some wooden kitchen chairs for us to sit on. People packed into the room, pointing to us and staring, or exclaiming loudly to each other. The old lady bustled from one corner of the room to another. The long day on buses and the struggle to communicate had worn us out and we sank into the chairs exhausted. The room was growing dusky and someone lit an oil lamp. That morning we had been in Syntagma Square in cosmopolitan Athens. The contrast between the two worlds was startling. It was as if we had stepped behind a stage set and found a whole new world and weren't sure which was real and which not.

Eventually the old lady shooed out most of the people and a woman appeared with a tray of tiny cups of thick sweet coffee, glasses of water and a small plate of hard candies. A middle-aged man with a gentle, kind look about him sat beside us and told us his name was Adonis. With gestures and the dictionary we learned that not only was this Yorgo's house, but the old lady was Yorgo's great, great aunt and she came with the house, a fact Yorgo had failed to mention. The

17

children kept staring at her. Heather sidled up to me and whispered, "Is she a witch, Mommy?"

"I think she's just an old lady. But if she is a witch, she's a friendly one," I whispered back and Heather relaxed.

Little Dave had to use the bathroom and taking him by the hand I followed a woman carrying a candle as she led us down a passageway. We entered an arched doorway and for a moment I thought I had stepped into a cave.

The door opened on to a narrow stone pathway in a room with a high arched ceiling. A half-wall made of Masonite, about three feet high separated the narrow stone walkway from what appeared to be a precipice on one side of the room. I realized a wooden floor on that side had rotted away. At the far end of the room some women stood in a cluster around a single gas burner cooking. The scene was lit by a wick stuck in a saucer of olive oil. It looked not just like a scene from the ancient past, but from cave-man days.

The women all smiled and chattered as we walked by. I followed our guide into the back yard where we finally found an outhouse complete with a porcelain toilet and a bucket of water with which to flush it. Little Dave's eyes were wide with wonder at all the new sights.

When we were back with the others in the big room the women began carrying in dishes from the strange kitchen we had seen. They set out plates of scrambled eggs, great chunks of coarse barley bread, bowls piled high with sliced lettuce, and mounds of macaroni and porridge laced liberally with olive oil. There were profuse apologies about there not being any meat. The porridge was tangy and salty. It was very hearty and we didn't miss meat.

After the meal was cleared we were told that the large room was ours and a smaller one next to it the children's.

Adonis shook our hands formally and the women bid us good night.

I unpacked the children's night clothes, then carrying a flashlight, navigated the way to the outhouse and back with them, and finally tucked them into their new bed. They fell asleep immediately. David and I, alone at last, embraced in relief, then explored our room. The walls were painted a flaking aquamarine. A fading design had been carefully painted around the tarnished brass chandelier. There was a table and chest of drawers and an old massive low chest made of a dark varnished wood. The ornate iron bed sagged with a thin mattress. The walls were three feet thick and each window was arched with the thick walls forming spacious window seats. There was an iron-railed balcony overlooking the main street. We went outside and looked at our new home. The moon lit up the white walls of the village. Here and there the soft glow of an oil lamp shone through a window.

We stood there admiring the scene. It was very quiet and we spoke to each other in whispers. Suddenly a loud sound cut the silence. A lugubrious sobbing echoed across the valley. There was an answering sob, then another. The village donkeys were talking to each other.

Chapter 3

Louis and Thia

The donkeys of Vourvoura woke us up every morning except on Sundays when the church bells next door clanging at dawn were so loud they drowned out the animals.

"Should I make oatmeal for breakfast?" I asked and nestled closer to David under the thin covers. The mountain mornings were cold even though it was spring.

"It'll warm us, but you better move fast if you don't want Thia to find you in the kitchen," David cautioned.

Like the other villagers we called Yorgo's aged relative Thia, which meant aunt. The children came into our room. We rose and dressed quickly.

I tiptoed into the cavernous, dimly lit kitchen. At one time it had been quite large until two thirds of it collapsed decades before leaving a gaping pit. I was thankful for the low partition, flimsy as it was, that kept us from falling into the pit. One of the village irrigation sluices ran under the kitchen filling it with the sound of running water. There was actually a waterfall at one end which became thunderous during rain storms. Thia used it as a handy dump for her vegetable parings and sweepings, flinging them casually over the Masonite wall.

I filled a pot with water at the single spigot in the house and used the gas burner to cook our breakfast. I had been thrilled to discover a box of Quaker oats at one of the town's two shops. I had just congratulated myself on escaping notice when a storeroom door burst open and Thia came in.

"Ah, *kalimera,* good morning, Andrianni," she greeted me with the name the villagers had given me. Then she noticed the oatmeal. The children also had new names; Heather, impossible for the Greeks to pronounce, had become known by her middle name Alexandra, and little Dave was Davidaki, little Dave to distinguish him from his dad, the "aki" being diminutive that could be added to any word. Oh well, if an immigration official could change grandpa's name, I supposed the Greeks could change ours.

"*Ligo lathaki!*" Thia cried and reached for her olive oil pitcher. That's what we had been fearing. *Ligo lathaki* meant "just a wee bit of oil". She poured on a pint or so and smiled at me. I thanked her and went to our room.

"Oiled oatmeal again?" David asked and we both laughed. No matter how often I explained we didn't want a lot of oil on everything we ate, Thia would not believe me. She was convinced my protests were mere politeness.

We ate and returned to the kitchen to wash the dishes. Thia reminded us Louis was coming. We needed no reminding. We had been in the village almost two weeks and had innumerable problems communicating. Inevitably the villagers would say, "No matter Louis will come soon."

Louis apparently spoke English and when he returned from his work in the mountains he would be able to help us over any rough spots. We had just run into a very large rough spot.

There were lots of empty houses in the village from all the people who had moved to America or Australia. We wanted to live by ourselves away from Thia's forceful mothering and oilcan, in a place smaller and less dilapidated than Yorgo's ancient family manse. We had come to Greece, among other reasons, so that David could work on his sculpture and finish enough pieces for a one man show in the States on our return.

He also had a commission to create a huge bust, a portrait of his agent. We needed the money the commission would bring. He needed studio space as well as more peace and quiet than we could get in Thia's house.

Although Thia ostensibly lived alone in the great decaying house until our arrival, she had a niece Soteria. Adonis, whom we had met the first night, was Soteria's husband. They and their two daughters, twelve year old Athena and ten year old Yorghia, came daily to visit and share their meals with her. Sometimes the children spent the night with Thia, sleeping in her room. The house was the largest in the village and now housed us curious foreigners, so it became the gathering place of the town. We always had visitors underfoot. While it helped improve our Greek it was disconcerting and would not make for good working conditions for David.

We inquired about renting one of the empty houses and ran head on into Greek hospitality. The people said, "No!", clicked their tongues and threw back their heads emphatically in the Greek gesture for absolutely not.

Finally Thia had come to our room and told us in no uncertain terms, "You stay here!" She had promised we'd understand when Louis returned.

And at last Louis was coming back. We waited all day in vain. At sunset someone told us Louis was home and would be by later that night. Too eager to wait we asked the way to his house and set off.

Louis's home was at the farthest edge of the village, a tiny three roomed house tucked in an orchard. A lot of children were playing in the dusk outside. A young pregnant woman opened the door with a shy smile.

"Come in," she said proudly in English.

We started to answer her in English but she said in Greek she didn't understand, having already spoken all the words she knew. It was Poli, Louis's wife. She took us to the kitchen where, by lamplight, we had our first glimpse of Louis. He was washing his feet in a basin and looked up at us surprised. He was slightly built, dark and mustached, unlike most of the other taller, fairer village men. His smile spread to his ears and crinkled his eyes. For the first time since our arrival someone looked at us with comprehension. The villagers usually regarded us with friendly curiosity or bewilderment. At first glance we knew that we had not only found an interpreter but a friend. We smiled back.

"So you are here. I was coming to see you when I had cleaned up," he spoke after a few seconds of silent exchange.

Louis, we learned, had emigrated to Chicago and spent a few years there. Unlike most emigrants he had decided to return. We did not discuss the practicalities that had been plaguing us at first; we were too busy getting to know one another. At one point Louis, still washing his feet, looked up at us and asked, "Why Greece?"

People had been asking us that question ever since we had made up our minds to go. There were a lot of "practical" reasons we could list: the low cost of living, the mild winters, the ancient art and such, but we could never articulate the deeper reason, the real pull we felt to the country.

I remembered one afternoon in suburban Maryland passing shopping center after shopping center, entering a market only to find all their vegetables were wrapped in plastic. I held carrots barricaded behind packaging looking like more plastic themselves. I longed to feel the food, see dirt clinging to a root. "There has to be something better," I thought. We sighed and prepared to list our usual reasons, but Louis suddenly sat up.

"No matter," he said, waving his hand to dismiss the question. "I know why you have come. You came here for the same reason I returned. You are looking for simplicity." The word hung in the air for a moment. Simplicity. He had said what we had gropingly been trying to explain to everyone all along. He leaned forward and lovingly touched the plain, softly lit, whitewashed wall in front of him with the palm of his hand. We watched the silent, significant gesture.

"And here you will find it," he said at last with certainty.

We stayed until quite late. Poli came in to serve us coffee and candy. She was proud of her husband's English but would not join the conversation even when we tried to switch to our broken Greek. We eventually got around to our problems.

"You cannot move. That much is certain. The old lady's pride is at stake. If you leave she feels the villagers will say it is because her house is not good enough or so she thinks. She will die of the shame," Louis explained.

"But we need a place for David to work, and I want a place to cook. We don't want her or Soteria to take care of us."

"And we want a little privacy," David added.

At that Louis laughed. "Do you know there is no word for privacy in Greek? There is a word for loneliness only. You are the first foreigners the people have seen. They will always be around you. You are now prisoners of our hospitality."

In the morning Louis came and helped us make some face-saving arrangements with Thia. She would not hear of taking any rent, but we were given not only the two rooms we already had but a large storeroom downstairs which

David could convert into a studio. She agreed to let us pay for the gas for cooking.

We started clearing the junk of generations out of the studio room. The villagers showed up all day long to watch us and to help. Amidst rats' nests we found what were to us astonishing treasures: an old loom, urns full of olive oil, wooden soap molds, casks of feta cheese and wine, and a collection of very old looking, gracefully made vases. I asked Thia about the latter.

"No, they are not old," she replied. "Only four or five hundred years, maybe six"

"How old is the house Thia?"

"Ah, that is old. Nine hundred years, a thousand. No one knows for sure."

Eventually we had everything safely stowed away elsewhere in the old house and whitewashed the room. As I set up some things in the kitchen I asked where the oven was and she pointed to a brick cave in the courtyard.

Little by little we worked to restore the rest of the house, whitewashing soot blackened walls. We had seen how the other villagers used their white wash leaving a white border on the ground under everything they painted, and now we discovered that was because of the drips the heavy lime made. The border hid the drips and was decorative. We even white washed the tree trunks in the courtyard halfway up in Athenian fashion. We scrubbed musty corners, rehung doors and potted plants the neighbors happily gave us. We always had at least two or three townspeople and a half dozen or so children hanging around, and while we never got used to the constant audience, we gradually just accepted it.

Even David began to work despite the cluster of men that gathered in the studio every night to watch him gradually shape the huge bust, an oversized portrait of his agent and our good friend.

****

"How many kilos of milk?" I asked Soteria as she poured what looked like gallon sized can after can of goats milk into a large cauldron. It was her day to make the main staple of the village, a porridge called *trahana* and her neighbors were contributing their goats' milk to the project.

"Fifty, fifty two," she grunted. She stopped to stick some more twigs on the fire under the cauldron.

Our Greek was broken but constantly improving. I studied early each morning, poring over a grammar I had brought. David was not as studious, but we had been improving faster since we had each committed to learning five new words each day from our dictionary.

Because it was spring, the chickens and goats were at peak production and the village women worked frantically to prepare its staple foods: feta cheese, trahana and hilopita macaroni. Trahana was made from wheat and milk. Hilopita was an egg pasta cut into confetti sized squares which was boiled along with the trahana to make a really delicious and satisfying mixture. I was fascinated and asked questions and wrote down proportions as the women boiled up huge cauldrons of milk over wood fires and gently stirred in the whole wheat flour using great wooden paddles.

After the mixture thickened and solidified, they scooped it out and spread it on sheets to dry in the courtyards and on roofs. Over the next several days the air became pungent with the odor of souring milk. The women and children kept patrolling the laden sheets, constantly crumbling the lumps as they dried until the whole mass was a crumbly, crunchy cereal-like consistency. Then they tied it in clean rags to make little bundles and hung it from lines strung in their "*apothikis*" or storerooms.

Soteria was amused that I wrote down the things she told me.

The hilopita was much simpler and easier to make and was less of a communal effort because the eggs could be saved up for a few days and so the task was more up to the individual housewife. The batch of white flour and eggs was kneaded and kneaded then rolled out with broom handles and cut into the tiny squares to dry and be hung next to the trahana. I went to Soteria's house when she and a neighbor made it together.

The feta making brought the cauldrons back into use. Once the milk in the great pots had boiled and women stirred in rennet harvested from a gland of a young kid or lamb, they let it curdle and lifted the chunks of cheese carefully out of the whey and hung them in bags in all the doorways to drip into tin pans beneath them. Every time we went in or out of a room, we had to dodge our way around the huge, bulbous wet, bags. The entire village stank of feta. It was stored in casks of brine.

The women were amused by my ignorance, curiosity and interest. Because I had earned their respect by sprucing up Thia's dilapidated house, they good-naturedly showed me their skills.

I had noticed that the lovely icons in her family shrine were an inch thick in dirt. Fearful of committing sacrilege I asked the neighbor ladies if they thought Thia would mind if I cleaned them and earned roars of laughter for such a silly question. Relieved, I surprised Thia by polishing the whole lot of them one morning. She happily crossed herself, and later that day gave me sack of her own store of trahana, a very generous gift, I knew after having witnessed the work that went into creating it.

David took to working late at night by the light of a spirit lamp we had bought at the store, in hopes of less chance of interruption. But the men of the village thought of the studio as the newest watering hole, lugging in jugs of wine and socializing with each other as they watched him. Slowly we settled into a routine.

The lady across the road began delivering a can of goats' milk to us every morning at Thia's suggestion. Thia taught me to boil it and sweeten it with honey from a villager who kept bees. We dipped large chunks of the coarse country bread in it and found it a vastly superior breakfast to olive-oiled oatmeal.

****

"It's your turn. I went yesterday."

"But I'm in the middle of this project," David argued.

"Let's go together and leave the kids with Thia. That way we can say we have to get home to them and get away sooner."

"Good idea."

Once a day we went to the stores to buy the day's food. We always got stopped and yanked to a table where some men who did not have work in the fields that day would insist on buying us some wine. If we had the children with us they'd buy them soft drinks. Since the soft drinks, kept cold in a sink of running water, were expensive and we didn't like the villagers spending their money on us, we usually didn't bring the children. We had tried to take turns treating the villagers, but they wouldn't hear of it.

"Maybe when the novelty wears off, we can buy our own drinks," David mused hopefully. But it didn't look like the novelty would ever wear off. It made the shopping take a lot longer.

There were two stores. In both a small stock of groceries and dry goods were at one end, chairs and tables scattered elsewhere. A tall stool and a mirror stood in the corner of one of the stores because the shopkeeper, Dimitri, was not only the postmaster and mayor of Vourvoura, but also the barber. He also occasionally pulled teeth.

The stores that also served as "tavernas" of a sort serving drinks or coffee at their few tables, were lively gathering places for the men at night when their farming was done for the day. They sat and drank wine and ordered plates of tinned fish. On the weekends the shopkeepers butchered a lamb or a goat and hung the carcass outside as an advertisement and the men ordered bits of fried meat, lamb or goat usually, with their wine. We could buy whatever section of the animal came next as they hacked their way up the carcass; there was no choice of cuts. We always made sure to wait until someone else bought the head and neck before making our purchases.

More than once we saw a man bringing in an animal for slaughter, carrying the lamb or kid draped tenderly around his shoulders. I had always admired the ancient statue of the man carrying a young calf in that manner. I had always thought of him as caring for the animal. I now knew what he was really doing.

The groceries were extremely limited as the villagers were very self-sufficient and there was no necessity to stock much. We ate mostly macaroni or tinned fish. If a fish monger came from up from the sea, we bought fresh fish. The fish was usually tiny smelt called *marithes*, which I learned from Thia to dredge in flour and fry whole, heads, guts and all. They were delicious and tasted like fish-flavored

French fries. The villagers learned we were eager to buy their garden produce and showed up to sell us their tomatoes, cucumbers and onions. They gave us as much as we bought it seemed.

One of our favorite dishes was a huge plate of fresh tomatoes, sprinkled with chopped anchovies which we learned we could buy in bulk at the shops, drizzled with some of the good local olive oil and flavored with the fresh basil that grew all over the backyard and terrace. That and a chunk of the lovely country bread was meal fit for the king of Greece, and far too good for a colonel.

We purchased a large straw-wrapped flagon and used it to buy our wine after the shopkeepers warned us it was not a good idea to keep the retsina in our metal canteens. We were pleasantly surprised to find that retsina *in situ*, unlike the bottled stuff we had learned to drink in the States, was an excellent wine. The turpentine quality imparted by the resin that was added to it was gone, and instead there was just a hint of pine aftertaste that we learned to appreciate.

Thia taught me to gather wild greens. Heather and I followed her through fields and meadows as she bent over each piece of greenery, cackling all the while.

"*Horta, horta*," she laughed triumphantly in her fairy tale witch voice, "greens, greens."

One day a neighbor delivered a real treat to us, a small basket of tiny new potatoes. I picked parsley that grew in the back yard and we feasted on the lovely tubers.

Every few days we built a small fire under a big black cauldron in the back yard so as to wash laundry and bathe. David rigged lines for me to drape blankets around for privacy, but I discovered the village boys spying on me from the terrace above. Even thrown rocks and swear words wouldn't dislodge them, so David stood guard by the wall above when I bathed. Thia wrung her hands and exclaimed over our wild waste of wood and water although David carefully cut more wood each time and there was plenty of water. So much bathing, she told us sternly, was unhealthy. She didn't bathe the entire five months we were there although it was summer.

Sometimes in the evening a few of the men showed up and took us down to the shops to share some wine. They were very pleased and amused that I was willing to accompany David as the Vourvoura women never went with their husbands at night, only very infrequently on a Sunday after church for a tiny cup of coffee, usually on a high holiday or their saint's name day. I was always enthusiastically welcomed.

On most weekends when Louis was in town. We'd go to the store with him. He'd bring his clarinet and play mournful mountain songs as we sipped our retsina and nibbled on the dried olives the shop keepers always served with the drinks, and tried to learn the lyrics from the other men who seemed to know all the tunes.

While our cooking and housekeeping routines didn't seem too complicated, Thia's were simplicity itself. In the morning she'd empty her chamber pot over the kitchen wall into the irrigation stream, wash her hands and face, boil up some milk, and then put on a pot of greens she had gathered to cook, or make a pot of porridge. That was it. She seldom left her bed, so there was no need to make it. We never saw her wear anything but her long dark dress and scarf. They didn't show any dirt so she never washed them.

Throughout the day she and Soteria and the rest of the family would help themselves from the pot of food, breaking off large chunks of the huge loaves of bread that sat on a shelf in the kitchen and steadily grew more stale until the next baking day.

When it was time to bake more bread, Soteria and Athena came the night before to prepare a preliminary dough, then the next morning she and the girls would knead up the loaves, cover them with all the rugs from the house to rise, and then bake them in the brick oven. Athena always made up special braided little loaves sprinkled with sugar which she'd present with great ceremony to Heather and little Dave. The family generously gave us a loaf although we bought bakery bread from the stores that was brought in on the daily bus from Tripolis.

We got to know Soteria and Adonis well. While Thia was a tiny woman, about the size of ten-year-old, Soteria was strapping, almost six feet tall. We watched her lift up the hind end of stubborn donkey to get it moving on more than one occasion. Adonis was meek, mild, and round shouldered. He suffered from back trouble. The other men in the village said that was because he let Soteria on top when they made love. Just the announcement that Adonis's back was giving him problems again was enough to send the wineshop crowd into gales of laughter.

We roamed the village meeting more and more people, and went for long walks through the verdant countryside. Heather and little Dave made friends with the village children and spent their days playing in the courtyard of the old house. Little by little the curious stares began to be replaced by, if not understanding, at least a good humored acceptance.

Chapter 4

The Day That David Invented the Doorknob

The house lacked many conveniences, such as full plumbing and electricity, but the thing we missed most was a doorknob on the front door. All the houses in Vourvoura had handles and little thumb latches instead of doorknobs. Thia's latch was broken. When it was windy the only way to keep the door closed was to shoot the bolt, locking it from the inside.

We often came back from shopping or a walk and found it locked because when it was left unlocked it blew open and wind put out the lamps in front of Thia's icons, a matter of great concern to her. Then pound as hard as we could there was no way to get any response for Thia was hard of hearing and her room was at the back of the house. Unless she happened to leave her room, which wasn't often, or unless Athena or Yorghia were there, we had to go back down the steps, out the courtyard door, climb a steep hill to get to the back of the house, scale a four foot wall, clamber through a small storeroom window and walk through the house to finally unlock the front door. It was a windy summer and this happened frequently enough to be a real nuisance. One day after we had gone through the routine twice David announced he was going to make a doorknob.

He found a broken limb from the apple tree in back and carved it into the proper shape, with a tongue-like flange for a latch, and installed it. Thia came out to replenish the oil in the icon lamps and stayed for a few minutes to watch David at work puzzled. He tried to explain what he was doing by gestures. She walked back to her room shrugging, sure this was again proof we were crazy, a conclusion she had reached the day after we had arrived.

Later that day I was sitting in our room which overlooked the front door and saw Adonis come in from the fields. He mounted the steps, sighing when he saw the door closed, prepared to shout for one of us. Then he saw the doorknob and stopped dead.

He looked at it a long time before he slowly reached out to touch it. He pulled it, nothing happened. He turned it and the door opened. He closed and opened the door again and again. He looked at both knobs and the latch very carefully. Then he didn't come in; he went downstairs and out to the street where Soteria was unloading sacks of grain from the donkey.

She followed him back up and he showed her the doorknob. She looked at it suspiciously. Then he opened the door. He closed it again and tried to persuade Soteria to open it, but she balked. He went inside, closed the door, then opened it and came back out. Finally Soteria reached for the doorknob and turned it. When the door opened she threw her head back and screamed with laughter. Her laugh was as hearty as the rest of her. She started shouting for the neighbors.

A few of the women came to see what the fuss was about. Soteria demonstrated the door, and Maria, our milk lady crossed herself. She had been interrupted at her baking and was covered in flour, she wiped her hands on her apron and tried the knob herself. All of the women laughed and went to get Thia. She came out of her room grumbling at being disturbed. Then the crowd gathered to show her the new addition to her house. Adonis opened and closed the door a few times to demonstrate. Thia stepped back and like Maria, crossed herself, but was finally coaxed into trying it herself. She opened the door and grinned a big toothless grin.

Finally the women left to return to their chores but Adonis returned with all the men he had found in the wineshop. They were all fascinated and played with the door, talking excitedly together.

They found David in his studio, shook his hand, then dragged him down to the wineshop where they all took turns buying him a drink. Every time someone new drifted into the shop some of the men would take him to the house to show him the new wonder. Two of the men fetched the village priest and took him to the house as well, which impressed Thia enormously. He returned and bought David a drink, too.

That Sunday there was a wedding at the church and Adonis proudly showed the doorknob to all the guests. In fact, the doorknob became a tourist attraction and we grew used to having strangers show up from other villages to ask to try it out. Soteria laughed every time she saw it, but all the men were convinced that David was a genius.

Chapter 5

Celebrations

We were sitting on our balcony eating our breakfast, planning our day when Adonis appeared in the street below us.

"Tonight there is a name day party," he called up to us. The Greeks celebrated the saint's day connected to their names rather than their birthdays. We hadn't been to such a celebration yet.

"Soteria and I will come and get you this evening," Adonis promised as he left, heading for his fields with his hoe over his shoulder.

Soteria was in a clean, brown cotton dress and fresh head scarf when they appeared after supper. Adonis wore a white shirt but no tie and seemed very impressed by David's tie, which I had insisted he wear. We later learned from Louis that one had to earn the right to wear a tie by obtaining an education, becoming a professional or getting rich.

They led us through the village main street, then up a narrow alleyway. We climbed an exterior stairway to the second floor of a house. The lower floor was an animal stable; we could hear the chickens and goats stirring as we waited for someone to answer the door.

A middle-aged lady dressed in black greeted us with great formality and led us into a parlor that had just been whitewashed that afternoon as we could tell by the clean, tangy odor of the lime. There were people already there dressed in their Sunday best perched uncomfortably on the edges of some straight backed wooden kitchen chairs. Except for a small table, the chairs were the only furniture in the room. The table was covered with a heavily fringed and embroidered maroon tablecloth on which was displayed some name day cards and a bouquet of flowers.

We were given chairs. We had inquired and learned from Adonis the correct greeting for a name day was *"kronia polla"* so when the host appeared to shake hands with each of us, we formally wished him *"kronia polla"* earning his smile and friendly nods from the others.

He took a chair and sat beside us trying to converse. Our frequent use of the dictionary puzzled and delighted the villagers. Most of them could not read and none of them had heard of a dictionary before we came, but they quickly realized that if we didn't understand what they said before consulting it, we sometimes could afterwards, and it was like a game to them. If we looked puzzled, they'd gesture to the dictionary for us to look it up.

After a while our hostess appeared carrying a tray of two glasses hardly bigger than a thimble and a decanter of a heavy yellow liquid that turned out to be banana liqueur. She poured out glasses of it for me and David. She refilled the same glasses and served them to the other guests. I was glad she had served us first. We all toasted *"kronia polla"* before we drank. The hostess then disappeared without having tasted any of it herself, nor having served the host. A few minutes later she reappeared with a plate of *loukoumathes*, Turkish delight candies coated with powdered sugar. We each ate one and wiped our fingers on a cloth napkin she carried over her arm. We noticed people toasted the host with the candy before biting it so we did, too.

She left again and we resumed our attempts at conversation which was limited to the weather and to answering their questions about our friend Yorgo in the States whom they hadn't seen since he was little boy.

Everyone was behaving strangely. Even Soteria was oddly subdued and very stiff except when one of us made a mistake in pronunciation and she would slap her thighs and give a great belly laugh. After a while it occurred to me that this was what they considered aristocratic manners in the village. It was not our presence that made them all so formal, but the occasion.

The hostess appeared again, this time with a small plate of bony pieces of lamb and a fork. We each ate a piece using the fork in turn, again first lifting it in a toast. Most were careful not to touch the tines with their lips except for Soteria who slobbered all over it.

The stiff chat continued and we were proudly shown a name day card that had come from Australia where this family had relatives. It looked like a slightly oversized, gaudy birthday card with gilt edges. We admired it and were rewarded with more *loukoumathia*.

We spent another awkward hour at the "party" then left with Soteria and Adonis after shaking our host's hand and wishing him one last "*kronia polla*". He and his wife were very pleased with themselves. Soteria and Adonis murmured approvingly to each other as they walked us home. We had apparently passed muster and even added to their status.

The following Sunday there was a festival and we got out our best clothes again. The young village women teetered down rocky goat paths in spiky high heels to the center of town where the men gathered around a large truck they had procured for the day from another village. There were no cars in Vourvoura except for an ancient Ford that belonged to Louis and was never driven. We were herded in among the laughing, chatting people. We waved to Thia as she stood on our balcony seeing us off. She never went anywhere except to the fields to pick *horta*. Someone pulled a large canvas cover over us all to keep the dust off the revelers' clothing and out of the young ladies' curled and pomaded hair. In spite of the suffocating closeness under the cover everyone sang for the five mile, bumpy drive out of town.

We arrived at a tiny church. Louis was there already with his large family. He told us that years before Vourvoura and a neighboring village had been involved in a lawsuit over the land on which the church stood. The villagers erected a church in a single day thereby taking advantage of a loophole in the law and claiming title to the property. Ever since, both villages good humoredly forgot their quarrel and met to celebrate the name day of the church.

People spread out hand woven blankets and set out plates of cheese, olives, bread, bits of fried meat and hollowed out gourds of wine. We were, as usual, the focus of attention for quite a while. The Vourvoura folk, already somewhat used to us themselves, wanted to show us off to their neighbors. We were pulled from one blanket to another, toasted again and again from the wine flasks, and passed all sorts of dainties to eat.

While all this revelry was going on outside the church, a service was being conducted inside, the usual way with festivals we learned. The priest came out carrying an icon and led the people in a circle around the church chanting the whole time. Everyone crossed themselves, then the priest removed his vestments and joined the fun. A short time later a little truck appeared in the distance and a cheer broke out.

A group of musicians got out carrying a fiddle, a guitar and a clarinet. As they played the people formed into a circle and began dancing. We hung back not knowing the steps until someone pulled us into the line. Someone produced a handkerchief and then one by one the younger men took an end of it to free their bodies for more movement as they led the circle improvising wild leaps and fancy turns while the rest of us followed sedately. Once in a while one of the men tossed money at the feet of the musicians.

The handkerchief was passed to me as a joke, but I did a few turns before I passed it on and earned some cheers. David was given it and stumbled through a few steps, too. Afterwards he went to the musicians and tossed some money at their feet. Everyone was very pleased with us.

By late afternoon we wanted to leave the party and go for a walk but found ourselves being followed by a young woman. We chatted with her and then tried to leave her behind but she stuck to us closely. The villagers had obviously assigned her to look after us. We really wanted to be alone for a while and decided to walk the five miles back to the village assuming her high heels would discourage her from the long hike, but she determinedly stayed with us for a half mile. I had an inspiration. I suddenly turned and shook her hand vigorously.

"It has been a pleasure meeting you," I said very formally in the best name day fashion. "I hope to see you at the next festival."

Then we rapidly took off leaving her standing behind us on the path looking nonplused.

We were very tired by the time we reached the village. Heather and Davidaki were worn out from the long walk and full day, and went to sleep immediately. We undressed and got into bed ourselves. We were making love when the door to our room burst open and a group of men walked in nonchalantly with the village priest in tow.

The villagers were back and the men wanted to take us to the shop for wine to celebrate our first festival. I was put out because they hadn't knocked, but by then I should have learned that they never did. There was no saying no, and they insisted on my presence as well as David's, so chasing them out long enough to get dressed again, we joined the happy throng.

Chapter 6

From Stones, Bread

"But I don't understand, Louis. How can there be a factory up there in those hills? It's so remote," David had been talking about Louis' work which took him away from the village so much.

"My brother Anastasius and me, we are making it. It is an *azvesti* factory."

"What's *azvesti*?" I asked.

"The stuff that is used for whitewash. How do you call it? Lime. You come and see it one day soon, eh?"

"How do we get there?"

We were sitting in the courtyard watching the sunset with Louis. He rose and led us up a few steps to see over the walls to hills on the other side of the valley.

"See that path over there beyond Costas' house? It climbs the mountain like so?" he gestured for us "Follow that. In two, maybe three hours or so you will find it."

We had been in Vourvoura more than two months by then and, at first our need for some privacy, then our love of the beautiful countryside had driven us to taking long walks. We went on day-long explorations, climbing the hills, hiking the valleys, discovering wildflowers and birds that were new to us, and admiring the tiny chapels we found tucked into the folds of the valleys and capping the highest peaks.

They were long golden-colored days. At sunset we descended back into the village. The herds of goats that were also heading home made the hills come alive with the sound of bells they wore around their necks. The sheep were also belled and we came to associate the melodic sound with sunset, as if the rosy colored hills themselves were making the music. Once home Thia usually greeted us with disapproval, sure we'd get ourselves lost.

Early one morning we asked Thia and young Athena to watch Heather and Davidaki for us. They were delighted to learn we were going to visit Louis that day, and pleased that we trusted them with the children. Since we weren't taking the children with us we didn't bother to bring food or water as we usually did on our hikes. With empty hands we left the village and started climbing the path crushing the herbs beneath our feet as we walked. It seemed most of the paths were paved with chamomile making walking a fragrant experience.

The path wound its way through trees and flowery meadows, then out of the lush valley where Vourvoura was situated and up into the harsh, dry, burned-over hills. We climbed and climbed, then made our way through other little valleys and yet more hills.

We came upon some stone towers. We had seen others in our wanderings. Two or three stories high they were made out of dark stone and were always abandoned. Some looked scorched by fire. We had explored a few of them, having to climb as they had no ground floor entrances or were nailed shut if they did. They were all the same; one room on each floor, empty except for wind drifted leaves, dust and sleeping bats and they smelled musty. We had begun avoiding them, feeling they were sinister. Eventually we learned they really were sinister, having been used as forts in feuds or in the interminable wars with the Turks.

Before long we left behind any signs of cultivation and the last of the towers. The valleys were higher and the path grew harder to follow as it faded on the stony soil. Instead of chamomile the air began to smell of sage.

Once we came upon a tiny grotto where a spring surfaced. Someone had built an arched alcove over it. We stopped to drink from a tin cup someone had tied to a rock with a string and we rested in the icy cool shade as we had left all trees behind, too.

A while later we found ourselves at one end of a long shallow valley and we lost the trail altogether. We stopped and looked but could find no trace of it, so decided to walk the length of the valley to see if we could pick it up again.

David went ahead with his long rapid stride, absorbed in the search. I slowed down and gazed at the yellowish landscape around me. Some summer clouds were moving in over the mountains and I watched them against the sky which was so vivid a blue it seemed indigo.

I was feeling free and adventurous, enjoying our search for the lost way when I saw some tumbled remains of an ancient stone wall. I stopped. The wall was clearly very, very old as this valley was too remote from any villages for it to have been tilled in generations. I turned slowly in a circle and in that parched land, time circled.

The soil barely covering the rock that broke through in patches, the stone hills, and the great width of the sky was rooted in a past and linked to a future beyond conception. I suddenly felt I did not belong to any age, but was tied to all time. The present was a bird with wings reaching in either direction. It was beyond a *déjà vu* feeling, and once in a while in Greece I was to feel it again. I simply called such moments "time out of mind" and learned to prize them, fleeting though they were.

I heard a shout and saw David ahead of me in the distance, waving. He had found the path. The moment folded its wings and I was back.

The "two, three hours" stretched to four as we lost the trail again and again, but we didn't mind. At last we saw a tower ahead of us on a broad plateau. It was not one of the dark, forbidding fortresses, but a new, fresh, yellow stone structure with many window openings and chimneys coming out of it. We saw a man in the distance and the sun glinting on his red-gold hair told us it was Anastasius. He waved his arms excitedly. He was joined by smaller, darker Louis and the two brothers came loping to meet us.

"You came!" Louis exclaimed and grinned, showing his broken front teeth.

We walked back with them to the factory, marveling at it

"You built this yourselves?" I asked amazed

"Yes, me and Louis," Anastasius said proudly in his very broken English.

I lapsed into my very broken Greek, "But it's so big!"

Both men laughed uproariously at my mispronunciation.

"How long did it take you?" David wanted to know.

"Two years. We are almost done, six months, more maybe. It goes slower now that we have no car," Louis replied. "Before we could take that road and bring in stuff. Now it comes by the path on our backs."

He pointed to a faint tire track that led across the plateau in the opposite direction of the path. Louis and Anastasius showed us around and David asked questions.

"How come you don't use a car anymore?"

"The license. Here it is very expensive. You pay every month fifty, sixty dollars. The first year is free. Our free time ran out. All our money is in this now," Louis said pointing to his furnace.

"How did you make the chimneys?"

"From old oil drums. I learned to weld in the U.S. And I welded them together."

We went on being more and more impressed by Louis's ingenuity and the two men's determination to finish the factory.

After our tour we went back outside and they began cooking a meal. Louis started a small fire of brush. Anastasius poured water from a goatskin and boiled eggs in a tin can. Louis tucked some potatoes in the ashes and fried some eggs on a shovel he thrust into the coals.

"How did you pick this spot for your factory, Louis?" I wanted to know

"See these?" he held up a stone. "These are the right kind of rock to make *azvesti*. It was part of my wife Poli's dowry. Her parents were killed in the civil war. Just a field of stone her relatives thought they would give her, but she will be rich yet. From stones, we will get bread. They will see." He paused to check on the potatoes and went on. "First I will make lots of money and then I will become a priest."

"A priest?"

"Yes."

"But you are married and have children"

"Oh, not a monk, a priest. Here, in our Orthodox church, they are all married. They must be. But first I want to make money, lots of money, so that when I become a priest they will know it was not for the money."

"Do priests make a lot of money?"

"Enough. The government pays them a salary and in bribes for different things they get more. I will not take bribes. I want them to know that I don't need to."

The food was done and conversation came to a halt while we all ate. Satisfied, Louis sat back while Anastasius cleaned up. Anastasius was very proud of his older brother and was delighted we were there to admire his accomplishments.

"You see," Louis finally continued. "Back there," he gestured in the direction of the village, "they do not understand me any better than they understand you, and it is not because of my Greek. We smoke different pipes."

He fished around in a hand-woven bag and took out a wooden flute. He played while David, Anastasius and I sat back and listened. All of sudden he stopped playing and broke into a loud wailing song. His voice rose and filled the valley. When the song was done he asked if we knew what it meant and then explained.

"It is about an Albanian shepherd. He sings down into a valley where a young girl is taking care of her animals and he says, "Beautiful girl, I would like to hold your head in my lap and gaze into your face. And while I gazed I would want the days to be as long as the days of May and the nights to be as long as the nights of December,' but the girl tells him he must be crazy because she has a house full of older brothers to protect her honor and he should sing his songs elsewhere."

He sang us some more songs and finally broke into a grin. "I have a loud voice, eh? Like Kolokotronis, the Greek war hero in the Turkish war. He was small like me but his voice was big, very big, like this." Louis stood and cupped his hands around his mouth and gave a ululating shout that was truly startling as it echoed in the hills. "Kolokotronis's big voice scared the Turks."

He sat again, "That is why I sing the masses in the church. No one in town likes me, this different pipe I smoke, you see. But still I get to sing in church because of my big voice."

Anastasius had a turn with the flute. David played it a little, too. We were reluctant to stop but the brothers had work to do and we had a long hike back to the village. We turned to wave good-bye before we lost sight of the factory.

"Tell Poli I see her on Saturday," Louis called across the valley in his big, big voice.

Chapter 7

Ta Pethia
(The Children)

Heather and young David, or Alexandra and Davidaki as the villagers named them, had adjusted to life in Vourvoura quickly. The children, *"ta pethia"*, won everyone's hearts. They made friends with Yorghia immediately, who being a few years older tried to lead them into mischief or blame them for her pranks, like the time she loosed some chickens in the same room as Thia's icon shrine. No one bought it. Yorghia's reputation in the village as an imp was too well established, and since she was the older one, she had to bear the consequences for her own misbehavior, primarily scoldings as far as we could see. Good-natured Adonis called her his "little devil" and since she was so much like her mother, shrugged her antics off. Soteria shouted loud enough to make our ears ring, but not loud enough to get Yorghia's attention. Heather and Davidaki were fascinated by Yorghia but had her number and refused to follow her lead.

Sweet maternal Athena mothered the children and enjoyed thinking up treats for them like the fancy breads she made for them or little bracelets and garlands woven out of the wheat from the fields.

After breakfast each day, unless we had a hike planned, I spent a couple hours schooling the kids in math and reading. Davidaki had only just turned five but was already reading well. Heather had begun writing and illustrating her own stories.

They learned their science on our walks. I was teaching them how seeds travel and we became so enchanted with the idea that David began teasing us by referring to anything vaguely scientific as "how seeds travel."

History and social studies were easy since we were surrounded with ancient artifacts and whole new culture. After lessons the kids were free to play with the village children who always showed up during their lessons and sat respectfully in the background until they were over. Once I came upon them watching the Greek children their age conducting a mock baptism. Heather and Davidaki watched intrigued as the child playing the priest dipped Heather's doll in a basin of water. Thia walked out of her room and laughed to my relief. I had been afraid she'd be offended.

Heather's doll had prompted the ceremony. She had the only doll I saw in the village. The kids' toys were one reason for their popularity. We also owned the only books in the village except for an English primer that Athena had from her high school. The family was proud that they had started to send her to a boarding school in Tripolis, the closest town, for several months a year. Most children only got the eight years of education the government provided for free.

I found I was also popular because I often amused the village children and practiced my Greek by drawing crude cartoons and describing the action in Greek with their help. The cartoon character in greatest demand was Yorghia who always was up to no good. Yorghia would proudly watch and suggest new escapades for the cartoon Yorghia. I was a little careful, not wanting to put any more ideas in Yorghia's head than she had already.

I read "chapter books" to Heather and Davidaki and if they did something I wanted to reward, they got an extra chapter. I had brought all the Tolkien books and we spent hours following Bilbo and Frodo on their adventures. I also told them the ancient myths, such as the labors of Hercules, as on-going sagas - "to be continued" when I tucked them in at night.

Our only problem was that Davidaki occasionally wet the bed still. We bought a sheet of noisy plastic the kids hated after Thia kept wailing, "He rains, he rains." We had cleaned the mattress but she fretted until the sheet was installed.

To keep our family dental problems to a minimum I had a Saturday candy rule. All the candy the kids got they could keep but had to save until Saturday to eat. On Saturdays they gorged themselves and I pursued them all day with their toothbrushes.

"*Yia Savato* - for Saturday," the kids would say, "Thank you," when handed sweets. They carefully tucked their candy away in a pocket. The villagers were charmed by their discipline and gave them even more candy to my chagrin, just to see them put it away. On Saturdays they'd call out to the children "Candy today?" and laugh when Heather and Davidaki would happily produce a piece and eat it. The other village kids quickly learned to put in an appearance on Saturday to share the wealth, a practice I encouraged, but guiltily thought of as sharing the tooth decay.

Heather got a toothache once despite the Saturday rule. That prompted a trip to the small city of Tripolis to find a dentist. We were at a loss to find a dentist and finally went to the police station to ask. The police were utterly swept away by the presence of foreigners in their provincial office. They insisted on escorting us to the only dentist in Tripolis.

It was a very quiet town and at the mid-day siesta there was no one on the streets. The policeman, David and the kids were walking rapidly but I lollygagged behind looking at the town. I stepped on a sidewalk grate and it collapsed under me sending me plummeting six feet down.

I was slightly bruised and scraped but not injured. While David was concerned and helped me up the policeman seemed to go into a panic. He asked me if I wanted an ambulance to a hospital in Sparta. He was greatly relieved when I assured him I would survive without emergency medical aid. When we reached the dentist office he took off at a run to share the story with his colleagues.

We were pleased to find the dentist office looked like any other we had seen, but the patients waiting their turn insisted, as did the dentist, that we go in first despite out willingness to wait.

The dentist was surprised we wanted her baby teeth fixed. He just wanted to pull the tooth. But he drilled and filled the cavity instead when we stood firm.

Back in Vourvoura the villagers had seen me help Heather with a tiny cotton ball of clove oil until I could get her to Tripolis. Word spread that I had medicine that could deaden the pain of a toothache and suddenly I became a dentist of sorts. People walked from neighboring villages clutching their aching jaws until I gave them an oil-soaked piece of cotton. I carefully explained that this was only temporary relief. They had to see a dentist. They'd promise they would but I always feared the next step was the mayor's barber shop where he kept a special pair of pliers ready.

Heather showed off her new filling to the village kids and impressed them.

Heather and Davidaki took being the prince and princess of the village in their stride and were generous with the other kids when it came to their toys, books and games as well as their sweets after we explained, and they could see, how little the Greek children had.

The children became a major resource for all the Vourvourans under twelve and David and I were proud of them.

Chapter 8

Gypsy Invasion

One morning Vourvoura was invaded by a caravan of Gypsies. A boy was immediately dispatched to the church to clang the bells excitedly and warn the villagers to come in from the fields. We walked to the store and saw the Gypsies' brilliant figures everywhere. A group of children dressed in dirty, but brightly colored rags followed us home.

"Ai, *gitanes*," Thia was moaning in the kitchen. "While you go to get them bread they steal your flour," she told us.

Adonis, rushing in from his fields, assured us the Gypsies no longer stole in Greece. "In Greece they steal and..." he made a throat slitting gesture. "Killing you can get away with, not stealing." Nonetheless, we noticed no one left their house unprotected.

After a while, once they were sure of an audience, the Gypsy men stampeded their animals through the town from one end to the other and back again twice. The clatter from their hooves below our balcony was deafening. Heather and Davidaki were very excited and jumped up and down, clapping their hands.

"Mommy, Daddy, see the pretty horsies!" Davidaki exclaimed.

The animals were beautiful, sleek and well-groomed horses and mules, unlike the poor neglected, over-worked beasts of the villagers. There was sharp interest in them among the village men, and it was clear some horse trading would be taking place before the Gypsies left.

A short time later our first Gypsy arrived. She was swarthy and solemn, dressed in a red satin blouse and a number of skirts and aprons, all printed with bright flowers and covered with many grease stains. She held herself very straight.

"Give me money," she said peremptorily.

David and I looked at each other. We tossed our heads back for no in the Greek fashion.

"Well, give me oil."

"We have no oil," I replied.

She was exasperated with us. "Then give me bread," she demanded.

I capitulated and went upstairs to get our last loaf. I wrapped it carefully in a clean piece of paper as the Greeks always wrapped everything. When I brought it downstairs she tore off the wrapper, threw it on the ground and walked off without a word. We weren't offended, nor was she offended by us. It was all part of her natural arrogance.

The next one was dressed even more colorfully than the first and she had her young daughter with her. They walked right up to us.

"Give me money," the girl said. She was no more than ten years old but already had two gold front teeth. Heather and Davidaki watched her fascinated from a corner. This time David fished in his pocket and came up with some small change. She took it without a word and her mother smiled at her. Her entire smile was a solid bar of gold with lines etched in it for teeth. This in a village where most of the people had missing teeth they could not afford to replace.

"Now, give me oil," the girl went on.

"No," I replied, annoyed at her greed.

"Then give us some bread."

"We have no more bread."

The mother interrupted, "Well, give us some old clothes."

She, too, seemed exasperated with us.

"We don't have any," David said. The woman spat on the floor and walked out. So it went throughout the day.

We saw their encampment at the edge of town, a bunch of wagons and blankets tied up to make lean-tos. None of the Gypsy men were begging; that was the women's work. They discussed mules and horses with the village men.

The villagers weren't happy about the Gypsies' presence but they tolerated them, except for old Plakoskefalos, which translated "flat head", our neighbor in back. He was aging and crotchety, and since he had spent some time in America, thought himself modern.

"Get out of here," he shouted to the women. "Why don't you work instead of beg?"

"God has forbidden us to work. You know that," one of the women called up to him indignantly.

"Then he forbids you to eat, too," the old man shouted back triumphantly. But his sister and niece were doling out food at the back of the house during the exchange. Everyone gave them something, although no one gave them much, and we were the only people who gave them any money.

There was an old Greek on crutches who had attached himself to the Gypsies. He begged, too, but at the first door, he was taken in and cared for until the Gypsies left and he went with them. Thia told us he had no family. Sometimes old or crippled people without younger relatives to care for them joined the Gypsies, who didn't mind their presence and were willing to feed and care for them.

I asked Thia why she fed the Gypsies if she didn't like them.

"But how else are they to eat? They are forbidden by God to work, Andrianni," she answered solemnly, surprised at my question.

Chapter 9

Different Pipes

Yorghia, Soteria's youngest daughter, came in the kitchen as I stood boiling some macaroni for our midday meal. She muttered a greeting then went into the storeroom. A moment later she darted out, slamming the door and screaming. "*Pointiki, pointiki!*" she shouted at the top of her lungs. "What is it?" I asked alarmed, but she had already run to the front room and was standing at the front door yelling for her parents.

Her shouts penetrated even Thia's ancient ears for she came grumbling out of her room. David came running from his studio and up the stair followed by both the children and two neighbors who had been watching him work all morning. Soteria and Adonis came running into the courtyard. The crowd gathered around Yorghia and she led the way to the storeroom. A gleeful predatory look had come over all the Greeks' faces. David and I looked at each other puzzled, then taking the kids by the hand we walked out back to look into the storeroom windows at the proceedings.

There was a wild chase scene in progress. Soteria stood on a bench jumping up and down waving a broom. Adonis ran puffing around the room with a basket chasing something at floor level. Thia had retreated to the bench with Soteria and clutched her long black skirts high enough to reveal that she wore long black bloomers, while she urged on Adonis and the other two men. Athena had appeared from somewhere and she and Yorghia were jumping and shouting and darting to the corners flicking rags with their hands while the men ran about with baskets. We lifted Heather and Davidaki up to the window so they could see the fun.

The slapstick chase went on until one of the men triumphantly raised the basket and clapped a rag over the top. The women climbed down from the bench and the girls cheered. They all trooped out to the back yard where we stood waiting to see their prize.

The girls crouched over the little fireplace which we used to heat our laundry and bath water, and they started a small fire. The men slapped each other on their backs and joked while Thia just stood there grinning. When the fire was going Soteria went inside and returned with a pair of fire tongs. Adonis carefully reached into the basket with them and pulled out a large squirming rat. I gasped, stepped back, pulling the kids with me.

Unbelieving, I stayed a few minutes, just long enough to see Adonis hand the tongs and rat over to Yorghia who crouched by the fire and held the rat over the flames. I hurried indoors to our room and got Heather and Davidaki interested in playing a game with each other. Later David joined me. We left the children and went out on our balcony.

"Did they really burn the thing?"

"It's horrible. They're torturing it. Whenever it looks like it's dying they pull it off for a while then stick it back on the fire."

"Why would they do such a thing?"

A while later I looked in back of the house and saw them dousing the fire. Yorghia flung the dead rat over the garden wall where the village dogs would find it. I came back to our room. Davidaki had forgotten the rat chase already, but Heather, older and wiser, had figured something was up.

"Why did they want to burn the rat, Mommy?"

I had known the question was coming and had been trying to come up with an answer. The Plague was all I could think of. I had already learned that here a hundred years was like yesterday.

"Rats eat a lot of people's food and they bring diseases. They can make people very sick. Long ago they made people so sick that lots of them died. I think the people around here remember that. They hate the rats so much they like to hurt and kill them. I think that must be why." The explanation I gave her was as much for myself as for her. I was still in a state of shock.

A few days later I caused a scene in the village when I stopped an eight year old boy from stoning a kitten. I grabbed his arm and made him put the stone down then carried the kitten home to nurse it. I was furious. No kitten ever caused a plague. That afternoon Thia and a neighbor pointed at me and laughed when I came in the front room.

"Crazy," said the neighbor.

"Maybe," I replied, surprising her that I understood. But Thia had called us that so often it was a familiar word. "Why this time?"

"To make a fuss over a cat. The village people are still laughing," said the neighbor.

"You shouldn't make such a fool of yourself, Andrianni," Thia admonished me seriously.

"You are the fools to teach your children to be so unkind," I burst out passionately and marched out of the room.

"See? Crazy," the neighbor said as I left.

That Sunday Louis came back to town and we talked about the rat incident and the kitten. He sat there thoughtful.

"Are all Greeks so hard-hearted, Louis?" I wanted to know.

"I do not know, Andrianni. I myself never let my children hurt anything helpless, and I know you Americans are generally more caring of animals than we are," he paused. "But I tell you, for three years I worked at a gas station in Chicago and maybe five times we were held up by people with guns. One time for no reason robbers beat up the old man who worked there in the mornings. They did not know him or have anything against him yet they hurt him enough he went to the hospital for a long time. That never happens in Greece."

"No armed robbery? Not even in Athens?" I asked incredulously.

"Never have I heard of even one. Killings maybe, but never without a cause, such as family honor, and even that very seldom."

"It's a value system we just don't understand," David put in diplomatically.

"Maybe," I shuddered remembering Yorghia with the rat over the fire. "It's like you say, Louis. We smoke different pipes from these people."

Chapter 10

No and Long Live,
Government Comes to Vourvoura

Not long after we arrived in Greece we had learned that the king and his wife had had a baby boy, the crown prince. While the colonels were running things, they were still paying lip service to the king, so the birth was a major official event. In Vourvoura no one seemed to pay attention to the outside world at all. But one day just about every man in the village met to shoulder shovels at one of the stores. Laughing and slapping each other on the back they prepared to head off to a mountain top nearby.

We were surprised to learn they were going to lay out rocks to spell "ZITO" which meant Long Live and outline a crown, in honor of the new prince's christening which was to happen soon. It hadn't seemed anyone in the village cared. But then we spied Louis and his brother Anastasius among the others and asked them about it.

"Ha!" Louis laughed bitterly. "The colonels are paying us to go into the hills and do this thing, this demonstration of joy by the people!"

I had read that during World War II the Axis powers had asked for permission to cross Greece, really making a demand that Greece decide to join them or the Allies. Although the dictator Metaxas wanted to join the Axis, the popular sentiment was extremely strong the other way. One way the people made that clear to Metaxas and the Axis was to spontaneously go into the hills and spell the word "NO", OXI in Greek, in rocks on the highest peaks and whitewash them. After OXIs appeared everywhere, Mextaxas caved and said no to the Axis, leading to the occupation of Greece and all the sorrows that followed, death and starvation and eventually a civil war among them.

I had seen the hills surrounding Athens and in our area bearing their proud OXI. It seemed to me this ZITO business was an insult to the Greeks' own history.

I asked Louis about that.

"Hey, we like the king and his family. It is no problem. But we would never do this except the government is paying well for that hill there to say ZITO. Nobody paid for OXI."

He pointed to the distant peak and everyone laughed. At the end of the day, sure enough, a large ZITO over a crown was emblazoned in whitewashed rocks on the mountain. The men came back and rang the church bells wildly so everyone would go outside and look at their work. Then they went in the taverna and drank a lot of wine. Everyone seemed to think it was a great joke. I learned the government had at first demanded that they remove the OXI on the higher mountain next to it and put the ZITO there, but no one would touch the OXIs anywhere in Greece. NO had become sacred, and ZITO would just have to take second best.

Nonetheless, regardless of the colonels and their rocks, Greece seemed genuinely happy about its new prince and prepared to celebrate making the baby a Christian. Unlike Catholics, Greeks waited up to six months to christen their infants because the baptism was a strenuous process and they wanted the baby strong enough to handle it safely.

A week later Louis was back in town from his factory in the mountains and we had joined him in the mayor's shop for a glass of wine when we saw a car drive into town. Everyone's attention was immediately riveted on the man who stepped out of it wearing a suit.

He came to the shop and announced he was from the government and would wait until all the men were in from the fields to discuss plans for the village. Curious, we stuck around. He introduced himself to us and then went and sat a table by himself. He was as curious about our presence as we were about his but didn't have time to indulge himself; he was here on serious business.

He ordered a large tin pitcher of wine and as men drifted in he offered them glasses of it, getting refills when necessary. Louis translated when our Greek faltered. The stranger told the men that other villages were currently in greater need than Vourvoura but that in six months the government hoped to bring them electricity. David and I looked at each other in dismay. We knew when refrigeration came to Vourvoura it would drastically change their diet in town, adding variety to the healthy, but bland monotony of trahana and hilopita varied with a few vegetables and once in a while some fried bony meat. But would the soft glow of lamp light we had learned to love in Vourvoura at night give way to fluorescent bulbs?

Most of the men just snorted at the announcement. They had heard promises before. However, they perked up at the announcement that a rich Australian Greek had offered to pay half the cost of extending the road to the next three villages that were currently only served by mule paths.

"Since the rich man will only pay his half if it is done soon enough to serve his ailing mother, this is possible," grinned Louis as he explained to us.

Then the man told the villagers they should not make feta cheese anymore because it did not keep as well as other cheeses. He was quite earnest about it and went on at such length at how the other types of cheeses could be made. We got bored and went home.

The next day we could see how well the suggestion had been received. Everyone in the village was making feta as usual.

Chapter 11

Hell With Company

"We have a proverb, 'Better hell with company than heaven alone'," Louis summed up the villagers' attitude towards us. Since we were their guests they had decided that we should never suffer from lack of company and they did not regard a family as company enough for itself. Our need for privacy was turning into an obsession, especially for David. To restore some sense of balance, we made up our minds to make some trips away from the village.

We first tried a "practice" trip to make sure our gear would be feasible with the children. We made up bundles and carried them. Heather insisted on carrying her own sleeping bag and sure she would give up, we were surprised that she determinedly packed it all the way to the campsite we had selected about three miles out of town.

"Too bad there's not a Girl Scout troupe here," I said to David.

"She doesn't need them. She'd put them to shame," David answered proudly.

The place we picked had a wide sweeping view of the next valley and was just lower enough in altitude to allow olive trees to grow. A shepherd out in the hills spotted us and eaten alive by curiosity he hiked up the mountain to visit us. He was wearing a foustanella, a traditional belted long shirt instead of trousers – a rare sight.

I was cooking our dinner of trahana and hilopita over a small fire of twigs and offered him some, but he laughingly turned it down although he accepted a glass of wine from us - against all advice we had filled one canteen with retsina, figuring we'd drink it before anything dreadful could happen to it. Our shepherd friend stayed with us until the sunset turned the sky red and then laughed at us again as he bid us good-night and left with his sheep, bells ringing melodically, behind him. He called his sheep with the soft "*ahaia, ahaia*" all the Greeks used to summon animals.

Pleased with our camping success, we planned a trip to the coast.

Thia had told us that the gravel road that wound through the village led to the sea. Old Plakoskefalos confirmed it when he visited us one afternoon.

"By foot it is one day away, but just a few hours by foot and you can meet a bus at a crossroad. It stops there early, five in the morning."

Visions of swimming in the blue Mediterranean were so strong that even the idea of an all-night hike did not daunt us. We packed some belongings into bundles we could carry and borrowed Thia's alarm clock. She had considered us peculiar before, now she thought us completely mad. The news spread throughout the village that we were leaving and all day we had to announce to everyone over and over again that we would return.

We woke at midnight and quietly made ourselves some coffee. We even let the children have some in their milk thinking they might need the caffeine under the circumstances. Then we shouldered our things and left. A full moon was shining and whitewashed Vourvoura looked snowy. We walked slowly admiring its beauty.

We felt very jubilant and adventurous. We talked in whispers until we left the last house well behind us. We had hiked this way before as far as an ancient Roman bridge where we had picnicked. We crossed the bridge entering new territory. Heather, Davidaki and I sang songs; they were thrilled by this great night time adventure. But David saved his breath as he was carrying the heaviest pack.

After a while the sky began to lighten. The road followed a little stream. The light grew stronger and mist began to rise off the stream and fields. Once I looked up and clutched David's arm in surprise. High above us, just catching the morning sun, was a big jet airliner. It seemed forever since we had seen one. We watched the silver flash of it until it was out of sight. At that moment it sunk in just how remote Vourvoura was and I felt a sense of isolation that was something of a shock, although not altogether unpleasant.

It occurred to me that although we might have come from the world of that jet, we belonged to Vourvoura now. If something terrible were to happen there was no way we could contact that airplane or that it could aid us. Even the nearest telephone was a two hour journey from the village by bus in Tripolis. We and the villagers were on our own absolutely. I then understood the Greek saying about hell with company. We were all silent for a while after the airplane had passed.

It was getting much lighter and we were concerned we were going to miss our bus so hurried our pace. We crested a hill and saw the crossroad below us and the bus still loading. We shouted for it and began to run down the hillside. Someone spotted us and the bus waited for the five minutes or so it took us to race down the mountain. All the passengers got out and surrounded us while we caught our breath.

They loaded on our things and insisted on giving up seats to us although the bus was filled to capacity. We were the center of everyone's curious attention. We would have been anyway but arriving in such dramatic fashion out of nowhere intensified the situation. We answered their questions all the way to the little seaside town where the bus stopped. They were astonished we were living in Vourvoura, and if someone had not heard of us in his village and confirmed it, might not have believed us. One of his neighbors had sought us out because of a toothache.

The coast was flat. The town of Astros and roofs of its houses were also flat rather than pitched and tiled as in Vourvoura. The whole place had a dusty, unfinished look that contrasted sharply with the pretty mountain villages.

By this time everyone on the bus considered us personal friends and they didn't want to see us leave. But firmly turning down all invitations, we began hiking out of town along the beach. We set up camp and made some breakfast.

We swam each day, cooked over a small driftwood fire and enjoyed our solitude. We walked into Astros during the hot, sleepy afternoons and drank lemonades at a cafe, writing letters while we waited for the day to cool before returning to camp with more supplies. Each day we went to the fishing boats and bought fish directly from the nets. We delighted in the pretty fish, brightly colored and elegantly shaped. Back at camp we fried them in olive oil briefly, squeezed lemon over them and tossed on herbs we found growing along the way, usually thyme. One afternoon we went to a little restaurant and ate in a garden beneath a grape arbor, stuffing ourselves with more fish.

At night Heather and Davidaki slept soundly after all their swimming, while David and I sat on the beach watching the fishing boats go out and listening to the music from the tavernas in town drift across the harbor. Sometimes I longed to go join the throng across the way, but settled for listening to the parties. David reveled in the solitude.

We were tanned and healthy and felt our sense of peace restored. We were ready to go back to Vourvoura.

We went back along a much longer route but one which involved no hiking. We arrived at sunset on the daily bus to our village. We'd been gone ten days. At the store word quickly spread that we were back and everyone in the village turned out to greet us. The men lined up to kiss David and shake my hand. The women lined up to kiss me and shake David's hand. They all insisted on taking us to the store to buy us wine and the children candy and soft drinks to celebrate our return. The village women clustered at the door to make sure the men treated us properly instead of just going home as they usually did at night.

At home Thia greeted us with chuckles and embraces. I was dismayed to discover that many of the improvements we had made had vanished. The flowered curtain I had hung beneath the sink was gone, as was the bright paper I had used to cover the dismal and dirty partition that separated the kitchen from the waterfall and stream that ran beside it. The trash can we had introduced was gone. Our glasses were also missing but Thia cheered me up by telling me they had been broken in a celebration of the crown prince's christening. I was sorry we missed the party and was glad someone had a good time even if it was at our expense. I made a shopping list for replacing everything then found all the things except the glasses on a shelf in the storeroom.

We had a quick meal and went to bed worn out from our day on the buses. The next day we treated ourselves to a hot bath in the back yard and washed our clothes over Thia's protests.

Chapter 12

Wedding

Louis's brother Anastasius was marrying Maria on Sunday. We had gone to their betrothal party soon after our arrival in Vourvoura. It had been a short engagement because Maria was having a baby and wanted to get married in church rather than the priest's house, which is the custom if the bride is so pregnant as to be obvious. While young girls are carefully guarded until their betrothals in Greece, once they are engaged, they are as good as married and allowed great freedoms with their future groom.

We saw Anastasius get off on the bus on Friday grinning and carrying a number of big boxes.

"The bride's dress," he said, indicating one of the parcels. We asked if she didn't get to pick out her own gown. We were reassured she had "reserved" it.

"Reserved it?"

Anastasius explained that Greek brides rented their dresses just as American grooms rent their tuxedos. It struck us as an admirably practical arrangement.

Sunday morning a carload of musicians drove into town looking for Louis's house. A while later we heard music coming from that direction. Thia hobbled out of her room smiling and nodding, and seeing we were dressed up in our best, she shooed us out of the house.

We walked slowly. We all enjoyed the walk through the village, across a high bridge that spanned the river and the verdant ravine between our house and Louis'.

There were many people milling around. The wailing mountain music was very loud and we saw that the musicians had cleverly amplified a bouzouki and violin using their car battery for power. Once again we were struck with admiration for Greek practicality. The little stone room was crowded. Anastasius was dancing with a few other men. Maria was nowhere in sight.

Poli, Louis' wife, came out of the kitchen carrying a tray of tiny glasses. We followed the example of the others and toasted the health of the couple with cherry liqueur. Then another woman came out of the kitchen with plates of little cakes drenched in powdered sugar that dusted all the guests and led to great flurries of whisked handkerchiefs. Every few minutes a woman circulated with plates of olives, fried meat or candies. All of us guests used a common fork, taking care to not let our lips touch it.

The music was getting louder and louder, and more people crowded in. We had been offered two of the few chairs, and when we tried to give them up to some of the older people, we were smilingly shoved back down. It made David very uncomfortable to be sitting when so many little old ladies were standing. I wanted to help Poli in the kitchen because she was near the end of her pregnancy, but she seemed shocked when I offered. We insisted on holding Heather and Davidaki on our laps, however, when people tried to give them chairs, too.

After a while the musicians unhooked their instruments from the battery and reinstalled it in the car. All but the violinist took off. A procession formed with Anastasius and the violinist leading. Anastasius danced as he walked and the people cheered him on. Two little boys followed them closely carrying flower-covered staves in very medieval fashion, one with the bride's veil on top and it floated gracefully as the boys waved it gaily in time to the music and spun around to show it off. At this point someone looked up at the sky and pointed. We all saw a huge thunderhead had blown in from nowhere. David pessimistically wondered if it would rain before we all reached the church, but I laughed at the thought. It had been sunny all day and for days before. We arrived at Maria's house and Anastasius pounded on the door shouting. I thought it peculiar that she wasn't ready as she had to hear us coming. Then from the giggles and laughter in the crowd I realized this was part of the ritual. Anastasius shouted louder, becoming positively abusive. Someone inside told him to go away. The shouting match continued a few more minutes, then Anastasius shoved the door open with a great kick and went in. A few minutes later he emerged grinning with his bride on his arm. There was a few minutes delay while her women relatives and friends fitted the veil over her elaborate, piled up hairdo. Then the procession continued down the road. Maria's heavy satin and lace gown had a long train which a little girl in white proudly held out of the dust for her.

The sky grew darker and a wind picked up. Maria looked up concerned and no longer smiled. We had reached the bridge now and there was no mistaking it; a storm was about to break. Someone ran ahead to fetch the musicians with their car. Everyone walked a little faster and the violinist speeded up his playing. There was a flash of lightning and a crack of thunder. All sense of decorum was given up as everyone fled for the nearest house. Maria was having a hard time of it as the little girl carrying her train could not keep up with her. Anastasius grabbed the train himself, flinging it over his shoulder and ran with his arm around Maria.

There was more thunder and lightning and it began pouring. Two of the men ran ahead to the only house between us and the rest of the village now, an old deserted place. They shoved at the door, breaking the lock and we all piled in. A farmer had been using the house to store his vegetables. There were two crates of tomatoes in the middle of the place that were too far gone and the place stank. It was so dirty and dusty no one could sit down and we all tried to avoid touching the filthy walls. Maria stood next to Anastasius fighting back tears. The bride's mother, exhausted from the mad dash sat down on a box only to find she had done so on a rotten tomato and ruined her dress. Heather and Davidaki began giggling, but we angrily shushed them since the woman was so upset even though we, too, could see the slapstick humor in it that had set them off. A few minutes later the car drove up. The wedding party left and the rest of us stayed there huddling together waiting for the rain to let up a little.

It poured as it hadn't since we had come to Vourvoura. It was almost tropical in intensity and it just didn't let up for an instant. The moisture in our clothes began to steam off; the room was getting unbearably uncomfortable. Still everyone waited for the car to return; it never did. After a while David and I and the kids decided to make a dash for it.

We ran as fast as we could and when we got to our house Thia burst into laughter at our sopping wet, bedraggled appearance. Adonis and Soteria were there having left Louis' party earlier. They helped us wring out our clothes. We changed and walked with Soteria and Adonis under their umbrella to the church. The wedding mass had just begun.

All the candles were lit and the priest was dressed in his most colorful robes, all red and gold. The ceremony was long and elaborate but cheerfully informal as most Orthodox ceremonies seemed to be. Once, the priest went to the bride, groom and best man with a chalice of wine. He casually took a sip of it himself as if he were just thirsty, not as if it were sacrificial wine at all. The best man's turn came last and when he handed the chalice back to the priest the latter glanced in it and handed it back to the man with a joke, twice. The people watching broke into laughter. The best man was famous for liking his wine.

At another point the priest, best man, bride and groom, and matron of honor all grabbed on to each other and with the priest in the lead swinging his censer they ran around and around the altar while everyone laughed and threw rose petals at them. "The dance of Isiah," Soteria told me. Maria smiled for the first time since she had seen the cloud in the sky.

When the ceremony was over and the church doors thrown open Maria stopped smiling. The town was flooded and the rain was still coming down. Usually the bride led a circle dance in front of the church after the mass, but she obviously wouldn't be able to do that. She and Anastasius drove off with the musicians back to Louis's house.

We went home deciding against walking back through the rain to the party. We could hear the music beginning again.

Thia thought the whole thing very funny and kept chuckling over how wet we had been. I asked her if she didn't think it was sad for Maria.

"No, no," Thia assured me. "It is a good omen. Now she will have lots of babies."

I wondered if that were any consolation for Maria when I remembered her in the dirty hovel in her beautiful gown.

Chapter 13

Wanderings

Our trip to the sea had been so successful we decided to go on more journeys. We began leaving Vourvoura for two or three weeks at a time. The villagers at first alarmed by each departure, grew used to our comings and goings, but it was always surprising to find how much we had been missed. Each of our returns was greeted with great enthusiasm, and we appreciated Vourvoura more after traveling.

I was also chagrined to find that each time after our travels more of the improvements we had made disappeared again. Plants that we had potted and arranged on the steps would have been moved to the backyard, the pretty curtains I would have hung would be gone, the partition needed repapering again. David and I conjectured.

He had the rather ominous idea that perhaps Soteria and Adonis wanted Thia to be depressed and die sooner so they could inherit the house. The rather more practical solution occurred to us that perhaps they didn't want the house to look good because they wanted to inherit it and were concerned the city relatives might come through and think it so charming they wanted to keep it. Whatever it was, I doggedly replaced things because I couldn't bear to live in a place that looked unloved.

We forgot all such cares while we traveled. We explored the famous areas of the Peloponesus: Sparta, Olympia, Corinth, and such, but it was the coast with its perfect beaches and warm blue waters that drew us most strongly.

We were camped in a lovely pine forest on a beach for a few days when a little motorcycle cart drove in. An older man got off, set up a camp and began working at something very industriously. This was unusual as we never saw Greeks camping, only the Gypsies. Heather and Davidaki went over to investigate and came back very excited.

"Puppets, Mommy and Daddy. He has puppets. Can we go to the show?" By this time their Greek was much better than ours and they communicated freely.

We went over and introduced ourselves. Sure enough, he did have puppets, the famous *Karaghiozhi* shadow puppets. We had read about them but never expected to find any.

All over Greece there were once itinerant shadow puppeteers. There was a standard cast of characters in their shows: a brave *evzone* (a Greek warrior), a sultan, a Moorish soldier, and Karaghiozhi, who was a lazy but canny Greek. He had a large family complete with a nagging wife and he possessed an incredibly long arm as his trademark, with which he'd smack his enemies. The shows were supposed to be full of social satire and coarse humor. The long arm was a phallic joke.

This puppeteer was very proud of his puppets which were carefully made from brightly dyed parchment and leather. He was doing some minor repairs on them and he told us he was doing a show on the beach outside of a cafe down the road. We promised to be there. He seemed flattered that foreigners were interested.

That evening there was a big crowd, as many adults as children, and we sat on the sand expectantly watching the white cotton screen that had been erected on the back of the man's cart. It was lit by a bulb powered by the vehicle's battery.

The puppeteer had a repertory of voices to match the colorful puppets. We could not understand much of the rapid patter but managed to follow the plot anyway. Karaghozhi wanted to get out of paying his debts that his wife nagged him about, so he pretended to be dead while each of the other characters came to his funeral and insulted him. Finally one insult was too much and Karaghozhi rose from his bier to punch the offender. The audience laughed and shouted at the characters, taking full part in the performance. It was a lovely evening.

One blazingly hot afternoon we arrived at Mycenae. There was not a speck of shade anywhere but in the great beehive shaped tombs. One was supposed to be Agamemnon's tomb. The stones that made up Mycenae were so different than any other ruins that it brought Homeric Greece home to us in a new way. This was ancient Greece to the classical Greeks that *we* considered ancient Greeks. The stones were so massive one could easily believe that titans had indeed built this stark and fierce place. By this time the children knew about the Trojan Wars and Odysseus, who was a favorite hero of theirs. I explained this was where it all began.

Inside Agamemnon's tomb the children were at first cowed and spoke in whispers, then they discovered there was an echo. We welcomed the cool darkness and I enjoyed hearing Heather and Davidaki shout aloud their youth and life in such an old place full of violent memories. While it didn't dispel the ghost of the bloodthirsty king, who in a thirst for power murdered his own daughter, it did add some balance to hear our daughter laugh..

David encouraged the children to shout loud enough to wake the old king.

Every ancient place had a completely different look and feel to it. The one thing we didn't like were the ugly little settlements that sprouted a couple miles from each of the sites. The prices of everything were always inflated, the services limited, and they never felt properly Greek to us. But they were Greek enough the shopkeepers cheerfully always let us stash our belongings with them as we hiked out to the old ruins. Once we came back to find the cafe with our things inside had closed but the shopkeeper had thoughtfully left his key in the lock for us. We found a tourist policeman and had him come back with us to open the shop, and relock it for us after we had collected our belongings.

We were always on the lookout for comfortable camp sites as we traveled. We found Nauplia (pronounced Nafplia) on the coast was a beautiful town crowned with a magnificent Venetian fort/castle. The Venetians were wonderful architects we decided. There were 1000 steps up to the top and we began climbing, counting as we went. Near the top David suddenly stopped.

"Oops, just lost count. We have to go back down and start again!" The children looked dismayed until they realized he was again teasing them.

At the peak we could see the tiny island with a small castle on it where the hangman of Nauplia had lived – not welcome in the town proper. We learned the Greek war hero Kolokotronis had been kept in one of the dungeons there for a while, and that the Germans had used it as a prison in World War II. David decided to go down into one of the dungeons and check it out. The kids and I waited on a terrace above.

When David came out he was ashen faced.

"It's no place any human should be," he told me. "Really frightening and totally dark."

We lazed on the beach at Nauplia but discovered the waters were too full of treacherous sea urchins to cool off and bathe after David got a spine in his foot. I had to pour hydrogen peroxide on his wound, but his foot still swelled up, so we decided to stay a few days until it healed.

We camped in a half constructed building that had been abandoned temporarily. There we passed the hot time of the day while I read aloud to the children. They were enjoying Jerome K. Jerome's "Three Men in a Boat." The spot was private with a view of the sea, clean, dry and had a water supply. That was all we needed.

We frequently passed Gypsy caravans on our travels. We had been told that the Gypsies roamed the Peloponesus in the summers but settled down in Athens for the winters, where, it was rumored they all owned expensive properties. It was too much of a contrast to imagine the wild clans becoming fashionable Athenians for half the year. Besides, we reasoned, what would they do with their bears?

Not all the caravans had dancing bears, but most did. They were usually kept tied to the back of a donkey cart and ambled along behind the family. When the Gypsies stopped to camp they tied the bears to trees or in towns to telephone poles.

Sometimes the animals seemed sad and bedraggled, other times they seemed as content as big, shaggy dogs. One rainy day on a bus, David pointed to a bear tied to an electric pole on the outskirts of a city, all by itself, dancing alone in the downpour, all its people having taken refuge in their carts. It seemed happy even without an audience.

There were usually a few young men that led the Gypsy caravans on motorcycles but most people rode donkeys or mules. The animals were covered with colorful bundles and some had huge cauldrons lashed to them filled with babies and toddlers. This always upset David.

"Imagine growing up in a cooking pot!" he said. I pointed out that when we had hiked in the hot sun a while on our way to the various ruins, our own children might appreciate a conveyance even if it was a cooking pot.

We usually camped well away from any Gypsies to avoid the constant begging.

We were something of Gypsies ourselves. We rode buses and accepted rides from whatever vehicles offered them as we traveled. We once rode in an ambulance; the driver insisted on treating us like guests and taking us out to lunch while we anxiously wondered if there was an emergency going on somewhere during the leisurely meal. A number of times fruit trucks gave us rides and the drivers always insisted on giving us some of the produce they carried. Our pockets were filled with lemons many times, and once a grinning, cheerful man thrust a big watermelon into Heather and Davidaki's arms, then still not satisfied gave David and I each one as well.

On one of our trips we were a day away from Vourvoura and eager to get back. The hottest part of the day found us sitting beside a dusty road. We had been waiting for two hours for a bus that was supposed to come by or for any kind of vehicle we could flag down. The children, usually good humored travelers, were cranky and uncomfortable. We were all thirsty but had drunk all our water, so there was nothing to do but wait.

A young woman appeared, walking over a low hill in the fields beside us. She was dressed in a full length dress and her hair was bound by a white scarf. Long black braids hung below her waist and her lips had the chiseled line that the ancient artists loved, called the archaic smile. She was taller than most Greek women and moved very gracefully. She walked to us smiling carrying a big platter on her head. When she reached us we saw the platter was heaped with black, wet, cool grapes. We greeted her. She smiled but said not a word. She just emptied the grapes into our laps and left, slowly gliding back over the rise and out of sight.

The grapes were unlike any we had seen before. They grew so closely together we couldn't break them from the stem. We just held the bunches in our hands and bit into them letting the juice run down our chins.

"Who was she Mommy?" Davidaki wanted to know.

"Demeter."

"Who's Demeter?" asked Heather.

"The lady who gave us the grapes," I replied and David and I smiled at each other.

Chapter 14

Rocks of Ages

"Room," The man said in English, grabbing David's arm as soon as we stepped from the bus. "You rent room."

"No thank you," David replied in Greek.

"Nice room," the man insisted, still pulling on David's arm. He was a big man, middle aged with a broad paunch and bald head.

David tried to pull his arm back but the man wouldn't let go.

"We are camping," I explained in Greek.

"Camping no good," the man switched to Greek. "I show you my nice room."

"No," David said emphatically and finally yanked his arm free. The man followed us a few blocks talking about his room non-stop.

This was another squalid settlement outside an ancient site, this time Ancient Corinth. We finally got rid of our unwelcome escort when we entered a shop and asked if we could leave our things there a short time.

Disencumbered of our gear and the intrusive would-be landlord, we began strolling out of town looking for a camp site. Corinth, we discovered, wasn't a single site like the other ancient places. It was a vast complex of ruin upon ruin and settlement after settlement from ancient Greece, ancient Rome and layers of invaders since. It always amazed us that the excavations were so recent. Since we had heard about these places for years we assumed they'd been dug up for years. Not so, and many times, like here at Corinth the job was far from done.

Just at the outskirts of the small modern settlement we found ruins that weren't fenced in and that were still only partly excavated. We found ourselves at the bottom of what looked to be a Roman circular arena and decided it would make an ideal camp site. We wandered around trying to decipher the Latin inscriptions on the walls, then went back to fetch our things.

We were all excited at being able to actually camp in a ruin. David and the kids started exploring while I began peeling and chopping vegetables for our dinner. They came back as I began cooking over our small one burner stove. The sky was turning a lovely twilight color when some local Greek boys discovered us camping.

They were immediately fascinated but didn't come down to the camp site right away. Up on the walls of the ruins against the purple and orange sky they began to stage a mock battle to show off.

We watched their silhouettes as they used sticks as swords and two groups played at attacking each other. One of the boys had picked up something to use as a shield and defended himself as well as an ancient hero. They could have been Athenians and Spartans battling and we all enjoyed the spectacle.

Finally it ended and they all poured down the slope to invade our campsite for a while. They sat on pieces of ancient columns to watch us get ready for the night until I finally shooed them all home. We reveled in the privacy of a place to ourselves without being the center of attention for a change.

David began to set up the tent when suddenly a gust of wind almost blew it from his hands. There was a sudden crack of thunder and as we looked up a flash of lightning startled us. Down in the bottom of the arena we hadn't seen the storm approaching.

We quickly tossed everything into the tent, hastily rolled it up and, leaving the cook pot behind, dashed to town, ducking into the first cafe we found.

We were just in time for the first drops of rain. The thunder was clamorous. The cafe owner told us all he had was eggs. The children were tired after a long day of travel and our wild run to town.

"Fine, make us eggs," I said.

A group of French and Spanish students came into the cafe. A young Spanish man whom we had run into earlier spoke a few words of English.

"Good, you are here. I go to look for you in ruins when rain comes. You need room now?"

He and his friends also needed a room and leaving behind the tired 17 year old sister of one of the French boys, they all went to look for rooms, for them and us.

I wondered if the cook was waiting for the hen to lay our eggs, it was taking so long, then I realized why he wasn't cooking our dinner. He had decided to take advantage of the men's absence and was insisting the young French girl have some brandy. She was obviously not used to drinking but was politely downing the drinks he kept pouring for her.

Just then our old friend the aggressive man from the bus stop came in and pounced on us.

"It's raining. You need a room. My room is nice and cheap," he said.

"How much?" I asked. He and I bargained and finally settled on a price with the proviso that we had to see it first.

He grabbed David's arm again, "Come now."

I had had it with him. I stood up and pointed to the children, "Not now. My children are hungry. After they eat we will come. Go away now."

Much to my surprise he caved in and left. I was not about to leave until the kids had finally eaten and the students returned to protect the teenager from the sleazy cook.

I finally asked the cook if he was laying the eggs himself and he laughed and made our dinner. While we were eating the students returned to find the girl so drunk she didn't know where she was.

"It's not her fault," I tried to tell the Spanish boy in my dimly remembered high school Spanish so he could let the girl's brother know not to blame her.

We were just taking our last bites when the man with the room appeared again. I had low hopes about this famous room of his but he led us to a house and taking us up a flight of steps opened the door to a charming room. There were embroidered sheets on the three beds, and fresh flowers on a vase on the table.

"Nice room," I said. The man took our money, smiled and then proceeded to remove the sheets and flowers.

"Hey," I started to protest but he pointed to our sleeping bags and left.

I shrugged. It was still a nice room and actually had a shower in the bathroom next door.

The children were so tired they went right to sleep, but we reveled in the luxury of a shower and I did our laundry in the bathroom sink.

In the morning we went back to the ruins and collected our cooking pot, tossing the vegetables down an ancient well.

Before long we were ready to leave. Corinth, in ancient days, had a bad reputation for travelers, starting with Sinis who used to rob them then tie them to bent saplings so they'd be pulled apart until Theseus, another of the children's heroes, gave him a dose of his own medicine. We decided it was still keeping the ancient tradition of the place using visitors as victims.

Chapter 15

Where Shepherds Walk

We were on the road again, exploring the far western edge of the Peloponesus. There simply was no traffic in this part of Greece so we resigned ourselves to riding buses, and even they were few and far between. The roads were rough but we had seen rougher – the road to Vourvoura for example. This was just a less traveled part of the world. We had spent most of the day waiting for buses or riding them, which was like being in a coffin because, of course, the Greeks pulled down all the shades and closed all the windows.

We were regretting having left the pretty beach at the town of Kiafas, west of Olympia, that morning. But on the last bus, the conductor insisted we take the front seats so we could see out. We saw the town of Pylos and instantly wanted to get off. It was a pretty port town, one of the nicest we'd seen.

The conductor wouldn't let us.

"You must go to Methoni. It is much more beautiful. You cannot come here and not see Methoni."

So we followed his advice, actually his orders, and went the extra ten miles. Methoni was not more beautiful but it was well worth the trip.

Here was another place where layers of history intermingled. A huge Venetian fortress built on a Frankish fortress, Methoni fronted the sea, even intruded on it in some places, with walls jutting out. Moats laced parts not protected by the sea. Underneath the ground we walked on were vast cisterns. We lay on our bellies and peered into them through rain holes, finding another world below us of arched caverns. This was literally layers on layers of history.

The Turks had moved in on it and left mosques, in ruins now, and baths. Churches were also intermingled with the ruins but they were in use, lovingly looked after by pious Greeks.

After we spent what was left of the afternoon at Methoni, we tried to get back to Pylos to spend the night. We had been sitting by the roadside about a half hour when a small tractor pulling a trailer came by and the man driving it hailed us. We climbed on thinking he was going back to Pylos since that was the only town in that particular direction, but no, about half way he stopped at a narrow track leading off to the mountains, and dropped us off.

It was too late for a bus and twilight was coming on so we decided to stay where we were.

There was an olive grove of really ancient trees, and at the base of the trees someone had piled freshly cut hay. We made beds out of the fragrant hay and opened our packs.

We had stopped at a store and treated ourselves to a salami. We had bread, water, canned milk for the children and some cognac for ourselves. So we had the makings of a modest feast.

The sky turned orange, then pink, then lavender. Sitting on our aromatic perches we gazed out on a lovely scene. The valley stretched below us to the sea which had turned "wine dark" just as Homer described it. A mountain sloped down to it on one side with a small village on its slopes. Pylos shone its lights by the water.

I made us salami sandwiches, and we sat there perfectly contented. We heard the melodic sound of a herd of belled sheep, and a shepherd walked up.

"*Kali spera, kirios, kiria,*" he said. Good evening, sir, madam. He was a soft spoken man.

"*Kali spera, kathiste, parakalo,*" we greeted him and invited him to sit down. We offered him a salami sandwich. He looked at it curiously then took it gratefully, but he carefully separated the salami from the bread and ate them separately.

A passing farmer with a laden mule saw us all sitting there and came to add bunches of lovely grapes to the meal then waved as he continued on his way. The silence of the evening claimed us again.

David took out the cognac and poured us all a tot in our metal camping cups. The shepherd showed us the direction of his village, determined where we were from, then settled quietly beside us to simply watch the view. We all sat there sipping our cognac as the children settled into sleep and we watched darkness fill the valley. There was nothing to say. The shepherd simply accepted our presence in his world.

This was another time-out-of-mind moment, but this time we all shared it, wordlessly, and it was a sharing of all time and place at once. The sheep had quieted and only broke the silence to cough once in a while. I had never known before we lived in Greece that sheep cough. David took out our tiny flask, and without a word poured us each another finger of cognac.

The stars were shining brightly. It was much later than was normal for a shepherd to be out, but he, too, had been taken by the moment. When our guest finally rose and wished us a good night and good sleep we simply nodded our good-byes. We watched him take his flock back towards his village, and settled back into our hay to count shooting stars before we fell asleep.

Chapter 16

Hollywood Comes to Vourvoura

David was working in the studio down below with two locals looking on as usual. I was upstairs on the balcony writing letters while Yorghia and a friend of hers were looking through our belongings, a favorite pastime of theirs. Heather and Davidaki were playing in the courtyard with some village children. Except for an occasional donkey sobbing it was a quiet afternoon.

Suddenly the peace was shattered when a truck covered with lurid posters and bearing a blaring loudspeaker burst upon the village. The girls became very animated, running through the house and clapping hands and jumping up and down. David went into the courtyard and called up to me.

"Yiannis and Panayotis say there are movies tonight."

"Movies?" I was puzzled.

'Yeah, they even said Hollywood or something close to it. That's what the truck is all about."

Yorghia and her friend assured me it was so. The truck went back and forth on the main road for a half hour making announcements I probably couldn't have understood if they were in English; the loudspeaker was set so high it got everything garbled.

That evening the whole town turned out. The larger shop had been turned into a theater for the event. All the chairs in town had been confiscated, carried in and set in rows. Someone had hung a sheet at one end of the shop to use as a screen. Greek sheets were always striped, and this one was no exception, being yellow and white, but no one seemed to mind. The truck parked outside the shop door and using a generator so loud it almost drowned out the film the entrepreneur showed the movie that everyone in town, even the hard working women had paid a few drachmae per head to see.

Poli and I had become fast friends and I sat next to her as she held her new little daughter on her lap. She explained what was happening when I couldn't follow the dialogue. Then I turned to David and the kids to explain in whispers to them. The kids filled us in on some of the dialogue since their Greek was so much better than ours. It was a Greek dowry tragedy full of pathos and repressed sexuality.

Every so often a technical difficulty would develop and while the operator took care of it the oil lamps were lit and people bought wine for each other as they chatted about the film. The shop keeper was beaming at us all.

At one point in the film a couple was expecting a baby. The male lead asked the expectant father if he wanted a boy or a girl and the whole village burst into laughter. Nobody wanted a girl because that meant the family had to come up with the "prika", the all-important dowry, to get rid of her.

The film was scratched and the sound was off a little at times but everyone cheered and clapped loudly when the right couple finally got together.

We left for home, Poli walking with us part way.

"Next year he will be back. I hope he has a different film next time. I almost know this one by heart," she said as we parted ways.

"You've seen it before?"

"For three years now it has been the same film," Poli laughed "But no matter. It is nice to see a movie."

Chapter 17

War Scars

On one of our hikes outside the village we had come across a huge obelisk, obviously not an ancient one. The highly polished column had a plaque at its base but it was in Kathourevesa, the official Greek used by government officials and lawyers, a wholly different language, taught to the children as a second language beginning in third or fourth grade. We couldn't read it but asked about it when we got back to the village.

People clearly didn't like talking about it, but Louis clued us in finally.

"In the war with the Germans, some partisans captured a general then traded him for prisoners. For reprisals, the Germans then came and took boys from fifteen years old. They took fifteen hundred children from all these villages and where you saw the monument, they shot them."

We were horrified, and stayed well away from the monument from then on. In one of the tavernas we had seen photos of the owner when he was a young man being herded into a cage by a Nazi soldier along with some other men. We never found out who took the picture as no one in the village except us had a camera, but the owner told us he had spent two years in a prison then escaped.

"Partisan," he said proudly striking his chest. Then he looked downcast. "Before EOKA."

We had read that some partisan groups, particularly the powerful EOKA had been taken over by communists who then launched a civil war after the Nazis were conquered. Allied air power was lent to the other side and communists were forced to flee into communist states to the north. To be sure they weren't bombed the communists kidnapped 50,000 Greek children to mingle among themselves. Those children never saw their families again. Communists were not popular anywhere in Greece after that, so we understood the proprietor's desire to separate himself from them.

It mirrored our desire to not be mistaken for Germans as we traveled around. Feelings still ran deep, although younger Germans seemed to be perfectly charming travelers.

Once we were walking down a street in the city of Nauplia. Some men standing in the doorways nearby saw us and one commented to another as we passed, "Germans."

David wheeled around and said in perfect Greek, "We are not Germans. We are Americans."

The men looked at us in utter amazement, not only Americans, but Americans speaking Greek. They grabbed the children and beckoned for us to come inside the house. We were trying to catch a bus but they had our children so we followed. One man called out loudly to his wife and we were promptly served coffee and sweets. In the meantime another one of the men had taken off and returned with his whole family and half the neighborhood it seemed.

"You must stay for a party. We will have a big feast."

We thanked them politely but told them we had to catch our bus. Someone went out to find a friend who had a car to drive us to the bus stop. As we picked up our things and loaded them into the little pick-up truck they had found, all our new friends called out farewells and begged us to come back and stay for a visit.

Once when we were in a small city, we watched a group of older Germans take over a sidewalk cafe, claiming all the tables, one to a person and lining them up in a row so they could sit side by side and shout to each other loudly and happily and they peremptorily ordered around the cafe owner, who kept wringing his hands. Finally a younger man, the man's son, came out and told them to leave.

We sat at one of the tables when they were put back where the owner wanted them and the younger man told us his father had been a prisoner of the Germans in the war, and said he refused to see them distress his father any more.

We came back and told Thia about it and Thia cackled then told us that the German commander for the area, the one who had ordered the execution of the children, had taken over this very house for his quarters while he was in the village, and had stayed in our room because, at the time, like now, it was the grandest in the village. Until our arrival, he had been the only foreigner to visit the village.

David and I looked at each other in dismay, but Thia only laughed at us.

"No ghosts," she assured us.

But we weren't so sure.

Chapter 18

Estrangement and Reconciliation

It seemed like we were having a tempestuous affair with Vourvoura. We kept loving it, becoming estranged from it, and reconciling again. Absence definitely made our hearts, and those of the villagers, grow fonder for each other each time we left and then returned. We kept finding new treasures in the village that both delighted and horrified us.

One day when the skies were especially full of interesting clouds, we decided to take a picnic lunch to the top of the hill outside of town where the graveyard and a weather-beaten old church stood next to a stand of gloomy evergreens.

We had already learned some of the customs associated with death. There were regular celebrations, some a few weeks after a death, some a few months, others a few years later when the women would boil up whole kernels of wheat with sugar and bits of dried fruit. They'd take a basket of this death wheat and wander through the village handing out paper cones of it to everyone they saw, even going from door to door to distribute it. Since our arrival we had eaten the delicious wheat of a number of deceased we didn't know but whose generosity we appreciated.

I had read, and Thia had confirmed, that when someone died they were only buried for three years. After that, their bones were dug up, consecrated in a special ceremony and the grave emptied for the next occupant. I thought that was a practical arrangement considering how small Greece was, with so little arable land, and how many thousands of years it had been around. Without it they might not have any land left for the living to feed themselves.

I asked what was done with the bones, expecting to hear they were cremated but was told simply, "The boneyard."

I was puzzled. The boneyard to me was a dominoes term for turned over dominoes. But I didn't inquire further.

The view from the graveyard at the highest peak in town was spectacular. We roamed around after we ate our bread and cheese looking at the graves. Many had little glass-fronted compartments that held photos of the most recent deceased. At one grave I almost cried because there was a photo of a little boy and a little plastic truck, obviously a treasured toy. David and I looked at it for a long time and explained it to the children, who were taken aback and became very solemn.

We were so intently interested in looking at the graves we hadn't noticed one of the more ominous looking clouds had crept up on us. Suddenly there was a crack of thunder of another sudden mountain storm. David and I were alarmed. We were on a very high hill and not at all sure there was a lightning rod anywhere around. There was a doorway and steps leading down below the church. As rain suddenly began pouring down, we fled down the steps through an old open door.

We gazed out at the downpour then turned to see where we were. It was very dark and having learned to always carry matches, we lit one and found a candle stump next to the door. We lit it and turned to look, and I screamed. All around us were bones and human skulls. We had found the village boneyard.

After I calmed down, we saw that in amongst the human remains people had casually tossed trash, like orange peels and old paper. The bones were also just casually tossed, and if we could get in, so could rats and other animals. Rain or no rain, lightning or no lightning, I insisted we get out of there and the children agreed. We ran all the way home, arriving drenched as the rain stopped and rainbows formed over Vourvoura.

My heart settled down to a normal rhythm but we never revisited the graveyard or boneyard. Another day Soteria told me we were invited to go to the school for a special program. David was working on a tricky bit of sculpture so I just went.

The program seemed for the most part to be a boring recitation of poems and texts the children had memorized. I was charmed when the children who had won some sort of awards were crowned with laurel wreaths just as in ancient times, but I was horrified at the behavior of the adults as the program commenced.

They not only talked and laughed all through the children's performances, but when kids stumbled or were nervous, they jeered at them.

One little boy who couldn't take sitting still so long was spanked and yelled at loudly, but there was no attempt to remove him. Things reached a pitch for me when a little girl, obviously suffering from stage fright was jeered at so rudely she fled the stage in tears. Despite the childish behavior of the adults and noise, the program doggedly went on. I didn't know whether to feel sorrier for the kids or the teacher.

I went home in a towering rage.

"How could they be so rude to their own children?" I ranted to David.

"Different pipes," he began to say but I would have none of it.

"Different pipes, different schnipes. I don't give a damn. That was just plain cruel."

David let me vent for a while and then suggested we go to Delphi. It was time for another trip. Time to build some affection for Vourvoura again and get over my quarrel with the place I was learning to love.

Chapter 19

Gypsy Child

The ferry to Delphi was freshly painted and modern looking. That was a nice surprise after the battered old boats we had seen in other ports and we were alone when we first went to the top deck. We chose a bench up there in the shade and settled down with the children. Older Greeks usually avoided the top deck because they did not like the sun and the younger ones did likewise because the wind messed their pomaded hair, so we hoped to have it to ourselves. However, we were not so lucky; we were suddenly engulfed by a wave of French-speaking tourists.

We could not help staring at them. By this time we had been in Greece long enough we expected the women to wear sedate clothing, especially women of retirement age as these were, and the men to act with the quiet dignity of the Greeks. These people were loud.

The women, even an unusually obese one, wore skirts so short we could see their underpants. The men carried cameras, wore shorts and brightly flowered sports shirts. They all could have been in Hawaii. They were all freshly scrubbed and smelled of soaps and colognes which was a nice change from people smelling of feta cheese and goats as they did in Vourvoura. I began wondering uneasily if I smelled of feta cheese and goats. I stared at these exotic people much as the mountain people had stared at us.

The French were shouting and giggling and making what were obviously risqué remarks to each other as the women kept coyly slapping at the men. They were thoroughly enjoying themselves. They had bags and bags of snack foods, something we hadn't seen in ages. We had not had time for lunch before we caught the boat and were very hungry. Heather and Davidaki looked longingly at the goodies; we promised them a meal on the other side of the bay.

One of the women spoke a few words of English and came to us to say hello. We smiled back politely.

The boat sounded its whistle and we were off. A couple of the Frenchmen clutched at their stomachs comically and pretended to run for the rail with their hands over their mouths. Heather and Davidaki thought this was funny. The French ladies did, too. They held their sides and roared with laughter.

We were just out of port when a Gypsy girl about ten years old came up from the lower deck. It was easy to tell the Gypsies from the Greeks. Not only were they usually swarthier and their features a little different from Mediterranean types, but the bright ragged clothing was a dead giveaway. They also spoke with a heavy guttural accent. Besides, this little girl was filthy. She wasn't simply dirty as children get when they've been playing outside a while; she wore a carefully cultivated coat of dirt that had been weeks in collecting. She also had the unmistakable proud carriage of a Gypsy.

This time the French people stared. I had assumed there must be Gypsies in France, but if so they kept a low profile. The tourists made much of her. They tried to communicate with her in French and she laughed at their strange sounds. They were charmed. They offered her some of their food and she turned up her nose, although Heather and Davidaki looked on enviously.

She was interested in the children and came up to us. I said hello in Greek and she answered. We started a polite conversation. The French tourists turned on us. A heavy set pompous looking man whose authoritative air clashed oddly with his tight shorts and sunburned knees, instructed the woman who spoke some English to act as an interpreter to us who in turn were supposed to translate what they said into Greek for the girl. I didn't care much for the arrangement, neither did the girl. The woman didn't like it either as her English wasn't that good I asked a girl a few questions which she answered with a toss of her head. I told the woman, to her relief, I would not translate as it was useless.

The girl had grown bored with the whole thing by this time and she climbed on top of the canvas cover of a life boat. The Frenchman wasn't through with her, though. He talked with gestures and tried many times to get her to eat something. He took some pictures, which she didn't seem to mind.

We were in the middle of the bay when a sudden rain shower hit us. The French became quite animated, running for shelter under the awning, shouting to each other, and bustling everywhere with their bags of food. The Gypsy girl sat unperturbed on the life boat letting the rain pour over her, getting a little clean.

The Frenchman was most upset when he noticed her. He gesticulated, wanting her to get down and come under the awning with the rest of them. She laughed showing all her beautiful teeth, none of which were gold yet. He then went so far as to offer her money to get down. I knew that wouldn't work, remembering it was against their religion to do anything for wages. She tossed back her head and clicked her tongue in the Greek manner of saying no. When he persisted she hissed at him like an angry cat. He gave it up.

The rain ended as suddenly as it began and a rainbow formed off to our stern. The French all crowded the rail and looked at it smugly as though it had been especially produced for them. The remainder of the trip was uneventful except that the Frenchman kept trying to lure the girl down with chocolate bars.

We were near the harbor below Delphi when suddenly the girl leaped down. She went to each of the tourists in turn saying, "Give me money."

They turned to me to interpret. "She wants money."

They began obediently shelling out. The Frenchman made one last effort to exert his will and offered her money if she'd let him take her picture with some of the others. She spat on the deck and turned away. He finally had to pursue her to give her his money.

Then he went to the "interpreter" and demanded something from her. The woman came to me and told me to tell the girl to say thank you. I looked at her nonplussed. She wanted a Gypsy to thank her? Not only was that probably against their religion, too, but surely it was obvious that money was the least thing they could do for the girl after she had put up with them so patiently. I told the woman it would do no good. The woman insisted. So I shrugged and grinning told the child what they wanted. She threw back her head and laughed.

Then she came and asked us for money. I was offended, not because I was unwilling to give her money, but because she had put us in the same category as the tourists. I looked at her evenly and said, "No."

She flashed her beautiful smile and then disappeared below deck. We all went below and I saw the girl join up with her large family. The French people gaped at the family with all their bundles. The Greeks below gaped at the tourists. We went ashore.

There was a carefully tended lawn in front of a seaside cafe where tables with colorful umbrellas had been artistically arranged. We sat at one to order our hungry children something to eat at last. We weren't very happy when all the French tourists came and sat at the tables next to us They noisily shoved a bunch of tables together while the cafe proprietor looked on in distress. Evidently they were still hungry despite all their snacking.

Just then the Gypsy family came by. The French all started calling out to the girl and waving. She just ignored them. The last child straggling at the end of the entourage, a boy about six or seven years old, suddenly stopped, ran over until he was right in front of the French group and dropped his pants. Squatting briefly he defecated on the lawn, then casually pulled up his pants and strolled on. The French tourists were at last speechless. Not so the cafe owner who chased the family shaking a fist angrily. They kept walking and ignored him. The French tourists didn't even notice. They were all staring at the steaming turd on the bright lawn.

Chapter 20

Gal Friday

I made a new friend when Paraskevi came to town for a vacation. Paraskevi translated to Friday but it seemed to be an accepted woman's name. I was charmed by knowing a real gal Friday. Paraskevi was living in Australia, working hard at some menial job. She had traveled home ostensibly to visit her mother but also in hopes of finding a husband.

Her English was very sketchy so we spoke a mixture of both languages, and each of us practiced our skills on each other having agreed to correct each other. What Paraskevi had besides some knowledge of English, was exposure to another way of life. It made the other villagers view her with suspicion and her search for a mate was not going well.

"I come here with dowry I earn myself in Australia, but no good. Men here think I not a virgin because I go to Australia," she explained to me sadly.

"What about a man in Australia?" I asked.

"Greek man in Australia come here to find wife. Get one with dowry who will listen to them. I am daughter number seven in family. No *prika*, dowry."

The next time we visited with Louis I mentioned Paraskevi's dilemma.

"Yes, it is sad. She is a good person. But also she is skinny broad," Louis, with the best of intentions, always called women broads after having learned his English in the Chicago streets. "Greek men like some meat on the bones. If she was more beautiful perhaps someone marry her even with a small dowry and Australia. It is good she has you for a friend here. The villagers think this is very nice. She is now more important. Maybe someone will take notice."

Paraskevi and I took to meeting at the shops in the afternoon and ordering coffees for ourselves, alternating our patronage between the two shops in town. We'd sit outside at one of the tables to advertise our activity. This thrilled the shopkeepers who thought it the most sophisticated thing to have happened to their establishments ever. They always insisted their wives bring out cookies and sweets from the family kitchens to serve to us with our thimble sized cups of muddy coffee. Frequently they refused to charge us for our coffee.

Paraskevi was resigning herself to spinsterhood because of the stubborn male attitudes of her fellow villagers. Once she reminisced fondly.

"When I was born, daughter seven, and no sons, my father took me on his lap and sat in front of the house singing to me. The neighbor said to him, 'Why you sing, with one more dowry to find and no son to help?' And my father said to him, 'I sing because I have beautiful baby girl.' My mother and the neighbors tell me this many times," she told me proudly.

"I like your father," I replied.

"Me, too, but is dead now," she said sadly.

Paraskevi had her eye on a Greek fellow who had appeared briefly in the village also vacationing from Australia. She tried to get close to him during the festival dances but after less than two weeks he left after having betrothed one of the village girls.

"You see?" Paraskevi said. "Me he knows for five years in Australia. Her he knows not at all. Her dowry is bigger than what I have saved."

The all-important dowry seemed barbaric to me until Louis explained that it is the woman's share of the family inheritance but given at marriage instead of at the death of family head.

"And then the sons inherit what is left?"

"Yes. The men will divide the land and money into lots. Then they put the lots on pieces of paper into a hat and draw one out. That way it is fair."

"And the girls get a dowry instead?"

"Yes. The sons cannot marry until the sisters have dowries. They must help because some day they will get their share. The mother keeps the dowry she brought with her when the husband dies."

"Seems logical when you describe it, but it is so tragic when something like this, where there are no sons, happens."

"Or when the sons do not work for a dowry," Louis began to laugh. "In Athens if you walk the streets you can hear broads complaining to their fathers that their brothers are drinking away their dowries in the tavernas."

"Different pipes," David concluded. It had become our shorthand for cultural differences.

Chapter 21

The Mani

The bus was very crowded. The shades were drawn closed against the noonday sun and the windows were closed shut despite the heat to keep out the dust. Heather amused herself by playing with a set of worry beads we had bought her for her birthday. Greek men all played with the little bracelets of beads when they sat outside the shops and cafes, tossing them casually and with dexterity. The idea was that they were calming.

A young man standing in the aisle beside her smiled then broke into a popular song, "I'm going to turn in my watch for a set of worry beads and then just count my troubles." Others joined in the singing, and we all laughed.

The bus pulled up at a large treeless square in the center of Kalamata. The heat was staggering. Our first impression of Kalamata was bleak. Plain-fronted, flat-roofed houses and shops lined the streets in an unbroken line. No plants softened the stark lines. We took our back packs and asked the way to the sea. Someone pointed it out but warned that it was more than a kilometer away, and that there were no buses during the siesta time of day. There was no shady spot to wait out the heat in the square. Nothing was open during the hot mid-day. We were hoping to camp on the beach that night and were longing for a cool swim, so we promised the kids lemonades at a cafe enroute and set off.

We regretted the decision a while later. The road was a long, wide avenue with absolutely no shade and not a soul in sight, not even a dog. We walked a good three kilometers and still could not find the sea or a cafe. Everything was sealed behind iron or wood shutters. Heather and Davidaki were beginning to complain loudly, our backs were sore and our water canteens were empty. Finally we saw a tree in the distance and encouraged by the promise of shade and rest we hurried on.

The tree was at the sea's edge. We had reached a broad esplanade. A wide beach with trees planted at the sidewalk's edge framed the brilliant blue sea. We sank down in the shade, exhausted but relieved. Just then a group of men in business suits emerged from an office building next to us. One of the men asked politely if we were lost. David answered no.

"Are you Americans?" one of the men asked eagerly.

"Yes."

"Please wait here," he said urgently. "Don't go away. I'll be right back."

We were puzzled but not about to go away until we had rested anyway. The man concluded his business with his colleagues rapidly for he reappeared in just a few minutes. In perfect English he invited us into his office for some cold refreshments.

"Lemonade?" the kids asked eagerly.

"If you like," he smiled.

He told us his name was Soteris and he had an American friend he would like us to meet. We sat gratefully in the office that held three desks and was cooled by an electric fan. Our welcome lemonades arrived, fetched by someone from a cafe somewhere in the neighborhood that Soteris could magically open at will. While we sipped the lemonade David explained we were looking for a place to set up camp. Soteris told us firmly that we were not to worry about where we would spend the night, and then asked us where we were traveling.

"To the area called the Mani," David replied.

"The Mani! But this is wonderful," he said to our great surprise.

Most of our friends and neighbors had attempted to discourage us from taking the trip. The Mani was a section of Greece famous for its poverty. We had read of it in Patrick Lee Fermer's book "The Mani" and were determined to see it. The Maniots' constant feuding, as well as their mountainous, isolated location made them poor. They were considered unfriendly people if not downright hostile. We wanted to see the area because of its architecture.

Through the ages they had built themselves siege towers for homes because of the internecine wars. In ancient days they would try to build one story higher than their neighbors so they could launch boulders through the roof. Of, course, the neighbors would try to get higher and so the towers grew. Then guns and cannons were invented and the Maniots almost wiped each other out. Some of the towers were supposed to be spectacular.

There were few roads leading down into the Mani and none at all in the area called the Deep Mani. Even Louis thought we were foolish to want to visit it. Soteris' attitude was a pleasant change.

"My grandparents were born in the Mani, although I have never lived there," Soteris told us. "My American friend has been there several times. He will be able to tell you all about it."

This was unbelievable luck, as no one we knew had ever been there. We left the office and followed Soteris a few blocks along the seashore and found a young man sitting in a swim suit at a cafe table set out in the sand.

"Richard, please take care of these people for me until I close the office. Do not let them want for anything," Soteris said after introducing us. He apologized for still having business that needed his attention. Richard ordered us more cool drinks. He was short, stocky and blond. He was also very sunburned.

We spent the afternoon swimming, eating fried marithes, the tiny fish we had had just a couple times in Vourvoura, drinking lemonade and getting to know Richard. He had a small income from savings in the States and had moved to Kalamata. He rented a small apartment from Soteris's family, all of whom were now like relatives.

Later that afternoon Soteris and his fiancee Soula joined us. While Soteris was graying and bit dumpy, Soula was tall, stately, and very beautiful with flashing black eyes. In true Greek fashion Soteris was not married yet even though he was middle-aged because he still had unmarried sisters at home. No Greek male married until the women were safely dowried and wedded off. It was hard on the older brothers who had many younger sisters.

We went out to dinner at a busy corner restaurant and then Soteris insisted on taking us to an English speaking movie. The theater was set up outdoors on the roof of a building. Instead of popcorn, vendors sold roasted ears of field corn that they grilled over charcoal braziers. Heather and Davidaki were thrilled by the novelty of the experience and by being allowed to stay up late.

The film was a Wyatt Earp western with Greek subtitles. At one point a drunken Doc Holliday was fetched from a poker game in the saloon to tend a wounded man, and spotting a bottle of whiskey on the dresser he poured himself a glass and raised it to the wounded man and said, "To your health." That brought down the house.

We slept at Richard's place, which he turned over to us while he stayed at Soteris's mother's house. It was a simple one bedroom apartment that seemed luxurious to us after all our camping. It had a small kitchenette that Richard seldom used as he took most meals with Soteris' family. Soteris mother, now a widow, was clearly very fond of Richard, and since she enjoyed spending her days cooking, it was no trouble cooking extra for him. She took her apron off her ample form to greet us effusively. We, too, had become part of the family.

We spent three or four days lingering in Kalamata, seeing the sights of the town and learning all about it from Soteris and his family, swimming and exchanging tales of life in Greece with Richard. Both Richard and Soteris were greatly interested in our life in Vourvoura. They wanted to know all about Thia, Louis and the others.

"This is village life as I have never seen it," Soteris said.

Soteris told us he had been the mayor of Kalamata until the colonels took over. The current mayor that the colonels had installed was a laughing stock in town because he was missing both his ears.

"Missing his ears?" I asked puzzled.

Richard explained that if a man has an affair with a married woman the cuckholded husband took revenge by cutting off an ear of the lover. The usual setting for such attacks was a movie theater when the husband could stealthily sit behind the man. The Greeks had no respect for womanizers, considering it less than manly behavior (although womanizers definitely abounded in Athens), thus the reason the earless mayor was treated with such contempt.

Soteris was the only Greek we had met besides Louis who was willing to discuss politics in his own country. He hated the new government. Heather, whom all the Greeks called Alexandra, her middle name, was told that her name was the same as the Greek princess, and therefore made her very popular. She beamed.

Soteris also told us about Kalamata, including the story of how the Kalamatiano became the national dance.

"The men had gone to fight the Turks. They were all massacred but one boy escaped to run back here and tell the women that the Turks were coming to rape and murder them. Rather than wait for death, the women took their children and on the cliff over the sea, they danced the Kalamatiano. Two steps one way, three the other until every last one had danced off the cliff to their deaths."

I never again danced the Kalamatiano without thinking of the story. No Greek does either.

The cathedral in Kalamata is famous for its efficacy in bringing men safely home from wars. The only condition attached was that the woman praying for her man had to crawl the half mile up hill to it on her knees, and then leave her wedding ring at the icon as a pledge. We went to see it and were amazed at the strings and strings of wedding rings hung all over the front end of the cathedral. I wondered if the women could reclaim them if the men did not return, or if that many had come back through the centuries. Soteris told us his mother had made the pilgrimage during World War II for his father and on his father's return he had bought her a new ring. The steep tree-lined boulevard looked formidable. I couldn't imagine Soteris' plump mother doing that. I couldn't imagine myself doing it on my knees. But then, I looked fondly at my husband. My man was not off at war. I might change my mind if he were.

Soteris had memories of the war as a child.

"There wasn't much food. When the Italians occupied us they used to share their food with me. Then the Germans came, and one day an Italian was handing me his metal plate of food and a German officer kicked it out of his hand scattering the food in the dust."

Maybe because of the war scars, we learned that food was important in Kalamata, and Soteris was eager for us to learn the delights of Greek cuisine that weren't available in the village.

He took us out to dinner every night and ordered for us, insisting we sample everything. Since Kalamata was a sea port the sea food was plentiful.

"Here, try this," he passed us some of his dish.

"This is delicious. What is it?"

"Kalamarakia yemista - stuffed squid."

"How do you make it?"

"Come, let us ask the cook," he laughed and so we went and asked.

As we all cemented our friendship, Richard was laboriously drawing maps for us of the paths in the Mani, and he told us which were the most beautiful villages. He also told us about a secret special spot.

"There's a cove with a spring and a cave. Kazantakis lived in the cave for two years while he wrote Zorba."

"But I thought he wrote it in Crete."

"No. His family was Cretan, most of the Maniots are by origin. But actually the events in Zorba took place in the Mani. The lignite mine in the book is up in the hills behind the cove."

The lignite mine figured hugely in the book. Zorba was supposed to be a mining expert, but in reality knew nothing about it.

Finally, early one morning we said good-bye to Soteris, his mother, Soula and Richard as well as the cosmopolitan pleasures we had enjoyed in Kalamata, and set off for the Mani.

We took buses as far as we could. The road wound through miles of dry dusty olive groves glinting in the sun at first, then the landscape turned into just rocky barren country. We got off at the end and walked to the cove Richard had mapped out for us. In the middle of the dry land it was a little paradise with its spring, wildflowers, white sand and blue water. Kazantakis's cave proved to be a roomy place with a dry sandy floor and a low stone wall partitioning it. It looked out over the sea. There was no need to set up our tent; the cave was comfortable shelter enough. We stayed in the little Eden a couple days before setting off for the Deep Mani.

There was a rocky track along which an old truck made a weekly run to a little sea port. We were fortunate enough to get a ride on it. We stayed in the port overnight, camping at the edge of town on the rocky beach. As we were leaving I pointed at a boat tied up to the small dock. Women were unloading dirt from it in their aprons. I asked someone what they were doing.

"For the graveyard," was the gruff answer. David and I looked at each other in shock. They were so poor they had to import dirt to bury their dead.

As we walked out of the village, the Mani, at first, did not seem that different than the rest of Greece, except that it was more barren and the houses were all three stories high. But as the hours went by and we penetrated the Mani deeper we could see it was unique. We saw people eating prickly pear fruit for their main meal. It wasn't prepared in any way that was visible, just plain, cut up prickly pears.

When we saw a rare fig or olive tree even its shade was fenced in with stone and thorn barricades. Alarmingly, all the men carried guns, rifles slung over their shoulders. I remembered reading that the Maniots called a newborn boy baby a "new gun". Even more disconcerting, people avoided us for the first time in Greece.

We had walked all day when we came across a woman in a long black dress sitting on a wall with a child. We asked if we were following the path that led to the sea. Her eyes wide with fear, she grabbed the child, hid it in her shawl and spat three times, the ritual for warding off the evil eye. She crossed herself. Upset, I said, "May it live for us," the standard response to anyone concerning a child and another charm against the evil eye. She still stared at us wordlessly in fear.

"What if she goes and tells her village that devils are out here in the fields and they decide to get rid of us?" David worried. We both remembered the rifles.

It was getting dark now so we found an empty field. David was still concerned and wanted to ask permission to sleep in the field from someone, anyone, since even the shade was fenced in this hostile land.

Just then an old woman on a donkey came riding by. I called to her to ask if we could sleep in the field. She cackled insanely and then reached into her pocket to pelt us with something. It turned out to be dried figs. It was the most hospitable gesture we had earned from a Maniot. We took the figs as a yes and had a cold supper out of cans. Neither of us slept well, although the children were dead to the world. During the night we heard howling on the hillsides. Richard had told us there were wolves in the Mani but we had laughed at him, sure they were dogs. We weren't laughing now. Later two feral cats came and fought each other for the empty cans we had set aside from our meal for burial in the morning

At dawn we considered our situation. Our friends had been right to warn us away from the Mani, we decided. But we were just a short distance away from a village that Richard had described as the best example of Mani architecture - Vatheia. We decided to go that far. Our supplies were running low and we were sure we'd find a shop of some sort where we could get some food at Vatheia. We hiked for an hour and saw it at the crest of a hill. Its towers soared six and seven stories into the air.

"It looks like New York," I gasped.

The towers showed the ravages of the Maniots' insane warfare as we approached. They had fired cannons at each other from opposite ends of the village generations before and the holes still gaped, unrepaired. Not one tower was undamaged.

Expecting a large and busy place from the size of it we climbed the hill to the village. It was almost a ghost town. The few people stared at us as we walked by but without the friendly curiosity of the other Greeks. We saw tables outside a house, a sure sign of a wineshop or cafe, and knocked on the doors. It was locked. After repeated attempts at rousing someone a voice clearly called from inside, "Go away."

We turned and saw an old woman. I asked where we could find a shop. She turned on us screeching.

"You cannot come here and not bring food. There is no food here. Go back where you came from and buy food!"

She ranted on, the other townspeople gathered around and punctuated her tirade with agreeing nods. We apologized and hastily left, heading back immediately to the little sea port as fast as we could.

It was a long hungry walk, but we had seen all we wanted to see of the Deep Mani.

We were delighted to find the little truck still at the port. It had needed repairs which were just finished. We made arrangements to leave on it in the morning. We went to a little cafe where the only thing for sale to eat was string beans. They tasted just fine. The store keeper insisted on putting us up for the night. He showed us to a room in a Maniot tower, a cannon hole for a window.

At first we thought we had met a Maniot who was as hospitable as other Greeks, but during the night, after he was clearly drunk he tried to break into our room, with rape on his mind. David and I didn't sleep but sat against the door, scared but determined, with our backs and back packs barricading us inside. We got up before the storekeeper woke and climbed into the truck at dawn.

We wanted to stay at our cave again, but without a way to replenish our supplies we had to make our way home. I wanted to rest up in Kalamata, but David felt Soteris and his mother had been hospitable enough and voted for us heading back to Vourvoura.

Chapter 22

After They've Seen Pareeee......

Our delivery truck took us to where we could catch a bus north. Our heads were crammed with mixed impressions, the primitive Mani, like stepping into Europe a thousand years ago, and where the people were hostile, juxtaposed against cosmopolitan Kalamata, where life was easy and the people relaxed and warmly welcoming. We were taking all of this back to Vourvoura with us.

The bus stopped in Sparta. The kids, so disappointed at our not going back to Kalamata, were happy when we decided to stop in Sparta and do some more exploring. Sparta was a lovely city with two boulevards lined with palm trees and flowers crossing it. People were friendly and welcomed us despite our bedraggled appearance after a few weeks camping, the last bit in the Mani where water was too rare to spend on frivolities like laundry or shaving. We asked the way to the "*archaia*", the ancient part of the city, hoping to see the ruins of the warriors' city state.

The ruins had hardly been excavated at all and columns and sculpture were scattered throughout a very old olive grove. We found a few square feet where some column bases had been dug out. The pile of excavated dirt made the only place free of thorns or rocks. We decided to pitch our tent there. We had hoped for a public fountain to use to refresh ourselves by bathing and washing our clothes, but no such luck.

We strolled into town to visit the museum and buy our dinner. We found a comfortable looking restaurant and went into the kitchen to pick out what we wanted for dinner – the usual practice in small towns where menus were considered superfluous. While we were eating some wonderful stuffed tomatoes, who should show up but a man who introduced himself as Taki, Yorgo's brother, Thia's other great-nephew. He had seen us in a cafe and recognized us by descriptions.

He wanted to instantly take us to his house. I was appalled. We all looked far too grubby to meet the gentrified part of the family. We successfully begged off because the children had to go sleep and we had left our things at the ruins. He only accepted our refusal because we promised to meet him at the same cafe the next day in the afternoon.

We went back to camp and strolled around the ancient olive trees. David found a piece of marble sculpture that had grown up with a tree. The tree trunk had gnarled itself around the male head and torso about a foot and a half in length and made it an inextricable part of the tree. It was a remarkable piece of sculpture and a remarkable mingling of ancient and contemporary Greece - a magic bit of alchemy close to where we'd be sleeping.

We tried to communicate the magic of it to our now sleepy children, then tucked them into their sleeping bags and sat beside them in the Sparta nightfall, musing over the wonders of all we had seen from the fierce Mani to citified Kalamata, literally just a day's walk for a determined hiker from Kazantzakis' cave, and, now, Sparta, so gentle, despite its warlike history. Ferocity and peacefulness wrapped around each other here in this ancient grove where the statue and tree were now one.

We went to sleep and I was very put out the next morning because not one of us had had any dreams of ancient Greece.

"Here of all places, after all we've been through. How could we not?"

"Maybe we were too tired," my sweet husband comforted me.

After a stop for breakfast in town we caught a bus to Mystra just outside of town.

Mystra was impressive. It had been a Byzantine university town and was still laced with churches, schools, large houses and a nunnery. The latter was still in use, populated by sour faced, unpleasant nuns. We had yet to meet a cheerful Orthodox nun. I mused that they were all originally from the Mani where everyone was grouchy.

The buildings were largely in ruins, burned skeletons reaching for the sky except for the churches which had been restored. But the ruins were so well preserved and so much more recent than so many others we had seen that they seemed miraculous to us. The Turks had considered Mystra a hotbed of rebellion and burned it out, so it seemed the churches were a form of defiance.

We saw the cathedral and started to go inside, but saw a man so deeply into his devotions, his head was touching the floor. We motioned the children to be quiet and then tiptoed back out so as not to disturb him.

By this time David was having a rare attack of indigestion. He was clearly uncomfortable on the bus ride back to town. Neither of us was especially happy about meeting Taki and family in our present state of dishabille. The Greeks had trained us too well to be comfortable with putting forth any less than a respectable appearance. I suggested we leave a note at the cafe for Taki and tell him we'd be back in two weeks to visit the family, and that we just go home to Vourvoura.

We hitched a ride on a truck and David's stomach immediately began feeling better. There were two German students hitch hiking on the same truck who started a conversation with us. One was militant and was honestly perplexed at why Europe wouldn't let his country make guns or rockets. I felt like taking him to the obelisk for the dead Greek boys, but held my tongue. The other one was a sweet man who practiced his English on the children. The kids had learned to speak precisely and slowly when someone wanted to do that.

When the driver let us off on the road that led to Vourvoura he asked if David was the one making the "big head", clearly meaning the oversized bust David was working on. He was pleased to learn he was, and we marveled at the way news spread in Greece.

The bust had apparently developed a wide reputation. Back in the States people had surprised to learn the classic white statues from ancient Greece had originally been painted by the artists. We had to laugh and agreed they should have just asked the modern Greeks about it because one of the questions David was always asked when someone showed up from another village to see the wonder was "When are you going to paint it?".

Back at home in Vourvoura I realized we had become spoiled by the Kalamataianos and Spartans. Despite the warm welcome at first, neither of us could just rest or relax. No one in the family except Athena was able to speak in a normal tone of voice and shouted at each other and us even when just a foot apart. It grated on me.

Soteria and Thia fussed at me while I was trying to cook for us because I was cooking "wrong". While I tried to wash our clothes, someone took the washtub and then they shouted at me because I was taking too long to bathe and they wanted to dump the load of winter wood in the backyard.

It took us all about three days to adjust back. Then Adonis, with his bad back, came to ask if David could help him saw the winter wood.

David welcomed the chance to help out Adonis, whom he liked very much. He not only began sawing it with a vengeance, but split it, too. This overwhelmed Adonis who ran out to get a jug of wine to keep feeding to David as he worked. David didn't like to drink while he worked but couldn't refuse.

Each day, as he chopped the wood, Thia flustered and began cooking for us all. She interrupted David several times a day to feed him tomato salad, cheese, or other treats. In a week, David had cut, split and stacked all the wood the family would need the rest of the year. He loved physical labor and hadn't minded at all, in fact, welcomed the chance to do something for the family that had so welcomed, even if imprisoned, us. He became the town hero and Adonis was clearly greatly relieved.

I thought about asking if the strappingly strong Soteria couldn't have done the work the family so desperately needed, but had already learned wood was men's work just as the bread baking was women's work and Adonis, although much better suited to baking than cutting firewood with his bad back, would never in his life have thought of baking bread.

My ears gradually became accustomed to the village sound level and Kalamata and Sparta became a memory.

Chapter 23

Spies?

Louis had come down from the azvesti factory and visited us in David's studio one night as David put the finishing touches on a crate he had built to hold the large bust he had finally finished – earning great acclamation in the wineshop. Louis admired David's handiwork and we told him we'd have to travel to Athens to ship it. He knew it was time for us to leave Vourvoura. Most of the villagers themselves abandoned Vourvoura in the coldest months when it actually snowed, moving to tiny houses they had in their olive orchards at lower elevations.

We had decided we wanted to live near the sea and were going to explore the islands before winter really set in and find a place to settle down. As we discussed all this David stopped work long enough to pour us all a glass of wine from a jug he had refilled at the wineshop.

"This is good wine," Louis commented. "Where did you get it?"

"From Stellio. It's really cheap. In fact, the price recently went down."

Louis howled with laughter.

"What's so funny?" David demanded.

Louis wiped his eyes and said, "Old Stellio has made your wine cheaper, the skinflint. He believes the rumor that you are spies and wants to get in good with you."

He laughed until he held his sides, but we didn't think it was so funny. We looked at each other in consternation and as soon as Louis caught his breath again asked, "What rumor that we are spies?"

"Oh, when you first came to the village someone thought maybe you were spies because no foreigners had ever been here before."

"You mean for the government?" I was aghast

"At first...to find young men who hadn't been in the army. Now most think you are spies for the American government, coming to see if Vourvoura is good for tourists. Oh, it is too much. Tourists in Vourvoura!" he began laughing again.

"Does anybody still think that? After all, these people know us. We're not spies"

"Oh, now most don't think so, but your typewriter convinced some."

"My typewriter," I exclaimed. I had a light portable manual that I used for writing letters.

"Yes. The only typewriter that any of them have seen before is in the police station in Tripolis. Stellio must think it is true. He is so tight he'd take the coins from the eyes of his dead mother. The people say he has crabs in his pockets to hold his money."

"Who else believes this?"

"The school teacher. He started the rumor, in fact. Dimitri isn't sure." Dimitri was the mayor and postmaster. "The priest says no. The old lady," he gestured in the direction of Thia's room, " says you are crazy but you are not spies. I tell them they are fools but they never listen to me. Maybe they think I am a spy, too. But Stellio has never lowered the price of wine for me." He was laughing again.

That night in bed David and I talked about the spy rumor.

"Maybe we should tell Stellio to charge the right price for the wine."

"No, " David said after mulling it over. "That would just make him more suspicious. We're leaving in a few days anyway."

"I'm just as glad we didn't know about this before."

"Me, too."

"Honey," I said a while later as we sat there dour in the thought that at least some of our neighbors thought we were spies. "I just thought of another reason they think that."

"What's that?"

"My protest letters. Someone must be able to decipher some English words."

"Of course."

When we had left the States we had both been appalled by the war in Vietnam even though it wasn't a popular position then and marchers were often doused with red paint for their lack of patriotism. My one way of trying to fulfill what I regarded as a civic responsibility even though I was so far away was to write letters to our congressman, senator and even the president periodically. I had sent several such letters from Vourvoura. I could imagine the villagers thinking I was in direct correspondence with the president. I found myself laughing like Louis had.

A few days later we were ready to leave. We had sent the crate with the bust ahead on the bus and would claim it at the station in Tripolis and ship the bust back to the States from there. We had packed the rest of our things and made arrangements with Adonis to have them shipped when we had settled down. We took the barest necessities in our packs. Thia was very tearful and gave me a parting present of one of the old vases that I admired before we sealed our last trunk. It was about 700 years old she said, and there was an ancient chip in the lip, but it had the initial of the family's last name painted on it.

Soteria, Adonis and the girls bid us good-bye I gave them some scarves they had admired. David gave Adonis a tool he had borrowed frequently. We had said good-byes to

Louis and Poli and the family already and had a final glass of wine with our friends at the shop the night before.

Early in the morning we gave Thia a final embrace. She took us in front of her icons and gave us a blessing. We put our packs on our backs and walked down the street for the last time. I was sure Soteria was busy taking down my curtains and moving my plants even before I hit the edge of town.

Everyone seemed to know we were leaving at that moment. Many people leaned out of their windows waving and calling out blessings and farewells. Stellio called good-bye from his shop doorway looking relieved to see us go. One woman chased after us to press some final sweets into the children's hands. It was the only time in my life I ever literally walked away from a place where I had lived and the feeling was surreal, as if I were in a fairy tale or Fellini movie.

At the bend in the road at the top of the valley we stopped to look back at our beautiful Vourvoura one last time. Then we turned and walked on down the road looking for a new home.

Chapter 24

Ferries and Islands

It was three a.m. and the boat had come to a halt. We had learned that the ferries usually made no announcement of their ports at night, so we took it in turns sleeping when we knew we'd arrive at an island this late.

I shook David by the shoulder and we quickly put on our packs and lifted the children carefully from the crowded bench. We stepped around a snoring peasant woman who slept in the aisle with one hand around her daughter and the other clutching a handful of sage as a seasickness preventative. I now so associated sage with seasick Greeks, I could not use it as a seasoning any more. We bumped into a basket and heard the disturbed chickens rustle around inside it

A small motor launch pulled up alongside the gangplank and we handed sleepy Heather and Davidaki into the arms of the boatman below us then hopped down ourselves.

"Where are we?" Heather murmured.

"Mykonos," David replied.

As we neared shore we coaxed the children awake. It would be too hard to carry them and the packs while we searched for a place to sleep out the remainder of the night; they would have to walk. The boatman sang as we neared the dock. The town was built right into the harbor. I imagined all the grouchy Greeks being awakened by his loud voice. There was no beach in sight.

"Where is the edge of town?" we asked when we reached the shore.

"There isn't one," he laughed. "Good night. *Kali ipno* good sleep," he added.

The town was barely lit by a few scattered street lights but fortunately the moon was almost full. Mykonos seemed a solid mass of snowy forms in the moonlight, as all its surfaces had been liberally coated with whitewash on an almost daily basis for centuries softening and rounding all edges and forms. There were no single houses that we could see. The people lived in homes cut into the fantastic piece of sculpture that made up the town. Once we left the waterfront there were no streets, just turning and twisting alleyways that laced the mass of dwellings. We turned into one hopefully looking for the outskirts of the village.

Heather and Davidaki were fully awake now. They enjoyed the novelty of midnight landings. As we walked I told them stories to pass the time. They were learning more of the Greek myths. Since we were really in Odyssey country now, they especially liked those stories. I spoke in a whisper so as not to wake the townspeople. We could hear some lively music faintly in the distance. Some taverna was still going strong.

We made a turn in the alley and stepped into a circle of light from a lamp. A stone arch crossed the alley.

"Look!" I said, pointing out a piece of an ancient frieze that had been built into the side of the arch. A charioteer grasped the reins of two muscular horses running hard. The marble was scrubbed clean and the bougainvillea had been trained to grow around the frieze. It was a strikingly beautiful piece of art. We explained to Heather and Davidaki that it had come from one of the ancient temples we had seen throughout Greece. The children often learned their history lessons *in situ.* We left and plunged on through the twisting, confusing street. We had already been walking for an hour and were tired, although Heather and Davidaki were having a good time.

"This is a big town," Davidaki commented. We agreed.

A huddled shape beside a doorway startled us once.

"It's a pelican!" David said and we stopped to look at the enormous bird. The pelican woke, looked at us briefly then went back to sleep. I was envious of his sleep. We all looked another moment at the astonishing sight then went on.

It was getting later. The moon was lower in the sky and it was harder to see our way. We could still catch strains of the taverna music from time to time but we never seemed to get any closer to it. We rounded a corner and David stopped short, silently pointing. It was the arch with the frieze again.

Heather and Davidaki thought it was another frieze and we didn't mention that it was the same one. We tried a different route and in a half hour found ourselves back under the frieze again.

"We're lost aren't we, Daddy?" said Heather cheerfully.

"Yep," he admitted. "Listen let's make one more attempt and then just sleep right in the alleys if we can't get out of this maze."

We were all four dragging with sleepiness by then.

We followed a new alley. It was now getting easier to see as the sky was turning light in the east and the white walls of the town were turning rosy in the morning light. At last we found ourselves in a field. The taverna was right next to us. We could hear the glasses smashing, the Greeks applauding the dancers, as we unrolled our sleeping bags. The music lullabyed us to sleep.

Island travel wasn't always easy, but on the positive side it was interesting and David reveled in our privacy after the communal life we had led in Vourvoura.

Because we had promised Taki, after we had left Vourvoura, before commencing our island travels, we had made our obligatory stop in Sparta to visit the rich, city half of Thia's family and found not just Taki, but Yorgo, our acquaintance who had sent us to his family home in Vourvoura in the first place. He was back in Greece to visit his mother and father. His cousins were trying to persuade him to open a restaurant in Sparta. They weren't having much luck.

He was astonished we had lasted as long as we had in Vourvoura. He, himself, would rather be boiled in olive oil than live in the village. His twelve years running a restaurant in Georgetown in Washington, D.C. had even spoiled him for Sparta.

"The stupid colonels," he fumed. "They have passed a law saying how thick a steak can be cut. And not just in restaurants, even my butcher can't cut my meat the way I want."

We were convinced Yorgo would not last long in Sparta, but would soon be buying a one way ticket back to the States.

We were circumspect about giving out much information about the family in Vourvoura, not wanting to cause problems for anyone, but extolled the intelligence of Athena and Yorghia hoping the family might help with their school fees. George's family lived in a two story town house with a large terrace planted with flowering trees in back. They force-fed us steak, chicken and homemade baked pies until we felt like French geese. We sat on the terrace sipping ouzo with the family patriarch when bats started flying in the dusky light.

"*Nictaritha* -Night birds," he said teaching us the delightful Greek word for bats.

Despite our objections the family insisted on paying for a hotel room for us because their home was crowded with relatives. We fled before they could start feeding us again the next day. We left the Peloponesus on our first island boat after surviving one last mountain electrical storm that drove us from our campsite at three a.m. and into a shed that reeked like a privy, a service it performed for waiting passengers. We had found the islanders much more relaxed than the mountain people of the Peloponesus had been. Fishermen sat on the benches mending nets chatting with each other. Both men and women sat outside the little cafes gossiping. The people were curious but mildly so, unlike the people on the mainland who had been demanding in extending their hospitality. The islanders also took time for pleasure and beauty in their lives more often than the mountaineers; every house was alive with flowers and even the cats, neglected and abused in Vourvoura, were fat and sleek, obviously used to affection.

We roamed the islands for more than six weeks, staying a week here, three days there, a day somewhere else, all depending on the erratic fall schedules of the inter-island ferries.

We traveled deck class with the majority of the Greek travelers and spent many days sitting in the sun with them sharing food and conversation, music and dancing.

We met many friendly people and sometimes found ourselves camping in rather peculiar places. On Rhodes, the night watchman of the athletic stadium allowed us to stay in the quarters for visiting athletes until a visiting soccer team came. In Kos we slept in the municipal park at the invitation of the local policeman.

Santorini was another midnight landing. This time David had been on watch and woke me from a sound sleep. After reaching the shore we looked up at a steep concrete path that hairpinned up the side of a cliff. A few lamplights illuminated a turn here or there. A few men with a train of mules were waiting for disembarking passengers. We were not the only ones to decide on a fall visit to the famous island the Greeks called Thera, and most of the visitors were Greeks.

A furious argument ensued as people began bargaining over the price of mule rides. The mules were skittish at the water's edge and the path was only a few feet wide. I didn't like heights and the thought of us being perched that much higher up on mule back, the mules being nervous and the path narrow didn't strike me as safe, nor David. We viewed the path again.

"It doesn't seem that far, maybe a half a kilometer," David ventured.

So we began trudging up hill. When we reached the light that seemed to be at the top we gasped with surprise. The path hairpinned up for at least as far again. Way below us we could hear the mule drivers still arguing with their potential customers. We rested briefly and started trudging again. After we again, this time with less surprise, found ourselves looking at another stretch of climb before us we suddenly heard a huge clatter coming up behind us. There was a niche in the cliff wall and we all crammed ourselves into it, huddling as the mule train came by at top speed from the bend below us.

We all looked at each other in relief at having missed a catastrophe and suddenly understood why there had been so many niches in the cliff. As we watched the people hanging on for dear life as they wheeled around a turn above us I was just as glad we were taking the slow way.

At the top, a ghost town seemed to greet us. Anyone who had rooms to offer had already led off the new arrivals and gone to bed, there were no open tavernas. Like Mykonos, Thera's village was a narrow maze. We finally found an open space and settled down in our sleeping bags to catch up on our rest.

I woke to the sight of schoolgirls dressed in their bright blue uniforms clustered around us giggling. Shopkeepers were opening the shutters of their stores all around us. One jolly man with a very bushy mustache greeted us with a cheerful *"Kali mera!"* when he saw we were awake. Apparently the wide space we had chosen, small as it was, was the main town square in this tightly clustered village. Greatly embarrassed we dressed inside our sleeping bags and emerged as quickly as we could to go find a room to rent.

Heather did not like Thera. The four days we were there she was nervous about the volcano cone in the center of the harbor. All the shops sold postcards of it when it was smoking and she was sure it was ready to erupt any minute. The rest of us thoroughly enjoyed it. We discovered the *vin ordinaire* of Thera was not the ubiquitous restina of the rest of Greece, but an excellent dry vermouth from vineyards the Italians had planted while they held title to the island. Thera also prided itself on its cuisine and we discovered *Stifado,* Greece's answer to hasenpfeffer. We loved the steep little village and stayed in a room with a veranda over a cistern that provided a spectacular view.

But even if we thought Heather would get used to the volcano, we knew it was not our island. We had decided we liked the Cyclades with its lovely architecture like Mykonos better than Kos or Rhodes or the other islands we had visited. But which one? Thera had no beaches we could see and the population was confined to a limited part of the great hulk of rock. Mykonos was beautiful but too busy for us. While we enjoyed the dynamic village life behind the touristy waterfront we wanted something quieter. So we took a boat to another Cycladic island.

Some of the young men on board had a portable record player and played it at top volume. They put on a *Tsiftiteli*, a wild Turkish sounding type of song and an old man leaped up. He wore *vrakes*, the traditional full velvet trousers of Crete , and a sash and vest, an increasingly rare folk costume. He danced with spirit while the younger men clapped the rhythm and urged him on with shouts of "Come on, Uncle!" "Opa!" and "Bravo!" When the song ended gourds of wine were passed around and small flasks of potent homemade raki that the islanders loved. By the time we docked in Paros we, as well as the whole crowd, were more than a little tipsy. We had dinner at a little restaurant, unrolled our sleeping bags on the beach by the dock and slept.

The next morning we realized we had found our spot at last. The town was beautiful. The architecture, like Mykonos, was maze-like; all the buildings and alleyways formed a whole, connected by steps and arches. The paving stones of the streets were whitewashed around the edges and the lines of them and the buildings all flowed into each other. Where Mykonos had a lively atmosphere with people bustling everywhere and motorcycles zooming down the alleys, Paros was relaxed. People strolled rather than walked briskly, and donkeys, not motor traffic, prevailed. We were to learn that other than two taxis that usually didn't work, there wasn't a single car on the island and just one bus.

We sought out the barber, the best source of information in any town, and asked if there was a house we could rent. We were in luck as he had a place himself.

After lunch, Nikos the barber closed his shop and led us out of town for a mile or so up the side of a mountain along a goat path. The stony path twisted between stone walls that fenced in the terraced fields and vineyards. Wherever a stone was freshly chipped it blazed white – the rock of the island was Parian marble, prized by the ancient Greek sculptors. We reached a tiny stone house in the middle of vineyard. It was whitewashed, but not recently. Its trim was painted sky blue. There was a small terrace in front with an acacia tree providing shade, that had a spectacular view west overlooking the village below with its two windmills, and the sea. In the distance we could see the island of Yaros, a prison island full of the colonels' political prisoners. There was a larger terrace with a grape arbor over it on the side of the house and a table and benches below it. Below the house a stream ran down the mountain and bamboo and bushes grew beside it in profusion. There was a large circle of concrete in the field behind the house – a threshing floor we were to learn.

Inside there were two rooms, one small and older. The other room was newer, much larger with a higher ceiling. A third room in back had a separate entrance and housed a round brick oven. It was smoke darkened and used for storing brush. It obviously had not been used for habitation in some time.

There was a well in back, a small orchard of pomegranate bushes, almond and lemon trees, a privy beside the house. The privy had a water lock toilet we could flush with a bucket. We were warned to never throw paper in it. A waste basket next to it was for receiving paper. It had a lace curtain for privacy.

We bargained briefly and paid our first month's rent, twelve dollars.

Chapter 25

Nikki

Our house, like almost all of them that we had seen in Greece, was made of stone walls about two feet thick pierced by a few small windows. The roof was beamed, the beams backed by a layer of bamboo that made up the ceiling, the riverside just below the house having provided the bamboo. Behind the bamboo was a thick layer of seaweed then a foot of dirt. The whole was capped by a thin layer of cement that kept it rainproof or at least it did if it was in good repair. We were to learn ours was not.

The large room in front we decided to divide into a studio and bedroom for the children, a tiny room behind it could serve as our bedroom and living area. The smallest room in back we planned to turn into a kitchen. It would need a lot of cleaning and several coats of whitewash before we put it to use, in the meantime we'd cook in our bedroom.

We were delighted to have so much space all to ourselves.

The only furniture was a table with two chairs, a few pots and pans, some dishes, kerosene lamps, and a bed. There was also an old fashioned, screen-wrapped hanging food safe, about a two foot cube, to keep perishables away from bugs and mice. Nikos, our new landlord, agreed to pay for whitewash and promised to bring up two more chairs and a couple folding cots for the children the day we moved in.

Heather and Davidaki ran around exploring their new home while David and I sat on the front terrace enjoying the view and making plans about setting up the household. I was busily making a shopping list to take to the village. The children were especially pleased with the creek that ran down the hillside.

Before long we saw a figure toiling up the path to the house. A tall, lanky, young blond man with a smiling friendly face accented with a mustache stopped when he reached us. He was not dressed in the ubiquitous American uniform of jeans, but instead dressed like a Greek townsman in slacks and a business shirt.

"Hi," he said coming towards us with his hand outstretched. "I'm Brett. Nikos stopped to tell me and my wife Anna there were more Americans on the island now, so I thought I'd come up and meet you."

Brett was a painter and he and Anna, a tall, blonde young woman from Pennsylvania, had lived on the island for three years while they ran a small art school. The school was a moveable one, with Brett renting studio space in various places around town as they became available. He told us there was one other foreign couple in residence, another American painter and his British girlfriend, Tom and Nancy. They had been on the island even longer.

"Anna and I have a house at the very edge of town along this same path. Stop by for an ouzo later."

We promised we would. Ouzo was the Greek aperitif, a clear anise flavored drink that turned milky when it touched water.

Later that day in town, shopping for a gas burner to use for cooking, we met a slim, dark-haired girl with a British accent who turned out to be Nancy. She and I instantly liked each other. She was shopping with a Greek lady in her sixties wearing a patterned house dress, whom she introduced as Nikki. Nikki was as round as a pumpkin and her face was creased with smile lines. She cooed and exclaimed over the children and fished some sweets from her pocket for them.

Greek ladies were usually very attentive to Heather and Davidaki and the kids usually accepted their fawning with grudging good grace, but I could see that they honestly enjoyed Nikki's mothering.

"You come to my house for coffee tomorrow," Nikki insisted. "Nancy, you bring them."

At Brett and Nina's house we enjoyed looking at his cubist paintings in subdued colors that captured island life. The whitewashed flagstones crawled through his paintings. Anna was cooly hospitable. I got the distinct impression she wasn't happy about other Americans moving to the island.

In town we had discovered a store selling Greek children's books. We were delighted because we could use them to improve our Greek. I had dutifully studied all the time in Vourvoura using a language text I had bought in the States. David had not and relied on me for translating much of the time. Each day we had got in the habit of looking up at least five words we would use that day to bolster our vocabulary. The dictionary often let us down giving us the kathourevasa instead of what people actually used. Children's books would be a big help since they were in common Greek.

The next day found all four of us and Nancy in Nikki's kitchen. She was very excited and bustled about making coffee on a tiny alcohol burner. She was surprised and pleased that we had learned some Greek already but she teased us about our mountain accent, which until then we hadn't realized we had. We sat chatting and enjoying the room.

Like most Greek kitchens it was spotlessly clean. Each of the flagstones of the floor was bordered with fresh whitewash and the thick walls gave off the tangy odor of fresh lime. There were few furnishings: a table, four chairs, a cot heaped high with homemade blankets of bright colors. A stone shelf built into the wall served Nikki as a counter, a small fireplace as a stove. Nikki's kitchen had dozens and dozens of baskets in all sizes stacked in corners and hung from the low rafters making an almost solid ceiling of wickerwork. They were her cabinets. She took her coffee and sugar from one.

I watched her make coffee in the Greek fashion in a tiny pot called a *briki* over a spirit lamp. She mixed the coffee and sugar together and brought the mixture together in a boil, then let it settle, repeating the process three times. Greek coffee was served in tiny cups and the bottom third of it was grounds you didn't drink. The tablespoon or so of drinkable coffee packed a caffeine wallop. Nikki's coffee was very good.

Nikki's husband, Agapitos, came in from the fields to rest a bit. He was ten years older than Nikki, thin and bent over. The two of them were very talkative and filled us in on all the island gossip. They talked at length about the house we had rented which they didn't like because of its dampness problems when the winter rains began. Agapitos warned us to be stern with Nikos and his wife Tarsa about fixing the roof. After a while we rose to go to town to do our marketing. When Nikki learned our errand, she insisted on accompanying us.

"I can show you how to shop here," she told us and she did.

It was no small accomplishment. We strolled from store to store where she introduced us to everyone. One shopkeeper was known to carry the best dry cod, another the finest oil. One household in the country made the best hard cheese, another the best soft, still another made charcoal. She introduced us to *xinomizithra*, a soft goat cheese made daily that couldn't keep even overnight. A sour cream cheese was the best way I could describe it and we learned to relish it lavishly spread on bread with onions or fresh tomatoes. Nikki immediately became a fixture in our lives. Unlike Thia in Vourvoura who spent most of her time in her room, Nikki loved people and enjoyed life. She taught me the skills of housewifery on the island. She came daily to our house because she wanted to be sure I knew how to take care of my family.

"For baking, Andrianni, you carry things to the bakery in town. After the bread comes out they will bake things for you for half a drachma or so," she explained.

"No, no, no. Po-po-po. Don't throw rags away," she told us. "You cut them like so, in strips, then make a ball. When you get enough the weaver can make you a rug and your floors will not be so cold in winter."

"Ai-ee! Don't beat your laundry on the rocks like that. You will wear your things out. Po-po-po. This way: you lay a large thing like a shirt or a sheet on a flat rock, rub on soap, then take a small thing like a sock in your hand and scrub the shirt all over. See? They are both clean," she instructed me out by our well where there was a concrete tub large enough to get into for doing laundry and bathing.

Nikki would accept very little from us. I could offer her coffee made the way I had watched her do it, which she dearly loved but denied herself on a regular basis because it was too costly. From time to time she'd sample our "exotic" cooking. Mashed potatoes were a constant source of amusement to her and she liked pancakes. I served them to her with honey and margarine I could buy in town in bulk. But the only thing we could really do for Nikki was talk to her. The children frequently visited Nikki and Agapitos, who really loved them. I realized how they were missing their own grandparents in the States when they called her *yiayia*...grandmother.

Chapter 26

Dimitri

Not long after our arrival we were talking to Tom, Nancy's boyfriend. Tom was very tall, narrow shouldered and dark haired. He, like Anna, seemed a bit cautious about newcomers to the island at first, but warmed up a bit each time we met. We chatted about spear fishing when we heard someone hail us from our veranda. There was a middle-aged man on a donkey outside. His face was so leathered by the weather it was hard to tell his age; he could have been in his fifties or sixties or seventies. He was a handsome man with an erect carriage like a soldier. He was dressed in old and patched clothes like our mountain friends. Tom grinned.

"*Yia sou,*" he greeted the man. He turned to us. "Dimitri wants to meet you. Do you have some time?"

Tom was usually somewhat formal. We assured Dimitri he was very welcome.

He lived in the inland valley of Marathi and was a real xenophile. He was passionately curious about foreigners. He had come laden with gifts: homemade cheeses, figs, gourds of raki and wine he had made. He untied all his baskets and parcels from the donkey's back and came in. His friendliness and good humor won us over immediately. Tom and Nancy already knew him and even reserved Tom thawed out and became expressive in Dimitri's presence. While we liked Tom for his intelligence, we were tickled to see him warm up so much around the sweet older man.

We set out the food Dimitri had brought plus some of our own and sat down to a feast. Dimitri grinned broadly throughout the visit, obviously having a good time. He reminded us of Louis without the American experience but with added years of wisdom.

"I know this house," he cautioned us. "Make Nikos the Barber fix the roof. In the winter it is like this." He reached for our new sieve to show us.

When he finally left, as he mounted the donkey he said, "Come to my house on Sunday and we will have a party."

On Sunday we loaded our market basket with fish, crackers and other items we figured Dimitri would not have where he lived, and we set off. Tom and Nancy agreed to accompany us on this first trip inland. An aging bus made a Sunday run inland and Dimitri was there to meet us when it stopped in the valley. He led us over a few hills and fields to his house which was surrounded by animals. His chickens, a couple cows, a sheep and a goat as well as his donkey were waiting for him on his front terrace. He chased them all away and we set our things down on a table in the front room. He then took us on a tour of the valley.

At one end of the valley was the ancient marble quarry, the shafts plunging into the mountain like mysterious caves. Parian marble was highly desirable in the ancient world because of its pure white color and fine grain which when polished came the closest of all stone to resembling the texture of human skin. All the famous Greek statues in Athens were carved from it and the Cycladic school of sculpture in pre-classical times had been situated on Paros because of it.

We went inside the cool interior of the tunnel into the mountain. Outside, weather and dirt had darkened the stone but inside it was pure sugar white reflecting our lamplight. We flashed our lantern on the white walls, intrigued that we were in a sugar cavern. We explored for an hour until I became too concerned we might get lost, and was worried the children might fall down the sudden pits we ran into that held water in the bottom.

Outside the quarries there were ruins of stone buildings and remnants of small gauge rail system left from an Italian attempt to reopen the quarries a hundred years before. In and around the ruins pieces of marble sculpture were scattered, left by sculptors who had stayed a while, attracted by the marble, but who had found their works too heavy to carry with them when they left. In one roofless building a life-sized nude in a bathtub gazed pensively at the sky, her face complete although the rest of her was just roughed in. The walls of the building were covered with exuberant paintings of nudes dancing, slowly flaking away in the weather.

"A Frenchman came and stayed one summer about ten years ago. No woman, so he was lonely," chuckled Dimitri by way of explanation.

At the extreme end of the valley Dimitri took us to a monastery. It was a fortress of a place, long deserted but looked after by Dimitri's brother who lived in a small house near it. Dimitri obtained the foot-long key to the thick wooden doors. As he swung them open he pointed to a slot above us.

"For boiling oil," he told us.

"Whom did the monks fight?" I asked.

"Pirates and tax collectors."

The walls of the chapel were covered with elaborate frescoes which were clearly very old. Dimitri casually lit a candle as he chatted, stuck it in a four foot tall iron candelabra and crossed himself. Outside of the chapel, the building was very plain and sparsely furnished. Dimitri's brother and his family kept it clean and freshly whitewashed. One cell contained a cot, table and chair. The small window overlooked the valley. I could picture a writer living there.

We were all hungry and after locking up the monastery and returning the key, we headed back to Dimitri's house. His two room house was not freshly whitewashed. He was a widower so had no woman to tend to such chores. A small brazier served as a kitchen. He, like us, had a well for his water supply.

We unpacked the food we had brought and I began frying the fish we had brought over the small clay brazier Dimitri had carried outside on the terrace. He set out the round homemade cheeses, wine, raki, hard boiled eggs, raisins, dried figs and a big loaf of the heavy country bread made with barley flour and baked in stone ovens. We hadn't seen it since we had left Vourvoura and welcomed the sight of it again. It had spoiled us for the town bread from the professional bakeries which always seemed lacking after Vourvoura. Dimitri explained that his sister-in-law baked for him.

Dimitri's most prized possession was a battery operated record player, the "peek-op", and a collection of old scratched records, which he proudly turned on. We feasted and danced all afternoon as he showed us some special island dances.

By late afternoon we decided we had better leave to walk home before it got dark. Dimitri walked us to the road and said good-bye. It was eight kilometers back to town but it was a beautiful walk. Along the way we found wild caper plants and harvested a crop to salt down at home.

Chapter 27

To Kill an Octopus

While the mild autumn weather continued David took advantage of it to learn how to spearfish. Our money was running very low while we waited for the commission check to arrive and he was determined to stretch it out by bringing home some seafood.

His first trophy was an octopus with legs about two feet long. He came in with it like a triumphant warrior.

"When I shot it, it swam into a little cave and I had to pull on the cord to get it out. It came out fighting and squirting ink and crawled right up the cord on to my arm. I was scared, but I remembered what the Greeks do and I surfaced and grabbed the head and turned it inside out."

We were all spellbound but I became worried for his safety.

"No, I was scared at first for a minute, but if there was a problem I'd just drop the speargun and go."

We had all learned to love octopus. Properly cooked it tasted like lobster, and dried and cooked over charcoal, it made a tasty snack.

I had never quite got used to the Greek method of killing the animals. Smaller ones they bit between the eyes, crushing critical organs, larger ones they turned inside out, which seemed to confuse the animal more than injure it, but then they ripped off the viscera which killed it.

Turning what would otherwise be something the consistency of rubber bands into a tender dish also required work. First, after rinsing off the octopus, it was slammed against a rock, picked up and slammed again and again until it became quite limp. This could take five to ten minutes depending on the size. Then it was dipped in sea water and gently wiped against a rock again and again as a lather rose and had to be repeatedly rinsed off. The octopus stiffened, then finally became so tender its legs could be easily torn apart. It was then ready to cook or dry. Whenever we walked along the waterfront we'd hear the slap, slap of someone tenderizing an octopus. It was a staple on the island.

One tasty recipe called for reserving the animal's own ink sac for sauce. Another favorite, without the ink, used a tomato and wine sauce and a lot of onions. That was Thera style and was served over noodles. An even simpler style was to just boil it in water and marinate it with lemon and olive oil a few hours.

We always saved a tidbit for the cat that came with our house. He was a great tiger-striped tom whose origins were from off the island since he'd been brought by a traveler. That made him valuable because he could vary the local feline gene pool. He took this duty very seriously. The kids named him Gree-gree after the type of night fishing the islanders practiced where a large lead boat towed out smaller boats like a row of ducklings, delighting Heather and Davidaki enormously when we watched them from our front terrace.

Dimitri also loved octopus and when he came by to visit I was proud to see him enjoy it so much. He told us folk tales as we huddled by the fireplace burning grape prunings we had gathered in the fields, munching on the roasted dried delicacy.

"Once there was a man who was a 'magus', a fortune teller. He and a woman fell in love, but he said she should marry someone else first and have three children. She asked why and he said because her first three children would die, and she would blame him and they would never be able to live peacefully together otherwise. But she insisted they marry so they did.

"She became pregnant by and by and had a baby but it died when it was six months old. She remembered what her husband had said and so said nothing. But then she became pregnant again. When this child also died at six months she became angry and cooler. When she lost her third child at six months she became frantic. She shouted, she wailed, she threw things. Finally her husband said he would leave the village because they could not get along. She calmed down and said since they had been through so much together she would go with him. They went into the mountains. It was very hot and after a while she asked her husband for water.

";See, already we are not getting along,' he told her. 'But if you must have water call for your first son.' She did and boy appeared with a glass of water on a tray. It was clean and pure, and she drank it all up. The boy disappeared. The next day she was again thirsty and her husband told her to call on her second son. A younger boy appeared with a tray with a glass of water, but it was not clean, but murky and dirty. She was very thirsty so she took a few sips of it anyway. The next day she was frantic with thirst from having so little water the day before. ;Call your third son,' said the man. This time a boy appeared with a tray holding a glass of mud. She took it and poured it on the ground saying she could not drink it.

"'Husband what does this mean?' she asked him.

"'They are giving you what you gave to me,' he replied."

I didn't know what to make of the moral except that love is like clear water, but it was an awfully good story, so I passed it on in letters to the U.S.

We ate well until the weather got too cold for David to swim. We really suffered in the first cold snap because the family in Vourvoura had not sent our trunks on to us that held our warm clothes and we had just one change of summer things and our sandals.

We got desperate. We were cold. I had no books to tutor the children. To make matters worse, the roof leaked and our only source of heat was in the one small room that held the tiny fireplace. Our neighbors lent us some discards of very itchy wool and we wore a motley collection that made us look like Gypsies as we sent telegram after telegram, made call after call from the island telephone center.

The Parians were completely involved in the drama and once the man who ran the telegram and telephone office on or behalf even grabbed the phone from us to chew out the bus station director in the city of Tripolis who was now holding our things hostage.

Confined to the house in the winter storms I got the kids into spinning and dancing like the planets to keep warm.

"No, no, moon, you can't run away, back around the earth. Come on earth, you have to go around the sun - that's the chair."

Finally the word came that our things were arriving on the next boat. Brett borrowed a donkey from a friend to help us get it all up the mountain to the house.

It was like Christmas as we unpacked our warm clothes, our cooking gear, the kids' toys and books, and David's precious tools. He happily set up his studio, and I settled the children back into a regular teaching routine.

It was still cold, but the Ice Ages were over.

Chapter 28

Revolution

Living without a radio or newspaper, we had two sources of news. One was the English language newspaper and magazine sheets from the ferries that the shopkeepers thoughtfully saved to wrap our groceries in - each item individually wrapped like a present. We read them all voraciously and then recycled them in the privy.

The other source was Brett who had electricity and a short wave radio and listened to Voice of America. He'd let us know when something was brewing.

One day David had to go to town to buy more sculpture supplies. He was working in the abstract using soldered tin and laminated wood shapes intertwined with each other. He had bought a German made torch that burned gasoline for the soldering. He had run out of gas and of course I gave him a long list of things I needed as long as he was making the hike down the mountain.

On the way down he stopped at the Taylor house to see if Brett had any news.

"The king has apparently attempted a counter-coup. The colonels are in a panic and no one knows where the king is. If they catch him, he's toast. I think he's hoping for a royalist rebellion. You had better think about if they evacuate us, because the American state department is talking about getting Americans out of Greece."

David left worried about having to move just after we had got settled. He had got his gasoline and was on his way to the shop where I bought olive oil when he heard a great racket.

The school had held a special educational event that day, showing all the school kids a film at the boat office in town. David didn't know that and as he was walking down the narrow alley that served the village as a main street it was suddenly thronged with uniformed children all shouting and yelling because they'd just been released from the film and were heading home early.

The street was so jammed he couldn't get to a store, and full of the major news Brett had just imparted, he thought a rebellion had just started. He instantly turned and started hurrying to get home.

On the pathway he ran into Brett again who knew all about the film. David told him he was heading home fast because revolution must have started. Brett found out the reason why David thought so and burst into laughter.

Much abashed but greatly relieved David laughed at himself, and the two headed into town to celebrate the end of the "revolution" with a glass of ouzo and finish the shopping..

Over the next few days we had made a daily trip to the Taylors to listen to the news broadcasts. We had a few evenings of conjecture wondering if we were going to be evacuated to Italy.

One time while we were there a couple of townspeople stopped by. No one had located the king yet, although we later learned he had fled the country with his family. Recalling all the hills that said ZITO, long live, I tried to make a pun. Zito had the emphasis on the first syllable, and the word for "Look for" was also zito but with the emphasis on the last syllable. So I said, with a toast "Look for the king". The Greeks just looked at me puzzled although all the Americans laughed.

I wondered if it wasn't funny because of the political situation or if it was just that Greeks didn't pun and changing the emphasis was as dramatic as if we changed the consonants in an English word. I finally concluded the latter and never tried to make such a pun again.

One joke made the rounds among the Greeks that really was funny. A man and his wife board a bus that is crowded. She sits next to an army officer and her husband sits in front of her next to an old lady with an umbrella. The officer reaches over and feels the woman's thigh. She turns and slaps him, the husband turns around and punches him, and the old lady whacks him over the head with her umbrella. They all get hauled in for questioning.

"Why did you slap the officer, Madame?"

"Because he got fresh with me."

"Why did you punch the officer, sir?"

"That woman is my wife."

"And you, Grandmother, why did you hit him with your umbrella?"

"I thought the government changed!"

Chapter 29

Plowing

"Ha-lai, ha-lai, ha-lai, ha-lai."

It was Cross-Eyed Nikos our neighbor outside our bedroom window. I peered out. He was trying to plow the field right next to our house. We had learned the Parians planted in the fall and harvested their grain in the spring. Nikos was so cross-eyed it was hard to understand how he saw at all. He always wore a flat-topped billed cap and was very animated. Nikos' younger brother Haralambos was with him. They were both dressed in their most patched and repatched work clothes. The two men, both small of stature, were pushing at the rear end of Nikos's mule, Kitso, who not only greatly outsized them, but despite Nikos's cheering cry and the shoving, wasn't about to budge.

It was five thirty, just barely light. We yawned and dressed then I went to the door and called.

"Hey, Nikos, Haralambos. Want some coffee?"

"*Kalimera, Kiria Andrianni,*" Cross-Eyed Nikos called good morning. "No coffee."

He answered for himself and Haralambos. He bossed Haralambos around constantly, and never let him make any decisions when they were together despite the fact that Haralambos was in his late sixties or early seventies, just a year or two younger than Cross-Eyed Nikos.

By this time Heather and Davidaki were also wide awake with Nikos's swearing and shouting, and they came to watch the plowing. Before long we heard a radio playing soap operas in the distance. The sound grew louder and louder and soon Tarsa, our landlady, appeared. She never went anywhere without her transistor announcing her arrival. She had rented out the field to Cross-Eyed Nikos and wanted to make sure he did not extend the boundaries in his enthusiastic plowing.

Tarsa accepted some coffee and after I fixed the children some breakfast, we sat on the terrace to watch the action. Tarsa considered herself gentry and cut above her peasant neighbors since her barber husband was a professional. She dressed in polyester clothes like the Athenians, wore make-up, and wore her hair in a chignon adding to her statuesque figure.

The action was better than an old slapstick film. Cross-Eyed Nikos had just one mule but he needed two animals to pull his wooden plow. Haralambos had neglected to bring his donkey so Cross-Eyed Nikos had yoked up his milk cow while he stormed at Haralambos' absent-mindedness. The poor confused cow didn't know what to do. Kitso was so insulted at being yoked to her he was letting everyone know he wasn't going to cooperate.

Kitso was a gorgeous animal, and Cross-Eyed Nikos took as much pride in him as any playboy ever did in his Ferrari. He never beat Kitso and he even kept his dark coat groomed and gleaming. But Kitso could give the old adage "stubborn as a mule" a whole new meaning.

Cross-Eyed Nikos was beside himself with rage this morning. Haralambos ran back and forth smiling, getting in the way and generally making himself useless. So did Bisti, Cross-Eyed Nikos's, neglected, tick-covered dog. She was worse than useless because in her attempts to help, she'd bark and nip at Kitso, then jump back when he'd kick. Cross-Eyed Nikos swore at her repeatedly and told her to go away, but Bisti was determined to help.

We offered to help in any way we could, but Cross-Eyed Nikos just grunted that we couldn't help unless we were mules. He went on rampaging at his animals which only made them more skittish and difficult to handle.

At length Tarsa came and offered a handful of our breakfast oatmeal to Kitso and got him moving, and the field began to get plowed.

Tarsa and I sat over more coffee and chatted. I asked if Cross-Eyed Nikos was related to her husband Nikos. She was horrified at the suggestion.

All older first cousins in Greece had the same first names because first born boys are named after their paternal grandfather, second born after their maternal grandfather. The oldest girls are named after their maternal grandmothers, the second after their paternal grandmothers. So it takes a fifth child to introduce a new name to a family. One exception are the names Eleftheros or Eleftheria. The name means freedom or liberty, and lots of children were given the names during the German occupation in World War II in a patriotic gesture of defiance. It wasn't unreasonable to ask about the relationship between two Nikos.

The confusion that results from so many cousins having the same names is neatly avoided with nicknames. Cross-Eyed Nikos earned his because the cast in one eye was so bad. Tarsa objected to him because he had reportedly beaten his wife so badly in his younger years that she had dumped him, taking children and household to Athens, leaving him to fend for himself. Cross-Eyed Nikos told us he was a widower, so we never knew what story was true. Tarsa had such an inflated idea of her status, I suspected the two Nikos really were related despite or even because of her heated protest.

The mismatched animals were getting the job done despite Kitso's occasional balking. Cross-Eyed Nikos led the animals along the irregularly shaped borders of the terrace and circled the field. Haralambos followed the animals scattering seed from a skin pouch slung over his shoulder. The first rains had begun and soil was rich smelling and dark.

The plow cut black paths through the first greening of the wild grass. The wooden bladed plow easily turned up a wide swath. The last furrows were finally scored into the earth. Haralambos began to unyoke the cow as Cross-Eyed Nikos patted Kitso fondly. He fed the mule a handful of some weeds as a treat and strolled over to Tarsa, the children, David and I on the terrace.

"This will be a good crop," Cross-Eyed Nikos assured us, calm at last. He reached down for a handful of soil, smelled it deeply, sighing with pleasure, then passed it to us to share the pleasure.

"A god gift," he said.

Chapter 30

Tarsa

"Tarsa, the roof still leaks," I said as I finished darning the toe of one of the children's socks.

"Yes, I know," Tarsa clucked her tongue sympathetically. "We are going to fix it for you."

About once a week if it weren't raining Tarsa strolled up the mountainside to visit us. Carrying a bag full of knitting and the inevitable radio, she'd appear at our door, then claim the most comfortable chair on our terrace. I'd bring out some needlework or mending, or some yarn so she could show me how to knit socks, and we'd chat while we worked. Nikki didn't care much for the lordly Tarsa and would always absent herself when our landlady came.

Sometimes Nikos the Barber accompanied his wife and walked around the vineyards inspecting his grapes on the south side. Once or twice Tarsa brought relatives and proudly showed us off. She was very curious about us and watched David work with a sharp eye open to his many skills. She was a shrewd businesswoman and was always coaxing services out of him she'd otherwise have to hire.

"Can you put in new glass in my window in town?"

"Can you fix this leaking faucet in my sink?"

Tarsa had facilities in town we did not on the mountainside. She always gave us some home baked goodies when David did one of her chores. She was a skilled baker.

When the rent was due I would pay Tarsa a visit in town. She always made a point of serving me something cold. Tarsa owned one of the few refrigerators on the island and was very proud of it. She kept a vase of fresh flowers and a lace cloth on its highly polished top and a plastic rose tied to its handle. She also served us preserved fruit. She especially liked to serve candied kumquats, a fruit I like very much but not in thick sugary syrup. I always had a hard time eating my way through it but didn't want to insult Tarsa's hospitality. Fortunately the children loved it.

Once she came with six lady friends from town to show them how to gather wild greens. I made a big impression when I put the teaching I had had from old Thia in the mountains to work, knowing just what greens to gather, even one Tarsa overlooked. Heather liked to gather greens and also impressed the ladies with her knowledge. Afterwards we all sat outside under the grape arbor eating some snacks I fixed and cleaning the greens. A few farmers from the inland valleys passed by on their way to the village on their donkeys. They stopped to visit with us and the town ladies informed them of my foraging skills. All during their visit Tarsa kept her soap operas going to my annoyance, even shushing my guests rudely when the dramas became exciting so she wouldn't miss a word. When she and her friends left we could hear the radio going long after she was out of sight

Our battle over the roof had been going on since we arrived. It leaked as badly as we had been warned. Tarsa was always full of promises but did nothing. We had even visited poor henpecked Nikos in his barbershop several times. He was always going to take care of it *"methavrion"* which meant literally the day after tomorrow, and that meant even later than mañana meant in Latin countries. The last rainstorm had left us with an inch of water on the floor and mud streaks on the walls and I was determined on action. After all, I had been trained by Thia and Soteria, Tarsa was not going to intimidate me as much as she scared poor Nikki.

"Tarsa, " I said. "If I had a pot to put under very leak I would have more pots than the tinker does in town."

"Oh, yes, Andrianni. It is terrible. We will do something right away, but tomorrow I can't because I am visiting my sick mother-in-law," Tarsa said unperturbed. She had more sick relatives than there were people living on the island.

"But I have idea that will save you and Nikos the bother," I said, pulling out my trump card.

"What is it?" Tarsa said at once suspicious.

"David and I are going into town today and hire some workmen. Then we will pay them with the money we have for the rent." The rent was due in two days. Tarsa was quiet and I could see the calculations flitting through her mind. David and I would be sure to find the worst workers because we didn't know any better and we'd probably get fleeced in the bargaining as well. The workmen, without Tarsa around to keep an eye on them, would take longer and might even filch some materials.

Tarsa sighed, "I will go and visit my mother-in-law *methavrion*, Andrianni. In the morning the roof will be fixed. "Oh," she sighed again. "I must leave and find the workers. No time to enjoy the sun and your fine company, now." She stole a glance at me from the corner of her eye. But I was hard hearted and watched her go, the radio getting ever fainter in the distance.

The next morning, sure enough, Tarsa walked up with three men behind her. She installed herself on the front porch with her knitting and radio to watch them work.

Our thick ceilings of bamboo, seaweed and mud needed a new capping of cement. The men made a thin mixture and brushed it over the roof to fill in the cracks It took three of them all day to complete the simple task.

At noon Tarsa cooked them a complete meal over our gas burner. She was known to be an excellent cook and they had included the meal in the bargain. She made a green bean stew with tomatoes, oregano and potatoes, all liberally doused with olive oil, and heated up a fish stew she had brought. She cut up bread and served cheese and olives. We ate with the men as they leisurely enjoyed her cooking, then napped a half hour or so before resuming work.

"Dinner and a hundred drachmas; not bad for a day's labor," David laughed afterwards, thinking of the many days he had spent at Tarsa's repairing her windows and doing other odd jobs as a favor.

I didn't care. It was raining again and the new whitewash job I had completed that afternoon was holding up and the floors were dry. I could use my pots for cooking again.

Thia Vaso above.
The house in Vourvoura below. Andriani on the balcony

Laundry day in Vourvoura and Davidaki works at his lessons.

Making lunch for the kids in the garden in Vourvoura.

Soteria making feta cheese.

Camping in Delphi above. The house on Paros below.

Our backyard on Paros. Plowing with a wooden plow.

Cross-Eyed Nikos milking Lavitsa above. Produce shopping below. Cabbage soup, stuffed cabbage, coleslaw – lot of cabbage on the menu that week.

Dancing the Balos with Dimitri. At Marathi above. Our view of the "new" windmill at the village. It was just 300 years old.

Cross-Eyed Nikos celebrates the end of threshing.

A festival. Cross-Eyed Nikos, Haralambos and Mrs. Haralambos on the right in foreground. At Brett's house below. David on far right, finally in front of a camera instead of behind it. Brett, Stephanie, Papoo, the children and Adriani on the left.

Heather also known as Princess Alexandra on Paros.

Chapter 31

Kalo Nero (Good Water)

One day David came in and exclaimed, "There's an eel in our well!"

"An eel! How did it get there?"

"Beats me. There must be an underground river or something. Where's the fish line? I'll fish it out."

The kids and I went along to watch the process and looked in the well. Sure enough, an eel about two feet long was swimming around. David tied a hook on the line and baited it. A man rode by on a donkey, looked at us and burst out laughing. I knew we looked a little silly with a fishing pole at a well, but I wanted to get the eel out. I began wondering about diseases one could get from fish-tainted water and I was concerned about how long the eel had been in the well. We were all looking intently in the well to see if it would take the bait when we heard a loud belly laugh. I looked up and saw our landlord, Nikos the Barber

"There's no fish in there. Try the sea," he jeered.

"That's what you think, Nikos, "David told him. "Come look."

"We have a veritable whale of fish," I said. I knew my Greek was correct because on the ship I had worked hard to learn the word whale in hopes of seeing one, but never did.

He looked in the well, interested, then laughed again.

"It's the eel," he said. "I put him in there two years ago.Good, he is still working."

"You PUT him in there?"

"Yes, to eat bugs that fall in the well and mosquitoes and such. He keeps the water clean."

I looked at Nikos askance. "Really? This well is clean? We won't get sick from him being in there?"

"By the Virgin, Andrianni. This is the best well on the island. It is *kalo nero* - good water. I come on Sundays to get water for our dinner."

That was true; I had seen Nikos and Tarsa fetch water from the well many times. David shrugged and hauled up the line. Nikki, too, always stopped for a bottle of it on her way back home from our house.

"Oh, don't you want to catch your whale?" Nikos was still laughing at us.

"Not if he keeps the water clean," David replied.

"Oh, but if you want him for dinner, go ahead. I can bring up another someday."

"No," I said looking at our water purification system swimming below us. "I'm not hungry enough."

Periodically Nikos inquired after the eel, wanting to know if we had eaten him yet and laughing at us. For the most part the eel remained hidden which was fine with me. We had written family and friends about our well, joking that we only had running water when we ran from the well, generally preferring walking water. I thought about writing about our eel but David advised against it thinking we would worry them as I had worried when the eel was first discovered.

I was reassured about the water when I noticed that people frequently did stop to fetch a bottle of it to take home. But I was absolutely convinced when one day I saw a friend, Yorgo Kano, stop his donkey at the well and start to fill a wine flask at our well. He was from an inland valley about five miles over a steep mountain so we didn't see him often. I went out to talk to him.

"*Yia sou*, Yorgo. How's it going?"

"*Yia sou*, Andrianni It goes well. Tomorrow is Eleni's name day and my son and his new wife are coming to visit."

"Tell Eleni *kronia pola*, many years, from me."

He chatted a few minutes then remounted his donkey and started going back up the mountain.

"Yorgo, aren't you going to the village?"

"No, I just came to get a bottle of your water to offer my son and daughter-in-law tomorrow. It is a special occasion after all. *Adio*, Andrianni."

I offered glasses of our water to our guests with more pride after that.

"*Kalo nero*," I'd say.

Chapter 32

Saturday Night Bath

While the landscape looked like spring with daffodils and narcissi in bloom on the hills, winter was bearing down on us.

Keeping house without the amenities they had in town such as electricity and running water forced us to develop some very old fashioned routines. One was the Saturday night bath.

We'd fetch water from the well and using both the burners we had, heat up water in our cooking pots. We had a nice galvanized basin about four feet long. First the kids got bathed, with us mixing boiling water with cold to make it comfortable. After a scrubbing, they stood and we rinsed them off. We'd drag the basin to the doorway and empty it outside.

Then it was my turn. I'd wash my hair then luxuriate in the hot soapy water until it grew cold. Then David got his bath.

The glow from the bath would last a couple days. We treasured our bath time.

When it wasn't raining or too cold, things were simpler. There was a large vat or pool next to the well about six feet square with a washboard formed into the concrete that made it up. As long as the sun shone and the wind wasn't blowing we could bathe out there, and sometimes we all bathed together because it was so large. Any Greek neighbors going by on the donkey path could hear us, but not really see us well because our pomegranate bushes shielded us, but they'd laugh and call out, "Getting clean, eh?"

Nikki told me that during the winter, she washed one half of herself at a time rather than all of her at once. Top half one day, bottom half the next. She always smelled nice so it must have worked.

The first sunny day after a storm was devoted to laundry first, then baths. At first I tried doing it all, but one sunny afternoon while the rest of the family lounged on terrace relaxing and I was washing our cumbersome sheets, I decided I'd had it.

I walked down from the well and announced, "You know, while all of you are able to sit around and enjoy the sunshine I have to wash all our clothes and sheets and towels. It's very hard to wring them out alone. So I'm up there all by myself resenting you, and I don't like it."

David immediately rose to the occasion.

"Come on kids. We're all going to do laundry with Mom."

And from then on laundry time was a family occasion and we all flailed away at the clothes, David and I working together to wring out the sheets, all of us enjoying flinging handfuls of suds at one another from time to time. The laundry got done much faster so we could bathe sooner and I was much happier.

Another routine we had, a daily one, was cleaning the kerosene lamp chimneys. We saved the newspaper the shop keepers wrapped all our things in for this purpose (as well as for privy duty). Heather became the "lamp boss" and took over most of that chore. She also learned to trim the wicks, and when her grandparents sent us the Laura Ingalls Wilder series that included "Little House on the Prairie" we all understood Laura's lamp chores very well, and even often envied some of the amenities she had in early America that we didn't here on Paros like a heavy flat iron. My iron was a thin shell into which I'd put a lump of hot charcoal. Then I'd swing it to get flames going then while it was hot for a few seconds I'd iron a few inches of cloth before I had to start swinging again. A nice flat iron and a hand wringer sounded like lovely luxuries. A treadle sewing machine would have been a dream come true.

Once our things arrived David fixed my small folding camping oven into a permanent, insulated efficient box with his metal working tools, and I could bake at home in small quantities. A cake, a dozen biscuits or a small chicken could fit into it. It was an invaluable resource since to walk to the bakery for us was impossible in the storms.

Our path turned into a riverbed during those worst storms and all the terrace walls that held the fields turned into waterfalls. We tried to limit our trips down the mountain as much as possible when the weather was bad. The first day back from a winter storm trip we'd have fresh meat and vegetables. Some items we could keep cold in the well, lowering down the bucket. The second day anything frozen we would have bought would be thawed then we treated ourselves to *keftedes,* Greek meatballs. I learned how to cook them from Tarsa using little bundles of frozen meat we could buy at the one shop that had a small freezer. They'd last until the next day once they were cooked, and after that we were reduced to dried and canned items.

Keftedes became a favorite that winter, and by Lent we made them in little fish shapes hoping to tempt our Greek neighbors that dropped by. They'd laugh at the Lenten joke but never eat them, sticking to real fish.

We kept our food in the small food safe that hung from one of the ceiling rafters.

One of our winter staples was *baccallaro* - dried salt cod. The stuff looked unpalatable to us but Nikki taught me how to prepare it and it became a favorite.

The trick was not just to soak the stuff in water for 24 hours, but to keep changing the water. The hard, smelly cardboard looking thing then plumped up and became sweet and fresh.

I learned to fry it and serve it with *tsatsiki* , a tangy yoghurt sauce, or stew it with tomato sauce, lemon and oregano like the Greeks did.

Another basic food that got us through many a storm and lean financial period was my lentil stew.

I personally can attest to its ability to warm you through the bitterest storms and keep you going when you must work. However, I must warn you, excessive overdoses can result in rebellion by young children.

Chapter 33

Yianni Day

"Opa! Opa!" people shouted encouragement to the dancers. They didn't really need it.

As Yianni dipped, Yorgo suddenly leaped to his shoulders like an acrobat and held his balance with his arms out while Yianni continued to execute the stately steps of the Hasapikos, a favorite dance. The music came to an end and Yorgo leaped down, transformed once more into a staid householder.

It was Yianni Day, and since so many islanders were named Yianni, it was a big day for celebrations. Earlier we had happened on another Yianni party, this one given by a bachelor fisherman at a taverna. He had insisted we join the celebration for a while.

There was a lot of "spasta", the breaking of glasses and plates at a dancer's feet to show appreciation. The taverna's bus boy was kept busy sweeping the shards so no one would get cut. The taverna owner smiled gleefully as he charged glass after glass or stacks of plates to the bill. Some people would order a whole stack of empty plates just to keep handy as ammunition. The breakage fee at a good taverna party was always higher than anything else because glass and crockery was imported from France, taxed, and very expensive. No one ever broke glasses at a private party much to the hostess' relief I am sure.

Yianni the Fisherman was in for a big bill tonight but he didn't seem to care. One old man, perhaps his uncle, very drunk but graceful on his feet, picked up a small wooden table with his teeth as he danced sparking another round of broken glasses. We had noticed all the tables had teeth marks on the corners, the sign of a good taverna. Yianni himself did the great trick of picking up a glass of ouzo from the floor while he danced and drinking it without using his hands. After successfully drinking one, a friend gleefully rushed out to place another in front of him. By the end of the dance Yianni had downed four ouzos and staggered off the dance floor.

We finally managed to get away after promising to let Yianni the Fisherman come to our house and teach us the hasapikos. He said he'd bring the music with his battery record player.

We had then met Brett and Anna who were taking us to another Yianni name day party in town, this one for Tall Yianni. Yianni was so nicknamed because he was over six feet and carried his height proudly.

The rag rugs which carpeted the islanders' floors in the winter had been rolled up and the tables and chairs pushed to the edge of the room, the center cleared for dancing. Yianni's wife Louisa had let their children stay up late for the occasion because they knew we were bringing Heather and Davidaki. The children settled themselves in a corner to play a game of Lotto which our kids had brought down.

The tables were laden with roasted meats, fried fish, cakes and candies. People helped themselves or each other to tidbits and constantly toasted Yianni as he and Louisa liberally poured from wine flasks. Everyone was dressed in their best. The women all wore brightly printed dresses and heels and the men wore sports coats although only David, Brett and Spiros, the director of the island's tiny museum wore a tie.

Someone brought a small record player which provided the music, although many times people sang with the records or pre-empted it altogether as they sang their own songs as a group. The island music was not mournful and wailing like the mountain music and was much more rhythmic.

Because they lived in town instead of the countryside most of Brett and Anna's friends were townspeople; shopkeepers or professionals rather than farmers like Nikki and Agapitos or Dimitri. The mile between our two houses seemed to separate two worlds. Because of Vourvoura we felt perfectly at home in the world of peasantry, while the Taylors always seemed a little like tourists when they met our country friends. I'm sure their town friends thought of us as somewhat country-bumpkinish.

Brett led a pretty young Greek woman, Maria, in an advanced state of pregnancy on to the dance floor. Everyone shouted their approval. The island women we found took part in the animated gatherings, drinking wine and dancing freely with the men.

Brett danced the Balos with Maria. It was the favorite dance on Paros, in which two people wove around each other without ever touching. We had learned it from Dimitri. When the music ended Brett tried to persuade her to dance again but she clutched her belly and laughed.

"I'll deliver! I'll deliver, Kirios Brett," and she sat down.

"A tango," someone called out a request to Yianni who was looking through the records. A tango was an occasion of great glee and some raised eyebrows because it was the only dance done in which a man and woman made physical contact outside of holding hands in a circle dance, and even then there was often a handkerchief between them. The tango carried an enticing air of naughtiness with it.

Spiros asked his wife Eleni to dance with him. Short, very round Panayotis got tall, stately Anna and I danced with Nikos the Barber, our landlord. David tried to persuade Tarsa to dance but she was too prim and proper to tango, much preferring watching the rest of us closely for improprieties.

Panayotis led Anna through a very melodramatic exaggerated version of the dance as if he were in an old silent movie, keeping a straight poker face as he whirled her about and dipped her despite the shouts and teasing of the onlookers. When it ended, he bowed very formally to her and thanked her, still straight faced and serious. It wasn't until he sat down that he grinned broadly and bowed to a spontaneous burst of applause from us all.

The evening finally ended with a *Kalamatiano*. It was a circle dance involving three steps one way, two the other. It was a very beautiful dance and it was done at least once at every gathering to whatever music had the right beat.

We wished Tall Yianni *kronia pola* as we left the party, and shook his hand again.

"*Na pate sto kalo*," he called after us in the dark...go with the good.

Chapter 34

Papoo

Since the Taylor's house was right along our path to town we frequently stopped in when we made our shopping forays down the mountain.

One day while we were sitting on their terrace enjoying some sunshine we heard a drum beating. Old Papoo, which meant Grandpa, Brett's landlord who lived right next door, was coming across the small field that separated their homes, beating a small drum and singing.

Papoo was not quite a peasant, like Nikki or Dimitri, but neither was he a town person. His home was literally at the edge of town - the last one before the fields and terraces that surrounded the village began their climb up the mountain. He was eighty three years old and a satisfied man.

Today he was very drunk.

"Money, money. Give me money," he called.

"Papoo, do you think you are such a good musician we should pay you?" Brett laughed.

Papoo grinned, "No, if you give me money I will STOP playing!"

We all laughed and Papoo sat down. He thought we foreigners were endlessly amusing, and with Papoo, if he loved you, he spent hours thinking of tricks to play on you. He was pleased this one had worked so well.

We had seen one of his pranks when his favorite cousin had come to visit. Papoo had been coming back from his orange orchard where he had been harvesting the fruit when he got the word. His wife told him the cousin and his wife had gone to a wine shop to see other relatives until Papoo got back.

Taking a huge basket of oranges, Papoo set off to the wine shop. We were shopping when we heard a commotion and went outside the shop, along with everyone else.

There was Papoo at the door of a wine shop bellowing at the top of his lungs for everyone to come out. The cousin's wife was one of the first to step out. Papoo stepped up to her, bowed and handed her an orange.

"Thank you," she said.

Then he handed her another which she took in her other hand and thanked him again. Then he handed her another, so she put her first orange in her pocket to accept the third, then he handed her another, and another. Each time she thanked him nicely although she began to laugh when her pockets, her hands, her apron were all full. Everyone was laughing as he politely bowed and handed over oranges until they were laying at her feet and the basket was at last empty.

Today we sat in the sun and Papoo told us about how dumb his sheep was and how smart his goat was. Both animals were hobbled in the field in front of us and illustrated Papoo's contention. The sheep slavishly followed the goat around. Every time the goat ate alfalfa, the sheep ate alfalfa, every time the goat ate hay, the sheep ate hay. As we watched the goat peed. Sure enough, a moment later the sheep peed. The goat periodically became thoroughly frustrated with its dumb follower and would turn around and butt her. But, we gave the sheep credit for persistence because it doggedly began following the goat around again.

"This week is my name day," Papoo told us. "You must come and make a party, a *glendi* , at my house on Saturday."

"Yes, Papoo, we wouldn't miss it."

Papoo always regaled us with wisdom he had gleaned in his life. He had had sixteen children (actually twelve, we learned, but he considered a miscarriage a birth), and five of his children were daughters.

"And with each daughter's dowry, I gave her a house," he said proudly.

It was a remarkable accomplishment, and explained why he was so self-satisfied and why everyone in town, even the haughtiest gentry like Tarsa, looked up to him.

As we headed back up the hill we racked our brains to come up with an appropriate present to give to Papoo on his name day. We finally decided on a bamboo flute we could buy from a flute maker in town. Papoo might not be able to play it, but he could play all sorts of tricks on us all with it.

Chapter 35

Island Christmas

We were glad we had finally put our foot down about the roof repairs for the rains settled in with a vengeance. For five or six days downpours would alternate with heavy drizzle. We had finally bought a small kerosene heater. The mildew had threatened to take over if we didn't get the place warm and the tiny fireplace in the corner of the bedroom wasn't up to the job.

The week before Christmas an arctic cold spell set in. The rain became sleet and even occasional snow. The water on the path to town froze and the goat track which doubled as a stream bed in the rains, became a river of ice and dangerous to navigate. We managed to get to Nikki's house one afternoon to check on her and Agapitos. They were surviving well but Nikki told us it was the coldest winter she could remember.

We kept the children warm and entertained at home and took it in turns to brave the trip to the village as we made our Christmas preparations.

There were no Christmas trees. The Greeks prized their trees and would never sacrifice one for a single occasion, but they did prune their cypresses and used the boughs as decorations even though it was still a relatively new custom. We pruned a couple large acacia trees in front of our house for our "tree". The large boughs we cut were still covered with tiny yellow balls of blossom and it looked as though it were already decorated. The kids made decorations out of bread dough we dried and painted.

I searched the village for wrapping paper. It didn't exist. I finally unearthed some colored art paper in a tiny shop and bought the entire supply. There were few toys on the island and the ones we found were shoddily made and expensive. There was no income tax in Greece. Instead anything imported was taxed. Most Greek children didn't have toys, but improvised their own playthings except for marbles which were very popular. We found a supply of ceramic ones but never could find the large playing marbles made out of Parian marble that some of the village children had. We couldn't talk any of them into selling us one of theirs; they were too highly prized.

Instead we made toys for the children. David made a periscope and set of stilts. I sewed stuffed animals and toys. I had noticed that there were very few dolls around. In some houses we had noticed some very fancy and expensive Italian made dolls set on a mantel as an ornament in the place of honor, but never had we seen children playing with dolls. I decided to make all the children we knew rag dolls and spent many evenings on the project working by lamplight.

Tom and Nancy were spending the holidays in Athens but we invited Brett and Anna up for Christmas Eve dinner. We would go to their house on Christmas Day if the path was passable. The weather had warmed slightly so the ice melted but the evening was stormy when Brett and Anna toiled up the mountain and the wind was blowing a gale.

I had cooked a special dinner making as many traditional things as I could using our gas burner and small camping oven. We had roast chicken, stuffing, yams and such set out. We had just sat down when we heard a voice hailing us through the wind. David opened the door in the teeth of the howling gale and shouted, "*Yia sou, ela* ...come in."

Dimitri emerged from the dark, dripping wet and chilled. It had been three weeks since our last visit and he had missed us. He had heard that Christmas was a big celebration with the foreigners and had braved the storm to share it with us. Brett and Anna had met him briefly before but didn't really know him. We sat him by the tiny brush fire and wanted to give him a shot of raki to warm him but instead he pulled a bottle of aged Metaxa brandy from his coat, a special potable indeed.

By the end of dinner everyone was very jolly. We all sang Christmas carols while David played a recorder. Dimitri sat back grinning happily, thoroughly enjoying himself. We tried translating some of the carols into Greek for him but Greeks love talking so much that they would never use one syllable where five will do. Even "Oh, Christmas tree" came out "Oh *kristouganiatiko denthra*" a mouthful of syllables we couldn't squeeze into the tune. When I told him the legend of Good King Wenceslas he was utterly delighted. Dimitri loved a good story.

We finally tucked the kids into bed after answering Heather's question about if Santa Claus had a black mustache in Greece instead of a white beard. We didn't think so. The children safely asleep, we began to fill the stockings by the fireplace. Dimitri was instantly alert

"What are you doing?"

"This is an American custom. We put candies and little gifts in the stockings for the children to find in the morning when they wake up."

He was charmed, "But that is wonderful."

He insisted on adding some of his hard earned coins. He was equally charmed when he saw me wrap the last of the gifts in colored paper.

"Beautiful."

We invited him to stay the night rather than ride back to Marathi in the storm. He consented and Brett and Anna bid us all good-night, inviting him to the next day's feast. We gave him our sleeping bags.

In the morning he was gone before we woke up. The storm was over and the sun shone.

We had just finished opening our presents when Nikos the Barber and Tarsa walked in. They had come up the hill bringing walnuts and cakes. Nikos also carried a great basket full of oranges. I was sitting on our bed with Heather and Davidaki and he walked up to us and turned the basket upside-down over our heads, showering us with the fruit. The children laughed and the beautiful oranges rolled everywhere. I knew how Papoo's cousin must have felt when he had presented her with an abundance of fruit.

We took a walk later distributing the gifts we had made for all our friends. We had bought Nikki a fancy coffee set and she insisted on making some coffee for us in it and serving us in her new cups.

At Spiros and Eleni's house I gave their little girl a rag doll. Her eyes lit up when she saw it and she hugged it immediately. But then over my protests and her sorrow Eleni took it away and propped it up on the mantel next to a huge, elegantly gowned Italian doll. All the dolls I made the children suffered the same fate.

Chapter 36

The Elli

The ferry had become only as predictable as the sea conditions. From a few times a week, the schedule had been cut to once a week. The boat did more than pick up or disembark passengers. It brought the mail and was the supply life line for the island.

The Elli was the name of the boat that served Paros. In the winter she would start sounding her melodic whistle from the time she rounded the head across from the harbor even though it would take her a good twenty minutes more to tie up at the dock

Up on our hill, whenever we heard the Elli call we'd put a stop to everything and unless the path was dangerously icy we'd pelt down the mountainside as fast as we could to meet her. If she was carrying a special load of something, the boat office would hire the town crier to announce it to the villagers. The town crier got ten drachmae for each of his announcements and patrolled the docks and main street. He also rang the church bells for special occasions. We enjoyed trying to imagine him on the television program "What's My Line?" in America.

Everyone gathered at the dock to watch the vessel pull up and lower her ramps that let the eagerly anticipated bales and packages reach the shore. Once or twice the seas were so rough the Elli couldn't dock safely and small skiffs went out to unload her and deliver passengers.

The most welcome bundles to come ashore for us were the mail sacks and we faithfully followed the clerk to the post office where Stellio, the postmaster, would receive them with great dignity.

Stellio always wore a suit and tie, and considered himself a cut above the islanders because he was from Athens. Or so the islanders thought. David and I were convinced that his solemn exterior hid a quick wit and dry sense of humor. I, for one, was determined to get beyond his facade and tormented Stellio by asking him bizarre questions and telling him American jokes translated into Greek.

But when the winter mail sacks came Stellio could wreak his revenge, taking his time sorting the mail, holding ours until last to keep us prisoners at the post office.

This time the storms had kept the Elli from the island for three weeks. The stores ran so low on some supplies the shopkeepers began rationing them. There was no shampoo left on the island and certain feminine items were at an all-time low. David had begun sharpening his razor blades because there were no new ones to be found in the shops. Even toilet paper began running low.

One day a shop keeper joked that the population of the island was likely to see a big increase if the Elli didn't come soon. Brett was with us and burst into laughter when the shopkeeper told him something in a whisper.

Once outside the shop he said, "The island is running out of condoms and the island men are getting very worried because their wives refuse to have sex with them."

Every day that we went to town we stopped at the shipping office to ask if the Elli would make it to port. The shipping clerk, normally very polite, began to get grouchy because of the constant questions that he could not answer.

We were at home looking at the white capped sea when David pointed, "Here she comes," he announced a moment before she sounded her horn.

There was no need to tell the kids. They were ready to go. Candy supplies had also run low on the island and we had promised, Saturday or no, when the Elli came it was candy day. We ran pell mell, leaping from stone to stone over rivulets until we reached the flagstone streets of the village. Most of the shopkeepers in town had gathered eagerly at the docks. Brett, Anna, Tom and Nancy and a British couple that had become trapped on the island as they waited for the ferry all stood at the docks. The Brits carried their backpacks and bolted up the ramps even before they were completely lowered, waving hasty good-byes.

The first order of the day was the precious mail sacks. Stellio himself had come to claim them after the long dearth of mail. We followed him to the post office. This time it was no joke. The last boat before the storms had brought no mail for us, a fact Stellio had communicated with a cool, Athenian lifting of his eyebrows in an abbreviated gesture for no. We had been too long without news from home.

"Hey, Stellio," I said as we watched him sort through the sack of foreign mail. "There was a man in a taverna with green pants, purple shoes and yellow shirt. He bought drinks for everyone then asked the man next to him, 'How old do you think I am?'"

Stellio stopped his sorting and looked at me with bemused expectancy, waiting for the punchline.

"Oh, tell him," David said impatiently. "Or he'll never get the mail sorted."

"'Forty-four' the man replied. 'How did you know?' the brightly dressed man was surprised. 'I have a cousin who is twenty-two and he is half-crazy.'"

Stellio was unable to help himself, cracked a smile and actually emitted a chuckle. "Here," he said handing us a letter.

We were overjoyed but as we went to the door he told us, "No, wait. There may be more."

In short order he made it through a stack of letters and handed us two more.

"Go to the shops then come back in case there is more," Stellio waved us out.

In great glee we went to a cafe where the owner, happily unpacking his supplies, made us coffee and served the children some cookies and lemonade. A holiday mood had spread throughout the town and friends passing by seeing us with mail smiled happily, "From mamma and papa?" We'd wave our answer yes joyfully.

We read our mail aloud to each other and the children, then went shopping, buying Heather and Davidaki their candy first. One of our shopping rituals was to collect all our lepta and save them for our lepta-string. Lepta were coins with a hole in the middle. They were worth so little that many people used them as washers because washers cost more than the lepta. Because of the hole in the center the children liked to string them. Someday when the string was full we would treat ourselves to dinner in a restaurant with it and enjoy seeing the expression of the proprietor when we paid him with the string of coins.

When we were done shopping, our backpacks were bursting with the load but we didn't mind the weight a bit. Before we were ready to head up the hill we stopped back at the post office. Usually once the mail was sorted Stellio had one of his clerks hand it out but when he saw us he came over himself.

With a flourish he whipped out three more envelopes from his inner pocket and presented them to us with a bow. We were thrilled and I smiled at Stellio.

He broke his reserve a moment and grinned at our pleasure.

"Half crazy. Very good, Kiria Andrianni, very good," he shook his head in amusement and chuckled again as he waved us away.

Chapter 37

Swallow Days

"The swallow days are late this year," Nikki told me I was out by the well washing clothes. She sat on the low stone wall beside me holding a cup of coffee. Nancy was visiting, too, and was busily knitting. Knitting wasn't a hobby on Paros, it was a survival skill. If Tarsa hadn't taught me how to turn a heel, we wouldn't have had socks that winter.

"Swallow days?"

"Of course, *helithones meres*...swallow days."

Nancy quit counting stitches and looked up from the sweater she was making, "Halcyon days. Remember reading poems about them in school?"

"But what are they?"

"It's a period of ten days or a fortnight or so when it gets warm and sunny as in the summer. A sort of false spring. It's quite delightful."

I finished the washing and carried the clothes to the line David had strung between the lemon trees. The sheets I had washed earlier were dry and I took them down.

"Wait, Andrianni," Nikki said, and she darted to the front of our house and returned with a handful of fuzzy acacia blossoms. She tucked them into the folds of the sheets "Now they will smell nice when you use them."

Before long the swallow days did arrive and I saw how they got their name. The swallows in town were intoxicated with the weather and performed wild aerobatics and even daringly buzzed the island cats. Our cat, Gree-gree, was driven wild. He couldn't catch the speedy fliers and the swallows knew it. The weather was so mild we even went swimming one day.

Nancy told me saffron grew on the island and was blooming. David and the children and I took long walks keeping an eye out for the beautiful wild crocuses that grew on the north slopes of the hills. We carefully collected the stamens in a little jar, always leaving just a few stamens behind so the flowers could be fertilized. The island women didn't use saffron in their cooking so we had no competition gathering the spice.

The swallow days came to an end with a wild storm that kept us housebound for three days. The town lost its electricity for the duration of the storm we learned afterwards, but up on the mountainside we had been snug with our oil lamps and kerosene heater.

Chapter 38

Black Jim From Bad Rock

The winter days grew slowly longer and milder as we approached spring, and the rains were less frequent. Wildflowers turned the terraced fields rainbow colors. The untilled fields above our house were vivid with them. One morning while we were out for a walk we discovered a woman and her young daughter at work cutting the weeds and wildflowers.

"*Yia sas*," we greeted them, and seeing that they were having some problems tying up the bundles of weeds, we stopped to help them. We spent the rest of the day scything and gathering the weeds with them.

"For the animals," they explained.

In the late afternoon a man showed up leading a few donkeys. It was the town garbage collector who daily took one of his donkeys through the village to collect the refuse from the townspeople. His name was Dimitri Mavris and he was from Kakopetra. That translated as Black Jim from Bad Rock and we always called him that.

We fastened the bundles we had made to their donkeys' backs and turned to go home but the family wouldn't hear of it. Instead they led us through the hills to a small valley strewn with giant rock outcroppings.

Their house, built right up against one of the great boulders was drowning in flowers that Maria, Mrs. Black Jim, cultivated. There was delicate white lace stretched over each of the windows and lace curtains hung in each of the doors. We commented on how pretty it was.

"For flies. So many flies," Maria complained. "I kill them and kill them but still they come. I don't understand it."

We thought maybe the dump Black Jim had created below the house had something to do with it but held our tongues. We entered a newly whitewashed room and Maria began preparing a meal of meatballs and vegetables at a small fireplace built into the corner. Vasiliki helped her father unload the donkeys after she had served us the ritual sweet and glass of water as a welcome. She was thirteen and extraordinarily beautiful.

Black Jim was pleased to be entertaining us and when we sat down to eat he produced a large, dusty bottle of his finest black wine, *mavrodaphne*, a specialty of the island. We ate and drank and talked of many things: the weather, the next festival, their family history and ours. Jim and Maria got a bit tipsy and began telling us about their courtship which had been unusual and was famous throughout the island.

"Maria was pretty then, and not old and ugly as she is now," he said. I stole a glance at Maria who didn't seem in the least offended, and was having trouble suppressing her mirth at what was to come next.

"She had a good dowry, so men were bargaining every day with her parents to marry her. They didn't need a marriage broker," he alluded to the way the job of finding a mate was usually done in the towns.

"Me, I saw her looking at me in a certain way and I thought, 'this is the woman who is going to be my wife' but the others had more money or land and her parents would not consider me. Still I would catch her eye and know she felt differently.

"I was big and strong then. So one night I had some raki to make me brave and I went to the field above the house and hid. When I saw her come out of the house to go to the well, I ran down and picked her up."

At this point Maria could no longer hold back and she laughed until she had to hold her sides.

"Her parents came running and yelling, but they were old and I was young. I ran up the steep slope and before their eyes I took her. And you loved it, old lady, didn't you?" he asked Maria fondly. Tears were streaming down her face she was laughing so hard.

"There they were below, but afraid to attack me," he leaped up from the table holding his head yelling. "Ai, ai, ai. Ach, *Panagia mou*, Holy Virgin, help us!" He imitated his in-laws' distress.

"And I kept shouting 'Hey you, I have your daughter. No more virginity for sale!'"

"Didn't they call the police?" David asked.

"Ten miles by donkey from the nearest town, how could they? Besides a neighbor was there, so everyone would know. No, they had to accept me as their son-in-law." The two of them laughed together.

Vasiliki sat in the corner smiling quietly. She had heard her parents' story many times before. She was the youngest of their seven children, the child of their middle age and the only one left at home.

Late that night after more tales, she accompanied us part of the way home lighting our way with a candle lantern. Her flawless face, olive tinted, and her black braids as thick as her wrists were illuminated and she looked like a creature from a romantic painting. I wondered what her courtship would be like.

Chapter 39

Nikki's Bread

"Nikki, do you know how to bake bread?"

She and I were sitting on our terrace drinking cups of thick Greek coffee that I brewed each day when she came.

"Of course, Andrianni"

"Do you think you could show me?"

"Let's look at the oven and see if it is any good."

I took our flashlight and she and I went out back to the big, round brick oven that was in the back room of our little stone house. She peered in, shining the light around carefully, then approved it.

"Good, no cracks. First, Andrianni, you must take a sack to the windmill and buy flour. Then buy yeast from the bakery. Tonight you will start it and in the morning I will come and show you how to make bread. Also, send the children up the mountainside for brush."

That afternoon David and I and the children took two clean pillow cases and walked to the windmill at the edge of the harbor, the one the people in town called "the new mill". The Meltemi, the summer wind, was blowing and the noise at the mill was overpowering as the sails whipped around outside, and the creaking and groaning of timbers mingled with the flapping of canvas. The whole building shuddered with it.

The miller greeted us with a big grin. Heather and Davidaki were delighted because he was covered from head to toe with flour like a great snowman. He led us up the tiny spiraled staircase and shouted to us over the din.

"You make bread, eh? We'll fill the bags with the best flour."

The wind shifted directions slightly and the miller took the time to readjust the sails by rotating the entire thatched roof until they moved properly again. We knew the miller from the local cafes. He showed the children the sacks of grain and then the fine flour that trickled from the grooves in the big stone mill wheels. He lifted the children one at a time so they could feel the power in the turning of the huge wooden shaft that connected the mill stone to the sails.

"This was the mast of a ship that sunk in the harbor," he told us indicating the shaft.

"When was that?" asked David

"When the mill was built, three hundred years ago."

"But we thought this was the new mill."

"The other is much older," he explained.

At last he took our sacks and filled them grinning all the while.

"You laugh at us?" I asked.

"No," he said "I praise you. The 'moderna' town wives all buy from the bakery. Now the American bakes in her own oven."

We left and he called after us, "*Kali orexi*. Good appetite."

Our next stop was the bakery where Soula, the baker's daughter, was weighing out dough on a balance scale while her younger brother fired up the wood fueled oven. We asked for yeast.

"Ah, you bake. Good Now I have fewer loaves to make," she smiled.

"You are tired of baking, Soula?"

"Yes, with all my heart. In the fall I marry my betrothed when he gets out of engineering school in Athens. Then I will never bake a loaf of bread again as long as I live."

"Oh, the artists will lose their muse," I said.

We laughed together. All of Brett's male art students fell in love with beautiful Soula and spent their time hanging around the bakery buying bread they didn't need. She had a collection of portraits they had done of her. She handed me a lump of dough wrapped in paper.

"This is yeast?" I asked, expecting something in a little foil package.

"Of course," she replied. Then she gave me instructions on how I was to use it.

I took the dough home, dissolved it in a little warm water, added some flour and honey, then covered it with a clean folded blanket.

Early in the morning Nikki came and we uncovered the mixture which was now seething and bubbling. She exclaimed happily over it throwing back her hands appreciatively, and I felt absurdly proud. But she shook her head over our pile of brush.

"Po-po-po-po," she said in disapproval, and sent the children back into the hills in search of more.

In the meantime in lieu of a wooden kneading trough like other people owned, Nikki asked for the large galvanized tub we used for bathing. She planned to make a lot of bread. She scalded it carefully with boiling water. Then instead of adding the flour to the liquid in American fashion, Nikki economically decided how much flour she wanted to use and began adding the liquid to it after first adding the yeast mixture.

She had me heat a kettle of water and started kneading at one end of the tub, asking me to add a little warm water from time to time. More and more water went into the tub and little by little she incorporated all of the flour.

Nikki, in spite of her heavy body, was incredibly light on her tiny feet. She seemed to float as if daring us to see her touch the ground. It was as if she wouldn't leave as much of a footprint as a baby. Her gestures were delicate, too. Her butterfly-like hands worked over the dough, fists darting into it, twisting, then lightly withdrawing.

She did a little dance around the tub. Round and round she went rhythmically moving her whole body as she pushed, punched and cajoled the dough for almost an hour. Magically it began to grow. It glistened and swelled forming a tight, glossy skin. It came to life under her lightly moving, strong hands.

Once she stopped and asked me to try. Instantly the dough turned sluggish. I was exhausted in a few minutes and she scolded me.

"Po-po-po-po, Andrianni I am twice your weight and twice your age at least, and you knead like an old lady."

She took over again and the inert mass seemed to spring to her hands, taking life again from her little dance.

At length Nikki pronounced it ready and began forming loaves. She made them big enough to put her arms around them David and I clumsily followed her gestures but gave up and settled for smaller loaves, although I impressed Nikki by braiding one loaf like a challa. Then at her directions we carried the loaves in and laid them carefully between clean sheets on our bed. She covered them gently with all the blankets we had in the house and some of the rugs.

"In the winter tell the children to get in bed with the bread to keep it warm," she instructed me.

We washed the tub and swept out the oven as the bread rose and found the long handled wooden paddle that had come with the house. We also went to gather more brush for

Heather and Davidaki had returned scratched, sweaty and tired but still without enough brush to satisfy Nikki.

Nikki set fire to a big tumbleweed and thrust it into the oven. She shouted for David and I to work fast and one after another we shoved weeds or brush into the oven as rapidly as possible.

The small chimney in front of the oven could not handle all the smoke and it poured out from the opening, darkening the whitewashed walls of the room and blinding us, but Nikki kept calling for more brush until we used up the entire supply. She closed the opening with the heavy metal door and waited a few minutes. She then glanced inside and gave a crow of triumph.

"Look, David, Andrianni," she pointed to the walls of the oven which had turned snow white with ash. "Now it is ready."

She swept the coals to one side with a stick. We carried the loaves in on the paddle and again she had a touch we could not duplicate. The loaves we carried slumped while hers sat plump and happy on the paddle as if they hadn't been disturbed and were still sleeping in our bed. She closed the oven door and at last rested.

I made coffee for us and we sat outside under the grape arbor.

"And so now, Andrianni, you know how to bake bread."

She and I gossiped and had a discussion about donkeys, and how they do not get gray with age like people. We got philosophical about animals and their relation to people. She agreed with Cross-Eyed Nikos that people were the animals' gods, so we had better behave and be good to them if we wanted our god to be good to us.

We swirled the thick grounds left in the bottom of our tiny coffee cups and turned the cups upside-down for a few minutes. Then Nikki showed me how to tell fortunes from the patterns left by the dried grounds.

"See? Marks like fire mean passion. Tall shapes are men, round ones women. Tiny drops are children, and this," she pointed out a coin-like mark. "This one means money. You have a lucky future, full of them all."

An hour passed by and she looked in on the bread, calling for the paddle. One by one she removed the great round, crusty loaves, and washing the charcoal from the bottom crust with a clean, wet rag, set them on a stone wall outside to cool.

She nodded happily, "Good bread, Andrianni."

It was all I could do to persuade her to take a loaf of it home with her. She finally consented to take the fancy braided one, and said I could bring a big loaf that night when Agapitos, her husband, was home. We stacked our bread on a bamboo shelf we had made that hung from our ceiling and regarded it proudly.

That night we went to Nikki's house and found she had set up a table in their big room instead of her kitchen, a great honor. She had even spread the table with her fringed cloth that only came out on holidays. She laid out olives, cheese and sardines, and we placed the great loaf in the center of the table. Old Agapitos bragged about Nikki's baking abilities, then, first making the sign of the cross with the knife in hand, cut a slice of bread using a dramatic motion of his long dangerous looking knife. I was afraid he'd cut his face as he swept it dramatically towards himself, but he didn't.

He looked at the slice carefully and smelled it while Nikki looked on apprehensively. I sat on the edge of my seat as he tasted it judicially. A puzzled look came over his face at the first bite. He held the slice up to the light of the oil lamp and looked through it.

"Andrianni, " he said reproachfully. "You bought your flour at the new mill."

I looked at him astonished, "How did you know that, Agapitos?"

"I can see. I can taste."

"Is it important?"

"No, it doesn't matter. He gave you his best flour. But our cousin owns the big mill."

"Oh," I apologized. "I didn't know. I'm sorry"

He ate the slice of bread with a gourmet's satisfaction "It is not important. This is very good bread."

Nikki and I smiled at each other.

Chapter 40

Scandal

Brett and Anna had a friend named Adonis. He was older than they were, in his early fifties. He was a musician, playing the guitar and bouzouki in the tavernas. He was separated from his wife and child who lived in Athens. Nikki didn't like him.

"From Syros," she said and spat to ward off the evil eye. "And sly."

We attributed her dislike to inter-island prejudice. We were always being told that the people from Syros were sly, the ones from Naxos thieves and so on. On the other islands it was said the Parians were drunkards. But Nikki was right about one thing, and that was that Adonis refused to make eye contact when he talked to someone.

Adonis would sit in the corner during the frequent gatherings Brett and Anna had at their house, brooding over the proceedings and gazing a lot at Anna. She, aware of his attention, began to get more animated when he was around. David and I were uneasy over the situation which seemed to get more intense every time we saw Brett and Anna.

Adonis took to spending a lot of time at their house. Brett, who played classical guitar, was delighted to have a friend join him in playing duets. Sometimes Anna joined in the music, playing her recorder.

One night the three of them showed up at our house late. They had had dinner in town and decided to visit us. We sat outside so as to not wake Heather and Davidaki, and brought out a bottle of wine. Brett was already very drunk. As the strains in his relationship with Anna had developed he had taken to drinking more heavily. He didn't even notice when Adonis and Anna left the table, first one, then the other. I went around the house to use the privy and stumbled on them in each other's arms.

The next day I went to town to get the mail and ran into Anna at the post office. She took me aside.

"Brett must never know about last night," she warned me with fierce eyes. "He would never understand and would be very hurt. We were all just drunk."

That much was true. I simply nodded and turned away.

But she must have changed her mind about discretion because shortly afterwards things escalated. We began to avoid both Brett and Nina. His paintings stood on their easels half finished. Whenever we saw him he talked feverishly about how happily married they were. Anna was becoming more and more flagrant about Adonis. She was seen at the beach and in the cafes with him where they outraged the Greeks by holding hands in public.

Anna underwent a change. She began to glow with the consciousness of her own sexuality. Her features, usually a little coarse, lit up and became beautiful. Her movements became slower and more graceful. She walked through the village erect, her bosom thrust forward, the wind blowing her hair and molding the loose dresses she always wore to her body. She appeared to be fully conscious of her body even to the ends of her long hair. She looked as if she was always on her way to a tryst.

I was giving English lessons to the police chief's daughter at the time and would meet the family at a cafe. The girl's parents and the cafe owner would always greet me with new tales of Anna's infidelities. The entire village was violently upset. While the women pitied her, feeling she was being used by Adonis, the men responded with vehemence. I suspected that was partially because she aroused them as well and so threatened the status quo.

David and I were at the butcher's shop one day when the butcher closed the door and began raging to us.

"What does she want with an old man when she is married to a *palikari* (a young warrior, the highest praise for a man). Why doesn't Kirios Brett take her and beat her?"

He grew animated as he demonstrated what should be done. "He should hit her and throw her on the ground and kick her. Then he should grab her by the hair and drag her through the streets shouting for the people to come and spit on her."

We escaped the shop and agreed it was no wonder most Greek wives were faithful to their husbands.

Anna's affair began to have repercussions for us. She and I were both American, we both had blonde hair, were both married to artists. Although we really didn't look alike, people who didn't know us mistook me for her. One Sunday some people spat at me as they came out of church and I rushed home in tears. We had begun looking for a house closer to town but when we found one we liked the owner wouldn't rent to us because he thought I was Anna. Spiro and Eleni tried to intercede for us but it didn't help. If I looked like her I would probably act like her, the owner concluded.

One day I was at Nikki's house and a lady came to visit. She looked at me and asked Nikki if I was the adulteress. Nikki, shocked, told her I wasn't and I embarrassed the woman by explaining in Greek that I was most happily married to my own *palikari* and was not interested in a Syrian scoundrel.

Afterwards Nikki wrung her hands and wept, "You must dye your hair, Andrianni. This is no good."

"Let Anna dye her hair," I answered, upset.

Every time I saw Nikki after that she'd ask me to dye my hair. Nancy, who was fortunately a brunette, agreed with Nikki.

"How about red hair? It's pretty."

One morning Tarsa came up bearing her radio to tell us some news. Anna had left on the boat for Athens the night before with Adonis. My life became easier, but Brett wandered the streets like a wounded deer.

Chapter 41

Holy Week

The sound of bells woke us at dawn on Good Friday. Every bell in every church in the village below was ringing. After a vigorous clanging to mark the beginning of the litany, the bells slowed to a steady, sad toll.

The village had been bustling with preparations the first four days of Holy Week. Everyone had been whitewashing; the houses, the tree trunks and even the paving stones of the streets all gleamed in the sun with a new white coat. Nikos and Tarsa had sent up a load of whitewash for us and our little house looked like new. The stairways in town got another coat.

Donkeys bearing loads of whitewash met in the narrow alleyways causing noisy traffic jams. One stubborn donkey stopping or even sitting down in the narrows alleyways that made up the streets of the village caused a noisy backup with everyone yelling, one person tugging at the front end of the donkey while another pushed from the rear. The donkey owners carried whips made from the dried and twisted intestines of slaughtered animals and they plied their animals with them as a last resort. Eventually all the houses got their whitewash.

Everyone had carried pots of flowers out to adorn their terraces and balconies. Women industriously washed sheets and blankets, aired mattresses, beat rugs. The shops were full of people buying new clothes and shoes for their children. The young girls sat outside in the sun drying their just-washed hair, and they constantly pestered the dressmakers, worried their new dresses wouldn't be finished on time.

Most people had been keeping a strict fast throughout the seven weeks of Lent; each week they eliminated something else until they ate nothing but boiled vegetables. The joyful tension built up until the air was thick with it. We were as excited as children in a snowfall before Christmas.

On Holy Thursday the little girls of the village had gone from door to door in the village begging for flowers. Everyone gave them blossoms. We had been puzzled until Nikki had told us it was to decorate Christ's bier. It all seemed very festive, the laughing girls carrying baskets of flowers.

But now, suddenly with the ceaseless, mournful bells, a pall seemed to settle over the island. David and I walked to Nikki's house. She was sitting outside her doorway sobbing.

"Nikki! What's the matter," I cried.

"Oh, Andrianni, he is dead, he is dead," the tears fell.

"Who, Nikki" I asked alarmed, convinced something had happened to someone in her family.

"Christ is, Andrianni. Can't you hear the bells?"

I looked at old Agapitos and saw he was weeping, too

"It is true, Andrianni," he said. "He is dead."

We left a short while later feeling moved and bewildered by their honest grief. The people we passed in town didn't even smile. Everyone looked solemn and occasionally we'd see someone else weeping. The cafes were open but no one ordered anything but water. Everyone but the smallest children or the very ill was fasting completely today. The men sat in small groups listening to the ever present bells, barely speaking but taking comfort in one another's company.

In the afternoon everyone began heading towards the cathedral and we joined them. The bier the little girls had prepared was huge and people gathered around it, many openly crying now.

Behind the altar there was a huge cross with a life sized statue of Christ crucified on it. The priests climbed on stepladders and began to take down the statue. They handled it with great tenderness as though it were a real body. Slowly and gently they lowered it into a linen shroud held by some men below. One woman broke out into a wail and the oldest priest sobbed so hard he had to wipe his eyes with a corner of the shroud in order to see.

The statue was laid in the bier and procession formed. A priest bearing an icon led the chanting, sorrowing people out of the church and through the streets. The bells kept knelling. We left the crowd when we came to the path that led to our house and went home.

We were glad when the sun finally set and the bells were at last still.

The next day everything was transformed. Christ was still dead but the preparations for his resurrection reached a feverish pitch. In town all the shops were open although everyone was still fasting. Each butcher had dozens of little lamb and goat carcasses hung on hooks. People were eagerly buying them in anticipation of the next day's feast. Children scurried around with baskets of brilliant red eggs and bundles of white candles. Women dashed back and forth from the bakery carrying trays of bread with bright red eggs embedded in the loaves. Even Nikki was all flustered with activity and made us promise to come for a meal after midnight mass. It was hard to believe that the day before all these happy, excited people had been so grief stricken.

At eleven that night we went to the cathedral. It was thronged, and the crowd overflowed on to the steps and into the courtyard. Inside, the priests were singing one of their interminable masses. Everyone clutched unlit candles and someone pressed long white tapers into our hands when they

237

realized we had none. The church was fragrant with incense, but the children complained that all they could smell at their level was the people many of whom, despite being in Sunday clothes still carried the aromas of goats and garlic with them so we kept lifting the kids up. Shortly before midnight the lights were doused. The crowd was silent in the utter darkness.

Suddenly, a priest appeared from behind the altar with a lighted candle held high and he shouted, "From this light, let light be born."

People pressed forward to light their candles from his then quickly turned to light their neighbors'. As each person received the flame, he began half singing, half chanting a hymn. We watched the glow and the song gradually spread together throughout the cavernous stone cathedral until the building was blazing with light and everyone was singing. The priests, bearing icons and whole tiers of candles, moved down the length of the church and into the courtyard with the crowd following.

The hymn came to an end as one of the priests mounted a flower-covered platform that had been erected that day. He read for a moment from a Bible then ended his reading on the stroke of midnight by shouting, "Christ has risen!"

At that moment all the bells in the village began pealing, everyone started shouting, boys threw firecrackers and the priests shot off Roman candles. Everyone was freely embracing. People hugged us and clasped our hands exclaiming joyfully, "Christ has risen! Truly he has risen!"

Any solemnity was completely forgotten and the priest laughed and joked through the remainder of the service as he led the procession back into the church. Everyone hurried home trying to take their candles all the way still lit, some shielding the light with jars held over them, to light the oil lamps in front of the family icons and make a cross of soot on the lintel over the doorway. They called to each other as they went, "Christ has risen!"

Our candle blew out before we reached the house but we relit it and made the cross on our door even though we didn't have any icons to bless and weren't religious, but loved pageantry.

On the way to Nikki's we could hear the music and celebrating beginning all over town. The hungry Greeks were at last breaking the long fast.

Chapter 42

Pascha *(Easter)*

After having eaten at Nikki's we had made our way home and slept later than usual. Cross-eyed Nikos did not show up at dawn as usual to milk Lavitsa the goat for our breakfast so we had snored away. It didn't matter, so had most of the island it turned out.

Nikki had made us eat some of her *Magaritsa*, the traditional Easter soup, the night before despite our misgivings about its ingredients. She insisted that it was best for breaking a fast, even though we told her we had not fasted. We knew all the innards, including the salted, cleaned intestines of a lamb or kid went into *Magaritsa*. Our fears were groundless, sort of. It was delicious, but Nikki had tossed in the animal's eyes, and presented them to me as a guest of honor.

I just couldn't do it, but saved faced by telling her, "Oh, no, Nikki. These should go to the oldest."

Agapitos beamed at me as I handed him my plate, and took his, and Nikki smiled at my good manners. My dish now held a goat's ear, but that was easier to handle.

We strolled downtown to have breakfast at a cafe. Everywhere we saw people busy cooking.

"*Yia sou Christos anesti*," they all called as they waved – Christ has risen. We replied "*Alithos anesti!*" indeed, he has risen.

If there was a lamb or a kid still alive on the island they were gratefully huddling out of sight. The rest were on spits over charcoal fires.

My notebook was brimming with wonderful new recipes I had gleaned from our neighbors.

I had watched Tarsa make yoghurt cake that she was known for and had duplicated it at home. Hers was huge since she could carry it across the road to the bakery, while mine was small enough to fit into our small camp oven, but I was still pleased that it came out as well as hers.

Tarsa also showed me how to make *Koulourakia*, the Easter Cookies. She had a meat grinder which she could use to form them while most of our peasant neighbors did not and were forced to buy their cookies from the bakery if they wanted them. I made a batch with Tarsa, put them into a tin box I usually kept my sewing things in, and carried to them to everyone when the big day came, making myself very popular.

All day we roamed from feast to feast. We were handed scarlet eggs everywhere we went and challenged to egg wars. Each person held the egg firmly in one hand and two people hit the ends together. If your egg survived uncracked someone else would challenge you. Heather's egg held up all day and she clutched it proudly. She named it *Yperavgo* - Superegg.

Everyone wanted to feed us. We couldn't keep up with the Greeks' consumption. They out-ate us and teased us about our lack of appetite even when we groaning from having stuffed ourselves with roast lamb and so many sweets our teeth were spinning around in our heads.

Chapter 43

Valley of the Cherries

On one of our visits to Dimitri's house in Marathi he told us the *visino* were ripe.

"The *visino*, the cherries. You come back on Wednesday and bring Tom and Nancy. We will go to the visino valley."

When we gave the message to Tom and Nancy they became quite excited.

"Really, it is a remarkable place. You mustn't miss it," Nancy said." We shan't!"

So Wednesday morning all six of us took the bus past the place where we usually got off to visit Dimitri and rode to a village high in the hills. Dimitri met us there with his own donkey and one he had borrowed from his brother for the occasion. We tied the baskets we had been instructed to bring to the animals, put Heather and Davidaki on them and walked up into the mountains.

The stony path wound higher and higher. Dimitri sang as we climbed. The air smelled of sage that grew all around. In less than two hours we entered a valley green with trees and filled with the sound of flowing water. It reminded David and I of Vourvoura. When we drew closer to the center we saw the trees were cherry trees and loaded with fruit. Dimitri was still singing and we heard voices suddenly join in his song. The trees were full of people.

We went to the house of one of Dimitri's relatives and he, in turn, led us to an orchard that he owned. We joined the people in the trees, climbing a ladder, and began filling our baskets

At midday we all climbed down and gathered at a little church in the center of the valley. People spread blankets and we all ate bread and cheese and cherries. They were amazingly sweet and juicy.

Everyone had hung clusters of cherries over their ears like earrings. some children had prepared a cherry bough for Heather and Davidaki, hanging bunches of cherries on a branch until it looked like a great bunch of grapes but a deep scarlet.

Someone else cooked some cherries and sugar over a fire then stirred the jam-like mixture into a glass of water to make *visinada*. They came and offered us glasses of the tartly-sweet drink. Some of the cherries were so red they were almost black. We were soon covered with stains but didn't care. We washed up in one of the cold, bubbling streams.

By mid-afternoon we were full of cherries and so were our baskets, including a big one I intended to carry triumphantly to Nikki and Agapitos, and another for Nikos and Tarsa. We went back to the orchard owner's house to pay for what we had picked and left leading the donkeys loaded with the fragrant, full baskets. As we walked out of the valley the people called their farewells to us from the trees.

Chapter 44

New Faces

Now that the weather was warming up the ferry began to be more predictable. It now made daily trips instead a weekly run. The Elli was due in at three in the afternoon and we meandered down the hill to meet it and claim our mail. It was a sunny day and we were early. We hadn't seen Brett in a while so we dropped in at his house.

One reason we hadn't seen him was that he had been feverishly busy getting ready for his art students. About twenty of them showed up for each six week school session during the spring and summer months. Finding places for them to stay was not an easy task for Brett. Brett also had to persuade the shopkeepers to order the special supplies he thought the students would need. They always promised to do so and seldom did, but Brett never gave up. This season he was having a harder time than usual because Anna wasn't there to help him. He told us she was in Athens for a "vacation" and we didn't question him. But this day we found him drunk, unshaved, and half dressed in his kitchen.

"I'm expecting my first students today. I promised them dinner at my house their first night here. Anna and I always do that, but I can't handle it. Do you think you could come to the boat with me and help make excuses?"

We offered to cook for his guests and set about sobering him up and making him presentable before it was time to meet the boat. By the time we heard the Elli's whistle he was in much better condition.

We spotted Tina among those disembarking. Mini-skirted, heavily made up and sporting a head of bleached blonde curls, jaunty Tina would have looked more at home in a shopping mall than on a Greek island. She bounced down the gangplank, chatty, bubbly and flashed an expensive smile at the Greek fishermen who were watching her appreciatively.

Brett gave us a look of dismay then set about being the respectable art school director. We collected another five students and led them to their rooms then to Brett's house. We all made it through the evening and Brett pulled himself together for a summer of teaching.

We asked about Tina the next time we saw him only to learn that she had never showed up for class nor did anyone see her doing any work. She swam, wearing her pink bikini, she danced picking up the local dances at the tavernas where she partied, laughing and drinking until morning. She made a multitude of friends among the younger Greeks. When she ran low on money she rented a tiny house and began cooking for herself.

The handsome young teller at the bank began dating her. That surprised us. Costas was a serious, even somber, young man, totally unlike bubbly Tina. We often ran into them picnicking at the beach or sitting in the cafes. Art students came and went as the summer rolled on, but Tina stayed.

She was not the only one at the art school to become captivated by the island. Brett came to our house for help one day.

"Goddam poets," he muttered. "You got to help me."

"What's wrong?" David asked.

"Doug, the Welsh guy I hired to teach poetry this summer. He's on the island one day and already he's causing problems," Brett moaned.

We went down the hill with Brett to a cafe where we found the Welshman. He was short with dark curly hair and a lilting voice. His accent sounded like a rocking chair. Dylan Thomas immediately came to mind.

"Listen, Doug, Phillipas the tailor came to see me this morning and he was very upset. His daughter Eleni was taking care of his animals below your house this morning and..."

Doug broke in, "You mean her name is Eleni. That's wonderful. It's so musical."

"Doug, what happened?"

"I woke up after my first night on the island, Brett, to the most incredible sound, bells and singing. It was a wild forlorn song and discordant bells."

"Does he always talk like this?" I asked Brett.

Doug looked at me haughtily, "I am a poet," he said.

"Then you should know better," I retorted.

"Go on with your story," Brett said wearily.

"I didn't know where I was for a moment, then I remembered I was in Greece and I looked out the window. There was a flock of belled goats and a beautiful shepherdess sitting on a rock spinning. She was spinning, I tell you with a distaff and spindle," he sat back overcome by his vision.

I giggled. Almost every woman on Paros knew how to use a distaff and spindle just as they knew how to knit. Nikki had been laboriously teaching me how to use one. I was hopeless. My thread was always lumpy and I kept hurting my fingers.

"Okay, okay, I get the picture," Brett said. "What happened next?"

"What do you think? I threw on my clothes and dashed down the hillside to speak to her."

"And you scared the shit out of her," Brett said flatly.

"What do you mean?" Doug was genuinely puzzled.

"What did you say to her?" I asked.

247

"Just how she was beautiful and the embodiment of all I dreamed Greece would be and that I was in love with her," Doug said with dignity.

"You said all that in Greek?" David asked incredulously.

"Of course not. I don't know Greek. I told her in English. But our eyes met and I'm sure she understood."

I laughed out loud and David had a coughing fit.

"Then what?" demanded Brett.

"She gave me a startled glance like a nymph and ran off followed by her goats. But she'll return, I know."

"Oh shit!" Brett exclaimed. Then he explained, asking us to confirm it, that Greek girls were very, very sheltered and under no circumstances should Doug forget it. Phillipas had asked that Doug never speak to his daughter again. Doug started to protest but I interrupted.

"Besides Eleni is engaged. Her fiancé works in the police station. They are getting married next month when the druggist finds someone to replace her in the shop."

"Druggist?" Doug was puzzled again.

"Yes. Eleni only watches the animals once in a while. She's a salesgirl in the pharmacy the rest of the time."

"A ruddy shampoo clerk?" Doug was appalled.

Brett, David and I exchanged glances "I'm afraid so," I answered.

Doug slumped and his face sagged. "All right," he said as he rose muttering to himself, "A bloody salesgirl," as he walked down the street.

"Thanks," Brett said.

"I feel kind of mean," I answered.

Chapter 45

Around the Island

David and I had talked about hiking around the entire shore of Paros since we had moved there. We finally made up our minds to do it. Leaving the children with Nikki and Agapitos we packed our knapsacks and took our sleeping bags and David's spear fishing equipment.

We waved good-bye as we headed down the path from Nikki's house to the bus stop in the village. We decided to take the bus to Marathi and start our hike from there since we had covered that ground on foot many times going and coming from Dimitri's house. We left the bus, shouldered our packs and started hiking through the stony, barren hills. We came down to sea level and the landscape changed into a very fertile plain.

Not long after we found ourselves at a small harbor with a white sand beach. The weather was glorious and it was still early enough in the morning we felt we had the whole day before us. David donned his snorkel mask, grabbed his speargun, and went to look for fish while I swam, then sunned myself, reading a book, but looking up often to enjoy the sight of the brightly colored fishing boats tied to the small dock. The red, blue and yellow craft had the traditional large open eyes painted on the prows. The mountains of Naxos, the neighboring island on that side of Paros loomed high across a channel.

David surfaced and joined me on the beach resting. Some fishermen with their families walked by on their way to the dock. They called out to us advising us not to eat as we were taking sandwiches out of our knapsacks. They told us they were bringing back a giant fish, many of them, as they boarded two of the boats. Thinking it was a joke we laughed and ate our sandwiches. David went back in the sea afterwards and speared a grouper, the prize fish of the Mediterranean. We wrapped it carefully in wet seaweed and stowed it in our packs for our dinner.

We were about the leave when our fishermen friends returned. They swooped down on us, forming a small procession as they led us to a small house in a nearby vineyard. They were all triumphantly carrying fish. There were about six men and as many women and a half dozen children.

The house had no shaded terrace so more than twenty of us squeezed into a small room. They set up a table and proceeded to load it with food. They informed us they were holding a banquet in our honor. We were wishing we hadn't eaten the sandwiches. Our new friends fried and boiled fish, made salads out of grilled eggplant and beans, cooked potatoes in the fish broth with herbs and tomatoes, fried squash, cut loaves of homemade bread, cut up homemade *kaseri* cheese. They set out gourds of the inevitable wine and raki.

It was a long leisurely meal. We talked and sang songs with them. They knew a lot about us including that David was a sculptor and that we had two children. They even knew the children's ages. As we all chatted the conversation was suddenly interrupted by a heavy set, serious man sitting beside us who said, "Beet Lays" in a loud voice.

"What?" I asked.

"Beet lays," he repeated and then began to hum. "I Want to Hold Your Hand."

"Oh, the Beatles," I said, understanding at last.

He had worked on the ferries one summer, he explained and heard the American music played on the loud speaker system for the tourists. The others looked at their expert on American culture proudly.

The people told us they wanted to have a party for us that night and invite a lot of neighbors and maybe have some dancing. We told them we planned to walk around the island and wanted to be on our way so would have to regretfully decline the party this time, but perhaps another time. They made coffee and told us how far it was to the next village. They walked with us part way and said good-bye.

"Railing Stones," called the ex-ferry worker, and he began singing "Get offa my cloud."

We were full and sleepy. The sun was hot. We stopped to rest often. Soon we were in an irrigated valley totally unlike any other we had seen on the island. The fields were level and lined with trees and shrubs instead of the terraced fields everywhere else. Our view was limited to the road right in front of us because of hedgerows. The hedges also blocked the breeze and the air was stuffy. We saw a tree and gratefully sat in its shade to rest. A boy on a bicycle suddenly whizzed by us to our surprise. It was the only bicycle we had ever seen on Paros, and, indeed, this short stretch of road was one of the few places on the hilly island where one could be ridden comfortably.

We picked up our pace to get out of the hot, uncomfortable valley as quickly as possible. Soon the road climbed and at a break in the hedges we saw a village rising out of some steep rocky hills. Three sharp promontories rose above the town like great fangs, each capped with a windmill.

We made our way there and found a cafe where some old men were sitting out the heat of the day. We sat a green painted wooden table and watched the other customers toss their worry beads and chat. The tables had teeth marks on each corner where strong-jawed dancers had lifted them giving evidence of livelier nights and a younger clientele than the sleepy afternoon offered. We nursed an ouzo while we waited for the streets to cool and the sun to set.

At dusk we left the town for the beach below. We found a sheltered camp site between some sand dunes and cooked our grouper over a small driftwood fire. We unrolled our sleeping bags and fell asleep counting the shooting stars.

We woke when it was barely light, long before the village was stirring. We decided to have breakfast at a cafe in the next village which we hoped was not more than a couple hours ahead of us. We walked along feeling very light and content as we watched the sun rise.

Hearing a new bird song we were startled to see a bee-eater sitting on a tree beside the road. We had seen pictures of this exotic, colorful bird in books but this was our first glimpse of one in the flesh. He was every color of the rainbow. He was more colorful than a parrot although a good deal smaller, smaller than a robin. We stopped to watch him for a while and when we left he decided to watch us for a while. He followed us for a half hour or so until with a flash of purple, blue, green and red, he disappeared over the hills.

We came to a village of sorts but could find no cafe or store. We were hungry by this time and wanted breakfast but were told there was just one shop and it only opened in the evening when the owner came over from another village. We asked if there was a place where we could buy *paxamadia*, the twice baked chunks of bread that Greeks use on journeys. We were directed to a nearby house.

In a yard full of rose and jasmine bushes we found a young girl baking in an outdoor oven. She beamed when we asked if she had *paxamadia* for sale, and immediately began filling our packs until they were brimming with *paxamadia* still hot from the oven, fragrant with sugar and cinnamon, an elegant addition to the normally dull fare of the dried out twice baked rusks. Then she refused any payment. We filled our canteens with water from the well and left the village. The *paxamadia* was delicious and we munched it as we walked. It made us thirsty and we drank from our canteens freely.

We planned to refill them and perhaps purchase some supplies from a farmhouse, but to our growing apprehension we saw no farmhouses at all. The hills grew steeper and the scenery grew wilder and wilder. There were no terraced fields. Thorn bushes and wild sage competed for places to grow among the rocks that made up most of the landscape.

Although we could see the sea the road was high and the steep cliffs made the beaches inaccessible. By noon we had little water left. We walked on a couple more hours and still saw no place to get water. We stopped to rest and looked at the blue sea beneath us at the foot of impassible cliffs longingly, feeling hotter and sweatier than ever.

Finally we saw some men coming towards us in the distance. Relieved we hurried up to them. They had no water but they assured us there was a house with a well an hour's walk ahead of us. We walked on and saw the house by the side of the road at last.

The young housewife dressed in a dark, patched dress and headscarf was very hospitable. She asked us in and served us sweets and glasses of water as she filled our canteens. We had seen a little white sand cove edged with trees below the house and asked if we could camp there. She consented with enthusiasm then filled our remaining canteen with wine, not water, refusing any payment.

We hiked down to the cove and set up camp in the shade of trees beside the shore. David went spear fishing and disappeared around the cliffs that walled in the cove. I swam and lazed away the rest of the afternoon, reading poems by the Greek poet George Seferis.

Three times David returned to the cove triumphantly bearing something: some fish of a good size, an octopus, and finally with a great flourish he came ashore with a langouste, one of the Mediterranean lobsters. He lay in the sun to dry and I read him a poem.

"The sea cove, the hidden one
And white like a dove.
We thirsted at high noon,
But the water was salt."

The Greek word for salt or brine in the poem was "*glifo*" but David said we should change it to "*gliko*" which meant sweet. I decided that fit our cove better. At sundown we built a small fire and started to roast the langouste with a few small potatoes we had in the bottom of our knapsacks.

"All we need now is a salad and this would be a perfect meal," I said.

At that moment we heard a melodic whistling and turned to see a man striding down the hill. He was dressed in patched work clothes. He came up to us and with a smile dropped an armload of cucumbers and tomatoes at our feet.

It was the young woman's husband, come to meet us. He also brought more wine. He was accompanied by his young son who ran off shyly and watched us from a distance. We wanted him to share our meal with us but he refused. He looked at David's catch with great admiration. We drank some wine with him and I read him the poem in Greek, which he liked very much and memorized to tell his wife. We offered him the fish and the octopus. After a great deal of persuasion he took the octopus and carried it happily up the hill, whistling again.

Dusk filled up the cove and turned the sea dark purple. I rummaged in the knapsack pockets and found a candle. We stuck it in the sand beside our plates and ate our wonderful meal, then lay on the beach talking. There was no moon and the stars were very bright. We tried to find constellations.

In the morning we heated a tin of milk we still had in our packs and ate more of the spiced *paxamadia* for breakfast. We spent the day at the cove swimming and fishing, cooking the catch when we were hungry. The family visited us again and we chatted about their beautiful place. When we finally left the next day getting more water at the house, the couple begged us to return. We stopped up on the road looking down at the cove, the hidden one, and white like a dove, where we had spent such lovely, idle hours.

"And the water was sweet," I said in Greek, paraphrasing Seferis's poem again. We smiled at each other briefly before shouldering our packs and walking on.

A strong wind sprang up and we walked in the face of it. Dirt and dust blew into our eyes and took our breath away, so we were relieved when the road became paved. We walked faster. We missed the children and were eager to see them.

We got back to the village at sunset and made it to Nikki's house by dinner time. Davidaki had skinned his knee while we were gone, causing great consternation among the entire village and the doctor had treated him for free. We assured Nikki there was nothing to worry about. We were so obviously worn out from our hike that Nikki and Agapitos insisted on cooking for us. Heather and Davidaki were cheerful although Davidaki complained that Nikki made him wash his ears every day.

Chapter 46

Summer Bounty

Along with the warm weather, new foods became available. Everyone's garden started producing at once. *Kolokithia*, the zucchini squash was everywhere and Tarsa showed me how to make *"Papootsakia"* - Little Shoes out of the young small squash. My notebooks were filled with new recipes I collected from the women of the island.

The government sent over a new goat to the island to act as stud and enliven the local goat gene pool. In a few months Wonder Goat would be moved to the next island where the eager does were awaiting their gene injection. Everyone raved about the goat so much and talked of how the females were throwing triplets after mating with him, that we finally walked over to see the Wonder Goat at the agriculture office - a small stone hut with a few fields around it.

Wonder Goat was remarkable and we always thought of him with capital letters after we met him. His horns twisted and he was huge, the largest goat I had ever seen. The goat looked at me and suddenly I felt completely uneasy. It was as if he was sizing me up sexually and with arrogance. He reeked of his musk so much that David swore he could smell him all the way up the mountain at our house when the wind was right although we were over a mile away. I came away from him knowing how the ancients could think some gods came to earth in the form of animals and were looking for human females. I was relieved when he was moved on to the next island.

At any rate goats milk, one of our staples, was abundant and Nikki told me if I bought the right baskets she would teach me to make two cheeses I loved, *xinomizithra*, the soft cream cheese, and *tirovalia* which we liked best fried.

The baskets were small but deep and closely woven. I bought more than I needed because they were so pretty.

Xinomizithra was made with cold goat's milk. It took just a tiny pinch of rennet and a squeeze of lemon juice in a bowl of it. The milk stood until it became bubbly and puffed up. Then I lined a basket with muslin and let the stuff drain outside under the grape arbor until it became firm. Then the cheese was mashed with a spoon and a little salt added. This was delicious with fresh tomatoes on some of the coarse country bread. But it was not a keeper cheese. People made only as much as they would eat in a day.

Tirovalia was made with hot milk. It was also a cheese that was not kept long, although not as perishable as the *xinomizithra*. The cheese was patted with salt and left for a day before it was sliced, dipped in flour and then fried quickly in olive oil. It was especially good with eggs for breakfast.

If I wanted a hard cheese I had to make a brine with enough salt in it to float a fresh egg, and after drying the *tirovalia* for a week in the sun, I could soak it in the brine in a small cask. This was the country cheese that we were served everywhere. Once I learned to make my own it gave me an absurd sense of power, like learning to turn the heel of a sock when Tarsa taught me to knit. I could do this. I didn't need mysterious factories to make these basics for me and my family. Greece was always handing me these unexpected pleasures.

Chapter 47

Doug's World

Every time we saw Doug he was in raptures over something. We began to think it was a Welsh ailment.

"Come see my house. It is a jewel embedded in a hillside overlooking the wine-dark sea."

Such exclamations sent us all into spasms of laughter, but he didn't mind. And his house was lovely. It was a tiny flower-covered stone room that stood next to a detached kitchen, the two connected by a flagstone terrace shaded by a grape vine. He asked Brett and us over for a curry dinner one night.

"Curry?"

"Yes, indeed. It's my specialty," then he grinned. "Only thing I know how to cook, actually."

"Where did you find the spices?" I was curious.

"Oh, I brought curry powder with me. The customs man made rather a fuss over it because I had so much. He thought it was drugs," Doug laughed.

"How much did you bring?" David wanted to know.

"A two pound tin."

"What? I didn't know you could buy it by the pound!" I was impressed.

"Oh, yes. I like my curry spicy."

He certainly did. That evening after having eaten and over-eaten we soothed our burning mouths with retsina. Doug was carrying on about the Mediterranean stars and Brett asked him if he would read some of his poetry. His mood instantly shifted, becoming sober and serious. He agreed but requested, "I'll read but let's not talk about the bloody stuff tonight."

His poetry was so unlike the Doug we had seen so far we were shocked. It was gripping and strong stuff about the squalor and misery of a small mining town in Wales. It painted a poverty stricken, ugly world and the attempt to find beauty in it. We were so used to his pompous and cliché-ridden speeches the freshness and originality of his writing was a surprise.

We were silent when he was done reading for a while, then I asked, "Have you done any writing since you've been on the island?"

"Oh yes. The last four were written here. I'm working on some others. It's a great place for work. I write from sun-up to noon, then it's the sea, teaching and the cafes for me."

It was a two mile walk home and on the way we talked about Doug's life. He lived the reverse life of most poets. Instead of writing about beauty as he lived in misery, he lived in a paradise and wrote about hopeless ugliness. I forgave him for his romanticism.

But Brett didn't. A week later we ran into him in town.

"I finally talk him out of falling in love with all the Greek girls on the island and what does he do, but fall in love with a student," Brett groaned. "Next year I'll hire a farmer to teach poetry."

I realized he was talking about Doug. "If the Greeks are off limits who else is there to fall in love with here?" David answered Brett practically.

"Which student, Tina?" I asked.

"No, Sandra."

"Sandra!"

She was an American, in her early twenties married to her college professor more than twice her age. She had come to the island ostensibly to study writing at the school but also, as she frankly put it, "to have a little fling before settling down." She was young and scared behind a sophisticated, cynical mask. She was serious about her writing but she didn't seem Doug's type at all.

We sympathized with Brett and when we ran into Doug we saw what Brett meant. Doug was looking downcast and abstracted. We had to call him twice before he saw us. I reminded him he was coming up for dinner that night with Tom and Nancy.

"Would you mind if I brought a guest?" he asked.

"Of course not."

He came with Sandra and all evening long made sighing references to lovers wrenched apart by a sense of duty, boring all of us and embarrassing Sandra. When they finally left we heard their voices drifting back up the hillside. They were quarreling.

That used up a month of Doug's summer. Then Sandra left for home and husband. Doug strode the streets looking thunderous until two weeks later when Sandra sent us all a copy of a story she had written and was about to have published. It was a satire of their summer romance. Doug was jolted out of his depression and called her a Castrating American Bitch.

Chapter 48

Nikki's Night Out

Nikki refused to take payment for having watched the children while we were on our hike around the island even though she had said she would before we left. So we came up with a scheme to repay her in some way. We arranged to have the children stay the night with Tom and Nancy and told Nikki and Agapitos we were taking them out to a taverna for dinner.

Nikki was totally afluster at the idea but was also clearly thrilled. Agapitos looked at us sagely and told us that he had been to restaurants and tavernas in Athens as a young man. Nikki had never set foot in one.

We walked over to their house on the appointed night and found them in their very best clothes. Agapitos had borrowed a white shirt from his son for the occasion and wore a jacket and Nikki looked very pretty in her best flowered dress.

As we walked to town using the flashlight to guide us on the rocky path, Nikki would reach out and squeeze my hand from time to time with excitement. We went to our favorite place, Vasili's, where they knew us well, and when they saw our guests they went out of their way to be hospitable. Vasili himself waited on us with lavish gestures, even spreading Nikki's cloth napkin on her lap for her, making her blush.

Agapitos tried to act very dignified and sophisticated as he thought a city Greek should and embarrassed us by snapping his fingers impatiently at Vasili and calling him "Boy.". Fortunately Vasili took it in good stride and brought in the rest of his help to pitch in. I was afraid they'd be condescending, but everyone was genuinely kind and seemed very pleased to welcome an older peasant couple.

When we were served an especially good watermelon for dessert, Agapitos and Nikki exclaimed over it. Agapitos carefully collected the seeds and tucked them in his pocket for his garden while Nikki nodded in approval.

The atmosphere at the taverna was light and happy. People danced and others smashed glasses at their feet. Some dancers picked up tables in their teeth much to Agapitos's pleasure. Nikki just sat awed by everything. We persuaded Nikki and Agapitos to dance with us.

Some Greek men did belly dances, and David and I did the Hasapiko which we had painstakingly learned from Yianni the Fisherman. We earned some broken glasses, and even a beer bottle for our efforts. Beer bottles were very expensive to break. We could see the glassware and crockery bills mounting for most of the patrons. We expected Agapitos to smash a few but I think Nikki discreetly restrained him to keep our bill down.

An old man arose and with stately steps performed a solemn dance, picking up a platter at the end and breaking it over his own head. *Spasta* the breaking of glasses, had recently been outlawed, punishable by stiff fines, but as long as there was no policeman around no one paid any attention to the law.

Suddenly the local police chief appeared at the door and a silence fell on the crowd. Panayotis was his name but since he had plump, prominent jowls and cheeks, we all called him The Chipmunk. He was very mild mannered and hated enforcing the Gilbert and Sullivan type laws the colonels passed and repealed on a daily basis. He sat at a table and Vasili instantly ran over with a beer for him. I felt sorry for Panayotis. He knew he had rained on everyone's parade.

The musicians were taking a break just then and someone went and put money in the new jukebox, the pride of the island. A sinuous Mid-Eastern number came on and a young Athenian woman vacationing on the island rose to dance. It was unusual for a woman to dance alone but this woman was a professional dancer in the city at a nightclub we learned. She began doing a very sensual, slow dance, undulating her hips. Everyone was utterly silent in admiration as they watched her, even The Chipmunk. As the dance neared the end there was a pause in the music and the woman halted and did a shimmy that looked as if she were trembling. Then the music picked up and she began undulating her hips again. It was just too much to pay any heed to the colonels. One man picked up a full bottle of beer and smashed it at her feet. It was a grand gesture but we understood he just had to be able to live with himself after that performance, and we expected he'd pay a fine for it.

The music still played and The Chipmunk walked over to the man's table, looked him in the eye, then reached around and unplugged the jukebox, effectively ending the woman's dance. A gasp went up. Agapitos and Nikki looked at each other apprehensively. So did David and I, wondering if a riot would break out. But Vasili announced he was closing and people sullenly left as The Chipmunk sat and waited for the place to empty. The man who tossed the beer became the hero of the island from that night on although I thought The Chipmunk had done rather well, too. He'd been brave but hadn't fined the hero.

"Andrianni, such a night," exclaimed Nikki the next day when she came over for coffee.

"Too bad there was a fuss, Nikki," I told her "I wanted you to enjoy yourself."

"Oh, but I did. Such excitement," and she beamed at me "And now I have been to a taverna and can tell everyone."

Chapter 49

Cross-Eyed Nikos Takes a Day Off

Cross-Eyed Nikos lived a half mile away along the rocky hilly path that passed our house, making him our closest neighbor. His three room house was a hovel without a woman to look after it for him, that is except for the *apothiki*, the storeroom. His *apothiki* was magnificent. Dried cheeses and figs, and baskets of eggs hung from the rafters. Barrels of wine and oil stood along one wall, and casks of feta cheese and olives along the other. Hanging shelves held his fresh meat and bread. Haralambos' wife cooked for him. Nikos ruled his younger brother's family like a patriarch.

He didn't quite live alone; he had a cow, some sheep, chickens and three animals of whom he was very fond: his beautiful mule Kitso, his goat Lavitsa and the neglected dog Bisti.

Kitso and Lavitsa had personalities as stubborn, loud and determined as their master. Nikos constantly had problems with them. They would not do as he wanted and were always getting into forbidden fields. Cross-Eyed Nikos would swear at them, storm, throw his hat on the ground in rage, but they would do as they pleased until he got very close. He never beat them.

Nikos was a talented blasphemer and could use obscenity with real art. Once I heard him swearing at Kitso.

"Your mother, your father, your grandmother, your grandfather, your brothers, your sisters," his cadence grew pronounced and his voice got steadily louder. "Your cousins, your uncles, your aunts, your godmother, your godfather, your best friend. All of them, I f___!"

Tarsa was with me on our terrace cutting up beans. She looked up at him on the hill then at me.

"He swears at his animals because he has no wife," she said smiling.

Bisti, the dog, was a different type. She was friendly, affectionate and always getting in the way. We often fed her and I kept her de-ticked. Cross-Eyed Nikos had a grudging relationship with her. He threw her scraps once in a while, yelled at her often, seldom pet her, but he did not send her away and he took her with him when he went bird hunting once a year, an occasion for which Nikos wore his Sunday suit and a vest. Bisti was a stupid dog and never learned to herd the sheep or Lavitsa, but she was good friends with Kitso. They often played together, Kitso rearing up, Bisti leaping and barking. Nikos once solemnly told me that man was a god to animals, and he seemed to take that task seriously.

Cross-Eyed Nikos was a hard-working man, up at dawn, working until sunset, stopping only for a quick nap right out in the fields. But he played hard, too, as we found out.

He came by one day to tell us that the following week there was going to be a festival at the deserted monastery on the top of the mountain that towered over the harbor, the name day of the patron saint. He wanted us to go with him.

Two days before the festival people began arriving from other places on the island and climbing the mountain. When the wind was right we could hear music coming from the monastery. Early Sunday morning Nikos came by to see if we were going. He was in his Sunday best and was actually riding Kitso, a rare occurrence. Kitso had been brushed until he gleamed so we realized it was an important festival. We hiked a ways behind Nikos and Kitso watching Bisti follow and nip at Kitso's heels.

There were easily a hundred donkeys tied up in the fields below the monastery, a virtual parking lot. Kitso was one of the few mules, and certainly the handsomest with his dark, glossy coat. He was an aristocratic animal and not at all happy about being hobbled among the donkeys.

The monastery was surrounded by an olive grove that provided deep shade and people had spread blankets and set up their picnics under the boughs. Inside the walls of the monastery there were mobs of people eating and singing. The buildings had been whitewashed so much over the decades that the steps looked like they were piled with snow and footsteps had worn grooves down to the original stone only in the center of each stair. Tins planted with flowers and the sacred small leafed basil the Greeks loved were everywhere.

Cross-Eyed Nikos pounced on us at the gateway and led us to a tree where Haralambos and his family had spread out a picnic lunch. We had brought bread, cheese and salami which we added to the feast, but they seemed paltry offerings next to the roast lamb, stewed pigeon and other delicacies Mrs. Haralambos had prepared. At one end of the courtyard an enterprising shopkeeper had set up a little stand where he was selling raki for a drachma a shot.

At the end of the mass being chanted in the chapel a man strolled out and an informal type of communion was taken. He simply walked around with a large gourd of raki in lieu of sacrificial wine and made everyone take a shot of it from the same glass. I was a little concerned about germs until I tasted the raki and realized there was enough alcohol in it to sterilize an operating room.

Our old friend, Papoo, was there selling *tamata*, the little tin plates stamped with parts of the body that Greeks put before their icons for healings. Papoo was happy to see us and wanted to buy us a raki at the stand, but Cross-Eyed Nikos came by and insisted on paying for all the drinks. He had declared ownership of us for the day. The raki stand was doing brisk business in spite of the fellow behind the counter having sampled his own wares too often.

The monks' cells were filled with people who had been camping. Some musicians emerged from one and began playing. People began dancing. Nikos wanted to buy us more drinks but we escaped to Haralambos's spot. The family was having a delightful time and introduced us to their friends. More food was passed around and someone brought out a gourd of wine. In Greek style the children were handed glasses of water with just enough drops of the island's black wine in it to color it a little so they could toast with the adults.

The dancing grew more animated and we joined in. Cross-Eyed Nikos danced a solo. He wasn't as good as many of the other dancers, but as he seldom danced at all, everyone was pleased and urged him on with shouts of "Opa!" But Nikos soon stopped dancing and went back to the raki stand where many wanted to buy him drinks to celebrate his solo.

The afternoon wore on and more people came. There were gourds of wine everywhere. The raki seller fell asleep after having turned the business over to a friend who started selling the remaining stock at half price. We saw a mother standing beside her teenaged son who was drunk for the first time in his life after having visited the stand too many times, trying to persuade him to drink some lemonade.

"No, little Mama, I can't," he protested.

"But for your stomach. You will be sick tomorrow if you don't. I know. How many times have I seen your father like this? Come drink."

The sun grew hotter and by mid-afternoon we had had too much to drink and decided to go home. As we left I groggily noticed I didn't see Kitso but thought perhaps Nikos had moved him into the shade. We took a shorter but steeper path and I ran my last pair of nylons and was irritable. David was irritable, too, so we had the kids take a nap and went to bed ourselves.

We woke at sunset feeling much more cheerful and sober. We made ourselves some coffee and sat on the front porch watching the harbor grow dark until we had to light an oil lamp.

Suddenly we heard the sound of hooves next to the house and like a hurricane Kitso swept by us, leaped a terrace wall below us and continued galloping. A few minutes later Cross-Eyed Nikos arrived breathless with Bisti behind him.

"@#$% mule! What a lot of fuss."

We invited him to sit down and have some coffee with us. He was very, very drunk.

"No. No coffee. @#$# mule!"

"Do you want some wine, Nikos?" David asked.

"No. No wine. @#$% mule!"

"What happened?"

"@#$% mule. He ran away. @#$% mule!"

"Do you want us to help catch him?"

"No. The @#$% mule will listen only to me, and to me he will not listen."

Kitso had stopped at the terrace below us, right in the middle of a vineyard, and he stood looking at us, obviously enjoying himself. Bisti joined him and the two nuzzled each other. Cross-Eyed Nikos got up and staggered towards them but as soon as he came close Kitso took off again, galloping through another field, this time one of wheat. Bisti barked merrily.

"You are the son of a whore, and I f___ you and Bisti, too!" Nikos shouted. He staggered back and accepted a cup of coffee.

"You don't make good coffee," he told me

I apologized, giggling.

"It's not your fault. It's your landlord's."

"The landlord's?"

"Your landlord is very bad."

"Oh, no Nikos. He is a little careful of his money, but he is not a bad man"

"He is a bad landlord. Look at this house. He rents you this house and he doesn't give you any milk or machines."

"Machines?"

"Yes, machines, f____ him," he said glumly.

David and I looked at each other puzzled, then I went inside to get our dictionary to be sure I understood. It was machines, all right

"What kind of machines are you talking about, Nikos?"

"Machine machines. Can't you hear?"

Just then Kitso, annoyed that Nikos had quit chasing him, decided to liven up the game and came galloping across the porch, knocking over the table, chairs, and cups, almost running into us. We picked up the furniture and crockery and stepped back in the doorway to get out of Kitso's path but be handy to catch him if we could. Nikos chased him around our house a few times with Bisti excitedly getting in his way. Then Kitso set off across the fields again.

A while later Nikos came back even more tired and just as unsuccessful. We made more coffee and sat with him again. This time he accepted a cup.

"Did you enjoy yourself at the festival today, Nikos," I asked to make conversation.

"No. Yes. No. No, I didn't. Too much fuss. I had a fight. I gave Yorgo the Sly a black eye when he insulted my mule. Everyone made too much fuss over it. There was too much raki."

"When did all this happen?" David wanted to know.

"This afternoon, late. Weren't you there?"

"We left because we had too much to drink"

"You shouldn't have left. You could have seen the fight. There goes that @#$% mule, the son of @#$% parents," but he was too winded to chase it.

"You need machines," he was back to that theme.

We couldn't imagine what he was talking about. As far as we knew the only machine he owned was a corkscrew and not a very good one at that.

"You are good people. Tomorrow I am going to bring you machines."

He was rested up again and went off chasing Kitso. Much later we were ready to go to bed and he was still out in the fields calling Kitso. I went to the door and shouted.

"Nikos, did you get Kitso yet?"

"No," he called. "Don't forget. Tomorrow I am bringing some machines."

"Fine Nikos Good night."

"Good night. In the morning I will bring machines and I will bring your milk."

"Fine," I said. "Thanks."

"Machines and milk. But I may be late with the milk," he added. "My @#$% goat is loose too and I have to catch her."

The mysterious machines never materialized but Bisti, Lavitsa and Kitso finally went home.

A few days later when I went to pay Tarsa the rent she invited me for coffee. Before she brewed it in the tiny *briki*, she reached for the small coffee grinder all the Greek housewives had and exclaimed, "Oh, the machine is empty."

I finally understood Cross-Eyed Nikos's complaint.

Chapter 50

The Trees on the Acropolis

We made a short trip to Athens. While we were there we went to the Acropolis again. Everyone did when they went to Athens. To not go would be like visiting your childhood home and not bothering to say hello to your mother.

We went on a Thursday. That's not a good day to see the Acropolis because the Greek children are off from school and it is a free day so it is very crowded.

It was the middle of heat wave and it gets hot on the Acropolis, really hot. The top of the Acropolis has been worn smooth by all the foot traffic for thousands of years until it is almost one solid, shining sheet of rock. It gleams like water it is so smooth. We could see the heat waves pouring up off the stone.

There are two trees on top of the Acropolis growing in what little pockets of soil that are left at the summit. One is the little olive tree, all twisted and silver-leaved, that grows in the Erechtheum. I always enjoyed seeing that tree. An olive tree has grown there since the Erechtheum was built, but not always the same tree. During the revolution the Turks burned the houses that used to nestle between the columns of the temples. The tree was burned, too. But the Greeks insist that another young olive sapling was found amidst the debris the next day in the same place. Maybe it was since they are supposed to be deep rooted, and maybe it had a little help.

The other tree is a pine, windblown and misshapen, but a nice comfortable looking tree with dense shade.

As we had expected the place was full of tourists. The photographers with their big old cameras on tripods kept getting in everyone's way. Only the Greeks paid to have their pictures taken; the tourists all had their own cameras. There were children running everywhere and trying to unsuccessfully shinny up the broken columns of the temples whenever the guards weren't looking. Nothing was roped off then. Heather stood between the caryatids while we took her picture. There were big slices of columns littering the grounds.

It was clear and the view was fantastic. We sat on the walls and watched it until the heat got to us. The museum was closed for some reason and the crowd thinned out at siesta time. The pine tree made one tiny patch of shade. We sat on the fallen columns under it with the children in our laps and ate the picnic lunch we had brought with us.

A tour group arrived. It was led by a hard looking, big-bosomed woman in her late forties. She was obviously Greek but she lectured in French and English, switching effortlessly from one language to the other. She looked bored. The tourists she was leading all looked at her instead of at the Acropolis.

She spied us sitting in the only bit of shade and marched over with the entire group at her heels.

"It's time for you to move now," she told us in English.

My jaw dropped at her rudeness. But there was the whole group waiting expectantly and feeling like idiots we just picked up our things and left.

She sat where we had been, in the shade, while her tourists stood in front of her in the sun and she continued her lecture.

I was angry but David thought it was funny. That made me angrier. All the way back to our hotel I thought of the things I should have said to her.

I should have refused to understand her. I should have said, "It's time for YOU to move, you are blocking my view." I should have told her to kiss a donkey in Greek; no one would have known what I was saying but her. That's what any of our self-respecting Greek friends would have done. I could picture the tour guide confronting Tarsa, for example, or Soteria; now THAT would have been a match up. David kept laughing at my should haves. I told him to kiss a donkey in Greek. That upset the children. So then we all bought giant street pretzels from a vendor and made up.

The hot weather broke with an unseasonable and furious rainstorm. We went back to the Acropolis to see it in the different light and to see the stone top wetly reflecting the temples. I saw the poor pine tree, drenched and miserable, and remembered the woman sitting in the shade with all the sheepish tourists standing in the sun and I finally laughed.

Chapter 51

Making Wine

The vineyards around our house were loaded with ponderous bunches of black grapes. Early one morning Nikos the Barber and Tarsa knocked on our door

"David! Andrianni*!* *Ela!* *Sika!*" They called. Come on. Get up. "The grapes are ready. Come help us."

We dressed quickly and only stopping to give the kids some breakfast bread and milk, we joined them. They were already out in the fields. They handed us some baskets and wooden handled folding knives with hooked blades and indicated where we should start cutting. It was the first time I had ever seen Tarsa do farm work. Her hair was tied in a scarf, totally unlike the usually stylish chignon she wore, and she wore old clothes. I was impressed and was not about to be outdone.

The sun was hot and the work was harder than it looked. The wooden handles of the knives blistered our hands. We worked until noon and stopped to eat. Tarsa had brought some bread, cheese and fish. She and Nikos lay in the shade of our terrace and slept a short while. Then we all started in again and worked until sunset, filling the four-foot high baskets they had set here and there in the vineyard. We made a late dinner and ate it wearily. The next morning we were awakened at dawn again and spent another day at it until the vineyards around the house were stripped.

David and I were tired but jubilant with having worked in a grape harvest and relieved it was over. But the next day as we returned home from town Cross-Eyed Nikos was at our door.

"Get up early," he told us. "I need your help with my grapes."

That evening we walked to Brett's house and found him worn out from picking grapes, too. It seemed most of the island had burst into activity on the same day and any available labor was fair game. Some late lingering students had also been roped into the harvest. We left early to get a good night's sleep, dodging donkeys laden with the grape filled baskets as we climbed the path.

Cross-Eyed Nikos was harvesting white grapes for retsina and his vineyards were on a steep mountainside. Kitso hauled up loads of the big baskets and we set to work harvesting. Haralambos showed up on his donkey. It, too, was laden with baskets.

We picked grapes until our backs were sore and our blistered hands callused over. Cross-Eyed Nikos and Haralambos worked steadily at twice our pace. The next day we picked again. We asked the brothers if we could help them with the wine making as well once the hard work of the harvest was over. They gleefully accepted our offer. A few more days of work and Cross-Eyed Nikos's slopes were bare. We sighed with relief thinking the hard work was done.

The following morning we went to his house and found the two men scrubbing out stone vats, one above the other, behind Nikos's house that were used for grape crushing. When the vats were clean Cross-Eyed Nikos brought out the baskets of grapes and dumped them into the higher vat until it was a couple feet deep in grapes. Then he plugged the outlet to the lowest vat that would receive the juice with a bunch of herbs to strain out the debris of the crushing. He rolled up his pants legs, washed his feet in a basin, crossed himself and jumped in.

"Come on," he said "Hop in."

Haralambos rolled up his pants, repeated the procedure and then David and I washed our feet and followed them into the vat.

Up until that moment the experience had been a visual one, the two tough old Greeks looking very picturesque. The tactile sensation was a shock. The grapes squished up between my toes and when I put all my weight down on one foot the stems, seeds and debris hurt.

In the beginning I stomped and stomped and was soon out of breath. David, too, looked tired in no time. The kids tried to stomp but gave it up quickly and played with Bisti instead. Cross-Eyed Nikos and Haralambos were crushing three times as many grapes as we were. I watched them closely for a while.

They lifted each foot quite high and brought it down sharply, shifting their weight as they did so, then instantly lifting the other foot. It looked like a dance. In fact, periodically one or the other broke out in a little tune to the rhythm of their stomping. I tried to copy their movements and found I didn't get so easily winded but I was nowhere near as efficient as they were. An hour later David and I were tired out and had to rest but they were still crushing grapes. The cloudy grape juice flowed steadily into the vat below.

The first batch was just about done and I thought that was it for the day, but no. Nikos leaped out of the vat and after scraping some of the skins and stems into a barrel, he dumped in more grapes until it was as full as before. We groaned and began crushing again

"Hey, Nikos, what do you do with the skins and stuff?" I asked.

"We will make raki out if it and what's left of the wine that's too old. Then what's left from making raki I give to the chickens."

Back to work. Right foot high, plunge, shift weight, left foot high. Squish, stomp. I stopped often to clean the skins from between my toes. The two brothers never did. The level of the grapes went slowly down. The lower vat was full of must and the men left off crushing long enough to fill a few large goatskins with the cloudy liquid.

By mid-afternoon I could no longer lift my feet and I went home with the kids who had thought the whole process great fun. I detoured by way of town to buy some supplies for dinner. On the way I passed someone else's house where the crushing was in progress, but this time with the black grapes for making Paros's famous black wine. Everyone was reddish-purple to their thighs. The normally very modest women had tied their skirts up to their waists and the men had rolled their pants as high as possible, but even so their clothes were stained. They called out a greeting and invited me into their vat. They laughed when I said I was already worn out from making Nikos's retsina, but the joking didn't last long. This was serious business.

David came home that night exhausted and with a new respect for Cross-Eyed Nikos who was at least twice his age.

"I told them I couldn't possibly do it again tomorrow because my feet are too sore."

But the next morning Cross-Eyed Nikos was at our door. Apparently our labor, amateurish as it was, was still valuable. That day was a little easier, but I still left early.

On the way home some of our neighbors stopped us to give us *mustalevri* as a special treat. This was a sort of cross between pudding and jello made from the must of the red grapes and dusted with sesame seeds. I thanked them and took it home. I didn't like it but the children did and Heather ate so much of it she became ill. After that any time she even saw *mustalevri* she became nauseous.

282

When the crushing was finally done Cross-Eyed Nikos took us into his wonderful apothiki where he stored all his goods and we watched as he emptied his goatskins into huge hogsheads. Then he produced a plastic bag of ugly looking yellowish stuff about the consistency of snot mixed with chunks of wood and charcoal.

"The resin," he told us.

He poured the sticky mass into the barrel and sealed it.

"Now, we wait. In four months wine, nice and clear. Then we will have a little get-together, eh?" he grinned.

At home we took off our shoes and soaked our poor, tired feet in hot water. We poured ourselves a glass of wine and looked at it with new appreciation.

"Here's to the end of wine making"

"Thank God," David replied.

A while later we heard a donkey outside and a voice calling us. Dimitri came to the door smiling.

"*Yia sou*," he said enthusiastically. "My grapes on the north slopes are ripe now. In the morning you can take the bus. We have to harvest right away. There are lots and lots of fine fat grapes."

Chapter 52

Visitors

We had run through the money we had brought with us. David's parents sold a piano for us and my brother sold our car and sent us the money.

Nancy showed me a new way to earn some money. We had discovered that yachts sometimes put in to Paros for a few days at a time. Wealthy northern Europeans, Greeks and even Americans sometimes visited. They were looking for handcrafts which were not in great supply on the island. Nancy clued me in that if I used some local fabric and used Greek motifs I could sew and embroider sun dresses and sell them to the yacht people. That and teaching English kept a small trickle of money coming in during the summer.

Tarsa had also finally begun paying David for the chores he did for her, sometimes in money, sometimes in produce from their land.

David also spearfished for much of our food while the weather was good.

I continued the children's lessons and embroidered dresses as I taught them. We did a whole special study of spiders after a visitor left a few tomes on the subject behind on the island. Any visitor was a potential teacher and I eagerly ferreted out their skills. I traded meals and sewing for tutoring for the children. Once a woman came to visit and I asked her what she did. She told us she was a French tutor. Heather and Davidaki referred to farting as tooting, and they rolled on the floor in laughter much to her puzzlement when they heard she was a professional "tooter". I took lessons myself, cooking lessons from Nancy whom I had discovered was a Cordon Bleu graduate. We were all happily busy.

Our summer routine was often broken by visitors. Once we were entertaining a couple, he American, she Austrian on our terrace at night by lamplight. She was in ecstasy about our life style - "So Old Testament!" She kept saying. He described our way of life as "living in primitive luxury."

We were all engrossed in conversation when suddenly Kitso, Nikko's mule suddenly thrust his head over her shoulder and calmly began eating her salad. No amount of pushing, shoving or yelling would budge him until he was through. Then he strolled off to munch the barley in his master's field until Nikko caught up with him a short time later. Afterwards the couple insisted on entertaining us down in the village at a nice restaurant. Our "Old Testament" life was just a shade too primitively luxurious for the sophisticated Austrian.

We had stayed in touch with Soteris and Soula and with Richard in Kalamata. Richard came to visit us on Paros and fell in love with the island. He was considering moving to Athens for a semester while he signed up for classes at the university. He told us that Soteris and Soula were at last married, Soteris's last sister finally having found a husband, freeing him to wed his own fiancee. I roped Richard in to teach the children some math, since he had been an accountant. A Canadian scientist came to visit, as did an English composer. The children got physics lessons and learned some music basics.

David, who had studied ceramics in college decided to teach us all about pottery by doing a raku pottery firing. We traveled inland to where a potter lived to obtain some clay from him and we all made figurines. David thought the clay was a delicate type and to be sure the ware was not damaged during the firing, we collected empty tins from everyone. In a place where we all knew how many jars we owned and reused everything, it wasn't easy collecting empty tin cans, but we sent word out over the island and finally had enough to pack the things we had made into them surrounded by straw which we knew would also burn in the firing.

We dug a shallow pit and built a fire of grape clippings and charcoal which we fed for some time before burying it under a layer of dirt. A group of friends showed up for the disinterment the next evening. It was a grand success. Our pieces came out properly turned into stone and satisfyingly black.

Once a princess of sorts came to the island. She was one of Brett's art students. Cecilia was a tall, willowy girl of eighteen who spoke perfect English with a trace of an accent. Brett said she was Austrian. She came to study photography and roamed the village in very short shorts with a camera around her neck. Brett finally persuaded her that shorts weren't worn in the village and she switched to the tiniest of mini-skirts making matters worse.

She'd wander around dreamily then suddenly lean over to take a photo of a flagstone or such, oblivious to the crowd of grinning Greek men who had gathered behind her to watch the spectacle. She only saw the world through her camera lens and was saved from backing off a dock more than once by the quick intervention of onlookers when she aimed for shots of the fishing caiques.

One day Doug inadvertently stepped in front of her lens and the next day she signed up for creative writing classes as well. Doug was irate.

"Do I really have to teach this loony teenager?" Doug asked Brett.

"I'm afraid so."

Doug sighed deeply. He had been doing a lot of that since his disillusionment with Sandra. He complained that Cecilia never wrote a word, just gazed at him or wandered off to photograph his grape arbor.

She came to our house one day to take pictures of our terrace, and Doug happened by at the same time. After the photography session we all sat on the terrace with cups of coffee. Heather came to us with a book she wanted us to read to her and Cecilia volunteered for the task. She turned to a picture of a castle and exclaimed, "That's my home.!"

"Yes, let me see if the illustrator is Austrian."

Up to that moment Doug had been pointedly ignoring her but he turned now to ask, "Are you teasing the children, Cecilia?"

"No. I think it is really a picture of our castle," and she rattled off the German name of the estate. "My aunt lives there. My father is too busy in the city to run the estate but he has the title. My brothers and I spend weekends and vacations there."

Doug looked at her oddly and when she went to leave he offered to walk her home. Later he asked Brett about it.

"Yeah, she's the princess of something or other I forget what. Her father is some kind of baron or earl. Why?"

It was all Doug needed to complete his summer. Suddenly Cecilia was no longer a dingbat teenager. She was "dreamy and artistic." He seemed to notice for the first time that she was really a beautiful young woman. I threw up my hands in despair when she almost walked off Brett's balcony and Doug described her as "detached from reality like an Olympiad." It was all right for her to continue to study with him even if she didn't write a word because of her poetic sensitivity.

"You're just another snobbish Brit!" I accused him and he just grinned.

"I never met a princess before," he said sheepishly.

So he now spent his mornings in his dreary, sooty, rainy world writing out his bitterness, and his afternoons roaming a Greek island with a princess on his arm.

But all too soon Cecilia had to leave her simple room in the village and her Welsh poet to return to her castle. She mailed some Austrian chocolates to the children. Doug borrowed some money to make a quick trip to visit her, and the castle as well, he admitted.

He was back sooner than expected. It seemed the baron or earl, whichever he was, did not approve of the situation and sent him packing, and Cecilia had found someone new to photograph. Doug was downcast but his good humor returned quickly. After all, he had dated a princess and he laughed off his dismissal with references to the decadent aristocracy.

He spent the rest of the summer dating a long-legged American girl who shared his love of jazz.

When his long summer was finally over we had a farewell dinner for him at Vasili's restaurant. It was a riotous evening and ended up with everyone dancing and Doug imitating the Greeks by leaping to someone's shoulders as he was dancing.

Afterwards we saw him off at the dock. His head was bent over and he was weeping. The romance was over and it was back to urban grayness. Now it was time for him to spend time at his desk in the grimy Welsh town and write about the beautiful island.

Chapter 53

Another Harvest

Cross-Eyed Nikos had a fine grain crop. His wheat and barley were ripe and heavy headed. He began the harvesting at dawn, cutting it all by hand, one small terraced field at a time.

We'd wake and watch him at work until he took a break to provide the milk for our breakfast. We purchased Lavitsa's milk from him and it was always a gleeful start to the day for the children because of Niko's unique milking style. He always wore a pork-pie type hat and turned the brim around backwards then used his head to press down his goat's tail so she couldn't defile the milk as he milked her from the rear, pulling her udders between her hind legs.

While we ate our breakfast on the porch we watched him get back to work swinging his scythe and singing. We noticed he left a small section unharvested in the last field.

"Hey, Nikos," David called. "You forgot to harvest some."

"No, David, that patch is for the sake of God," he explained.

There was a circular stone threshing floor in the back of each house on the island. Heather and Davidaki played games, bounced balls and skinned knees in ours. We now learned their proper use.

Cross-Eyed Nikos invited us to his house to watch the threshing. As usual when there was any hard work about, Haralambos was there, and he smiled good-naturedly as his brother shouted orders at him and abused him if he was not behaving efficiently. Haralambos was often as efficient as

Bisti the dog, but was equally good-natured, if not very bright.

The grain was stacked on one side of the threshing floor. The men tossed on a layer about a foot thick with wooden pitchforks. Then they harnessed Kitso and a couple donkeys together along with a cow and began driving them in circles around and around the floor.

"Ha-lai, ha-lai, ha-lai," they shouted and clapped to make the animals move faster. Bisti, excited by all the activity, ran wildly barking and leaped at the animals.

Nikos and Haralambos laughed, encouraging her as they wanted as much speed as possible for the threshing. Whenever the animal in the center became too dizzy and started staggering, they stopped and switched them around. After a while they led the mule and donkeys off to the side and using flat wooden shovels, began tossing the grain high in the air. The steady sea breeze blew the chaff off to the side as they threw the grain. The cleaned grain fell in a shower back to the stone floor. When it had been cleaned enough they scooped it into sacks and shoveling more unthreshed grain on to the stones, they began the process all over again.

I had fixed a meal and offered it to them at midday but as much as Haralambos looked as though he wanted to eat, Cross-Eyed Nikos decided against it.

"Food is not good when you work hard, Andrianni," he told me apologetically. The men rested a while and I marveled that they wore cream colored coarse wool undershirts embroidered with a small red cross at the center of the neckline and with long sleeves under their work shirts. I asked if it wasn't hot but Nikos told me seriously it did not do to get chilled when working hard.

All day they worked and by late afternoon the pile of unthreshed grain was just a small mound. All of a sudden

Bisti went mad. She began barking and leaping at the mound, growling and snapping. I leaped back alarmed when she pulled out her head with a large rat held triumphantly in her teeth. The men laughed uproariously. They egged her on to try again and she unearthed two more rats and ate them with relish

"At least they didn't roast and torture the rats like in Vouvoura," I told David as we walked home.

A few days later Cross-Eyed Nikos invited us over to celebrate the harvest and try some aged black wine he judged ready. We sat in his kitchen while he proudly served us his own cheese and olives and bread made with his own wheat. He had also made a large pot of lentil soup. The wine he served was very, very fine. We thoroughly appreciated it and were glad we hadn't had to help make it. Nikos had apparently been sampling it throughout the day. He was mellow enough that he even petted Bisti when she sidled up against him affectionately.

All our Greek friends were philosophical when in their cups, full of thoughts about life and love they liked to share. Cross-Eyed Nikos was no exception.

"David, Andrianni," he began, clearing his throat.

"Yes, Nikos?"

"Beans are beans," he said meaningfully. There was no arguing with that.

"And lentils are lentils," He went on with a dramatic gesture.

"We understand, Nikos," we nodded solemnly.

"And," he paused for full impact and tried to fix his crossed eyes on our faces. We sat on the edge of our seats expectantly. "When they boil, they boil," he ended triumphantly.

Chapter 54

Sad Lovers

The summer was coming to an end. Most of the art students had deserted us but Tina still remained. She had a birthday party at Vasili's and we learned she was thirty, older than we had thought.

The house she rented in town had an electric outlet and she generously offered us all the use of it. Nancy and I spent days there together sewing with Nancy's machine, supplementing our meager wardrobes and making warm things for the children. I cut up an army blanket to make a coat for Heather with a pixie hood and lined it in red. Tina also had an electric heater and when a cold snap hit we'd all gather at her place to warm our perpetually cold fingers and toes.

Tina's affair with Costas the bank teller had become very serious but she was looking less and less lighthearted. Costas was a young man who had much to do in life. Not a Parian by birth, he had been assigned to his post at the bank on the island but his family lived in Athens. He wanted to finish his education. He did not want to get married, or rather, he could not even if he wished, if he were to meet his family's needs as they were poor and depended on him for support. If he were to marry it would have to be to a woman with a large dowry. Tina's dowry was her smile and her indomitable good nature. Costas loved her, and she him, but it was hopeless.

About this time Tom and Nancy began having domestic problems. She wanted to start having children after their eight years together but Tom was set against it. They seemed to have a stable relationship and we assumed they'd work out their difficulties. So we were surprised when Nancy showed up one day in tears.

"What's the matter?"

"He's left. He just up and left, the bloody man," she wept.

She was too upset to be alone and stayed with us for a few days. Then Tina learned the news, was all sympathy, and offered to let Nancy stay with her.

It didn't take long for word to spread. Tom wrote telling Nancy he had met an old girlfriend and was getting married. He expected her to leave Paros before he returned with his new wife. The Greeks grew incensed on Nancy's behalf.

Tina was getting more and more despondent. Costas's assignment was coming to an end. The day before he left he gave her a pet rabbit in the true Greek tradition of lovers parting. Nikki explained it. The men when leaving a woman gave her an animal, perhaps in lieu of the child she would never have. Tina waited and hoped and finally went to Athens to find him. She returned in despair and the rabbit died.

In the meantime Brett had finally heard from Anna. She had thrown over Adonis and was living in Crete with a new lover. She had no intentions of returning. Brett made a trip to Athens to begin divorce proceedings.

It was the autumn of tragic romances on the island. It exhausted us and made Nikki weep and wail. It brought up old memories for her and sitting with a cup of coffee she told me about her and Agapitos's marriage.

Nikki had been born on the poor island of Ithaca to an even poorer family who could provide no dowry for her at all. As a young woman she had hired herself out as a domestic to a wealthy Athenian family. In those days a girl who did that was looked down upon and considered unmarriageable, but it was survival for Nikki. She met Agapitos in the city and they fell in love, but his family had betrothed him to a woman from the island with a dowry and there was nothing to be done.

"So he married her, Andrianni, God rest her soul, and in her third labor, she died. Agapitos came back to Athens and found me and we were married, so I raised that poor woman's babies. And the people here said I had killed her by witchcraft," she said sadly. "But I didn't. I wouldn't do such a thing."

"I know you wouldn't, Nikki," I assured her.

The islanders also blamed Nikki's barrenness on God punishing her for the witchcraft. Nikki's step-children adored her as did her grandchildren, but she said it was a sorrow to her that "I never held a living child inside under my heart, Andrianni."

I sympathized. It must have been a burden for such a maternal soul as Nikki.

"Ah, Andrianni, if we think of all the sadness in the world it is too much, and we might as well drown ourselves like rats, so let's not."

There was one bright note. There was a German man who worked in Ethiopia but who had a villa on the island and spent his vacations there. We all knew Hans as he had spent some time during the summer on Paros. He returned for a late vacation. He heard of Nancy's plight from a cafe owner and the next day was at her door offering consolation. He took her out to dinner, bought her gifts and was very sympathetic. Nancy, swept off her feet by the rush of attention, allowed herself to be consoled. She still lived at Tina's but saw Hans daily.

Before long Hans confessed that he had a wife in Germany from whom he had been separated for five years. He offered to start a divorce if Nancy would marry him. She agreed. It seemed as if one romance might have a happy ending after all.

Chapter 55

Sophia Day

It was Sophia's name day and we were invited to her party. Nancy and Hans, who were now engaged and waiting for his final divorce papers to marry, were going to come, too. We found our way more by the sound of the music than by our flashlight.

Sophia was the village weaver. She was a good looking woman, statuesque like Tarsa, but with no snobbish attitude. She always dressed in colorful clothes. Her husband Yorgo was very proud of her skills. We were fond of her and her cheerful attitude. She had a beautiful home. It was in an orchard with a row of old cypress trees along one side. Skeins of brightly colored yarn hung from hooks in the ceiling, and stacks of carefully dyed and cut rags stood in the corners of her workroom. The rags were for making *kouralous*, the rugs that blanket all floors in the winter. We had saved our rags and our own *kouralou* was on the magnificent loom that stood with the same expectancy that awaits skilled hands as a grand piano. She often had a warp being measured out that was strung in patterns on spikes sticking out of an exterior wall. It made her house look like an exotic harp. There was always a sense of beautiful things about to burst into life that pervaded Sophia's home.

The music was coming from a battery operated record player turned on top volume and the guests singing along with the records. There were tables set in the courtyard and some inside in case the night grew chilly. The kitchen cooktop had been moved outdoors for the occasion and was at one end of the terrace under the cypress trees behind a bamboo screen. Sophia was there cooking assisted by a half dozen women relatives.

First they made us sit at the table with the men and served us some liqueur and sweets, but after the welcoming was over. I insisted on helping the women cook. Sophia knew me well and didn't protest too much. She let me carry plates to the table until Hans and Nancy arrived then shoved me back in my seat.

Sophia had just two burners and no oven, but the women managed to prepare an amazing variety of dishes. At one point I counted thirty different plates of food; there was fish of several sorts both fried and poached as well as grilled, chicken stewed with herbs, eggplant roasted and whipped into a mousse-like concoction, wild greens, green salads, beans stewed with tomatoes and potatoes, tiny meatballs with a toasty crust, sweets of all varieties. We all ate from the same plates although we each had our own forks and napkins. Periodically someone speared a special morsel for us with their own fork and handed it to us after ceremoniously toasting us with it. Everyone was quite dainty about how they ate from their forks to avoid spreading germs.

Yorgo, Sophia's husband, told a lot of very bad jokes. I told my "half-crazy" joke Stellio the postmaster had liked so much, and it was a grand success. Finally someone got up to dance, doing the favorite of the island, the Balos. The kitchen filled with women cooking again.

It bothered us foreigners that Sophia was doing so much work on her name day although she didn't seem to mind at all. At last we persuaded Yorgo to get her to come out and dance. He pulled her out from behind the kitchen screen by her hand and everyone laughed as she shyly struggled and giggled, blushing. But she did dance while everyone cheered her on with "Opa!" and "Bravo!" Then David got up to dance with her, then Hans, then a few other men until she fled laughing back to the kitchen.

As each plate was emptied it was whisked back and replaced by a new full one. Everyone complimented Sophia profusely whenever she put in an appearance.

The evening wore on and more wine gourds emptied. At last Sophia decided she had cooked enough and she and the other women really joined in. Everyone was dancing now. Some men did the Hasapiko and then cheered when David and I rose to do it although our dance was not as practiced as theirs and was a simpler version. Someone played a Kalamatiano. Then someone put on the inevitable tango. It was such a hit it was played over and over again. There was one couple that did it exceptionally well with graceful exaggerated movements. The crowd demanded repeat performances until they were worn out.

Someone put on an old favorite of mine which David and I had nicknamed "the jiggle dance" for the effect it had on the female anatomy. It was a dance only the women did. We all locked arms in a circle and then jumped high, one jump one way, two the other. It was rapid and energetic and the music got faster and faster. Soon we were all breathless but kept going. One lady collapsed but the circle of women just jumped over her until she could crawl out of the way. Another fell, then some others. The men shouted encouragement as they held their sides laughing. At last it was over and we all sat down laughing and panting.

Then men then took turns doing solos. Yorgo leaped high and slapped his heels to celebrate his wife's special day and she watched him proudly. The cypress trees sighed in the wind as they presided over the lamplit party.

Chapter 56

Foreign Invasion

The romance scene had improved on Paros. Hans and Nancy were very happy and the Greeks had accepted them as a couple. He was staying on extended leave from his job in Ethiopia where he ran a brewery while he waited for their wedding. He had a picture of himself bowing as he handed Haile Selassie a church key the day the brewery opened, the first in Ethiopia.

Tina, whom we had all learned to love, moved to Athens after a grand farewell party, so she could find a job and she wrote that she had begun dating again. Brett had brought back an exotically beautiful American girl from Athens on his last trip there. Her name was Stephanie, and although she had rented her own place, she spent most of her time at his house.

We had settled into our winter routine after one last trip to Athens. The storms were on us with full force.

In bed one night I heard someone banging on our door crying out for us over the fury of the wind and rain. I leaped up and opened the door to find Nancy on our doorstep, wet through and weeping. David lit the lamps and we brought her in and turned on our little kerosene heater. She was hysterical. I dried her hair and David poured her a glass of brandy. We finally got her calmed down enough to tell us what had happened.

"It's Hans's wife. She's a demon. She came while we were out and broke into the villa. She's burned everything I own." This started a new bout of weeping. "Hans had to jump her and prevent her from attacking me with a cosh."

"A cosh?"

"One of those things thugs and gangsters use. You know...a blackjack." Sometimes when Nancy was upset she got so British we couldn't understand her. "He told me to run away and come here. I don't know what to do."

She started crying again. I talked to her and calmed her again and didn't notice for a while that David had disappeared. He reappeared an hour later. He had been to see Hans and the woman.

"She's very upset. She ís saying she doesn't want a divorce and wants to live with him again."

"But he hasn't seen the bloody woman since she left him five years ago!" Nancy protested.

"She admitted that but she doesn't care. She looks like she's going through a change of life panic to me," David diagnosed. "She ran me off the property after having been civil at first."

"But what is Hans doing?" I asked.

"He looks scared. Said for me not to argue with her and that he'd be in touch."

"But she's burned Nancy's things. She can't do that It's against the law!"

"I know. I saw the bonfire she made. But it turns out the villa is community property and she has a right to do as she pleases in her own home. That's what she says anyway, and the policeman doesn't know."

"Policeman? What policeman?" I asked.

"I found The Chipmunk sitting in the field above the villa in the dark. He was watching the place and wanted to know what happened."

"It's bloody unfair!" Nancy put in.

"I agree. But let's all get some sleep and figure out what to do in the morning."

We tucked the sleeping kids into one cot to free up the other for Nancy.

In the morning a little boy delivered a formal letter to Nancy from Hans saying their intended marriage was off; he was reconciling with his wife. Nancy burst into tears again, then announced she didn't believe it.

"The man loves me and I know it. It must be to satisfy her that he wrote this thing. The divorce has already started and it's only two months until it's final."

We agreed with her assessment. "It's likely he's keeping her happy until it's final."

"But she still attempted to attack me," and Nancy marched off to the police station with us following her.

"Yes, we saw the lady arrive last night in a fury," our friend, The Chipmunk, told us. "We were afraid there would be problems. Does she have a gun?"

We all looked at each other. This was a new consideration. "We don't know."

"But she did have a weapon of some sort last night?"

"Yes, but Hans took it from her."

"Since she didn't actually do you any harm, there is nothing we can do, but we will keep an eye on things." It was clear that our mild-mannered police chief was terrified of the invading Valkyrie.

David decided he'd return to the villa and see if he could talk to Hans alone to discuss the matter but he returned discouraged.

"He's her prisoner. He couldn't say anything except that he'd sent the letter. She is crazy, I mean really disturbed. I don't think we ought to provoke her in any way."

When Nancy had run she had taken her purse with her so it had survived the bonfire with her passport fortunately intact. She moved in with us for a few days and I shared my wardrobe with her since we were about the same size. One afternoon while we were gone the crazy woman broke into our house. We came back and found a note triumphantly declaring she had taken Nancy's passport and money. She was going back to Germany with Hans and Nancy would be stuck on this island forever, the note said.

We went straight to the police. Breaking into our house was just too much and they promised to go get Nancy's things the following day. Still worried about whether the maniac had a gun or not we decided not to return to the house that night and stayed with Brett and Stephanie. Nancy spent most of the time weeping. She looked through her purse to see if anything else had been taken and discovered the woman had also stolen her address book.

The next day we accompanied Nancy and the police to the villa, leaving the children safe with Nikki. The woman scornfully threw the things at Nancy's feet and laughed at how little money she had.

"I have four kilos of gold jewelry, do you hear," and she cackled as she shook her many bracelets at Nancy. "You a pauper, tried to get my husband from me."

Hans stood there pale and quiet. The police were obviously scared and relieved Nancy had got back her things with so little fuss.

We all went to Brett's house again and tried to put together a dinner. I didn't want to return to the house while the German woman was on the island. Nancy was inconsolable.

"He just stood there and let her say those dreadful things to me."

"Nancy, he realizes she's nuts and is humoring her," Brett said.

"They're leaving on today's boat," Nancy cried. "I'll never see him again," and she sobbed again.

Stephanie and I began cooking and sent the men into town on an errand. We heard the ferry whistle.

"That's the boat. They'll be gone and I love that bloody man so," Nancy wailed.

The men burst into the house a short time later.

"We ran into Hans in an alley just before the boat left. He says to tell you not to worry. He'll be in touch shortly. He says he loves you, Nancy, and to trust him. He didn't have time for anything more."

"Oh, thank God," Nancy exclaimed and burst into a new fit of weeping. Then David gave her a wad of bills he said Hans had thrust into his hands for her. It was a lot of money. She shed fresh tears, but was a good deal happier.

It was a week later that the letters began to arrive. The lady had made good use of Nancy's address book while she had it and everyone Nancy knew now became a member of poison pen pal club. We got the first one. Tom, then her mother both wrote alarmed letters to Nancy. Nancy assured them both and asked them to ignore the obscene missives. The letters grew more and more abusive and disgusting as the weeks rolled by. We quit reading them but saved them in case Nancy ever needed them in a court of law. One peculiar thing we noticed was that the woman seemed to know what was happening on the island since her departure. At the post office one day we saw Constandinos, a merchant who knew some German, buying a stamp for a letter to Germany. Dinos was very uneasy and tried to hide the letter from us so all came clear. We had a paid spy in our midst.

Telegrams began to arrive for Nancy all signed with different names but all from Hans. He also wired her some more money. Nancy rented a room in town and settled down to await the outcome.

Chapter 57

School Days

We were back into a winter routine. We trekked up and down the hill as the weather allowed hauling supplies on our backs or on the old donkey Brett owned and lent to us on occasion. Marisal was officially retired and Brett had rescued him from the slaughterer that winter. He became the children's mascot and a trip down to town wasn't complete without visiting him and offering him a carrot or other treat. While we were in town we always treated the children to pastries or yoghurt and honey at the cafes where, when it was storming, the fishermen played cards and drank endless cups of coffee as they waited out the weather.

Once in drenching rain on the way back from town we came upon a goat giving birth next to the path. One of our neighbors was assisting her and was glad for our company, so we stayed and watched the whole process. The children touched the newborn kid in awe when it stood on wobbly legs to nurse for the first time.

We enrolled Heather and Davidaki in the local school thinking they needed more social contact with the local kids. I continued lessons and roping in tutors whenever possible for them, but now they were also learning whatever the Greek kids did as well, such as school songs and the national dances. I enjoyed buying them the little blue smocks that all Greek children wore as school uniforms. Even office workers wore the same sort of smocks to protect their expensive and precious clothes at work. The kids seemed to love school and their teacher was impressed with them. I was impressed by the school when on the first day the town declared a holiday and the archbishop came to bless the children, including Heather and Davidaki.

Heather's only complaint was the cheek pinching. On the way to school the children would be greeted by many neighbors who were delighted that the kids were going to school. Their way of expressing their approval was to grab Heather's cheeks with their thumbs and knuckles and squeeze them affectionately. Some of the ladies were so affectionate they hurt her, so she and David took to skirting houses, traipsing through streambeds and around fields to avoid the worst of the pinchers. They ran into stinging nettles on their detours but I had taught them to rub nettle stings with dock leaves to make it better.

The kids taught us all the songs they learned, and we helped them with their lessons. Heather told us when the fishermen were at sea the school flew one kind of flag and when they returned replaced it with another one. At Halloween a relative sent the children plastic skulls filled with candy. Stellio at the post office puzzled over them but finally declared it candy not a toy so the island customs officer could not charge us duty on them. The children, at my urging, decided to share the candy with their schoolmates and the following day the teacher accompanied them home, very excited. I served her the ritual sweets and water then made her some coffee. She had come to ask if she could use the plastic skulls to help teach the older children anatomy.

The skulls were very crude, hardly anatomically correct, but she didn't care. She was thrilled to have them. I promptly took out the books and teaching aids I used for the children and offered to let her use any she might find useful. She gratefully accepted some things including a map of Greece, promising to return them.

We sat talking about teaching.

"The schools were closed here during the war and the Civil War. Many people did not learn to read and write."

"So I have heard. My dear friend Nikki has learned to read and write some from her grandchildren, so your teaching has helped more than the children," I told her.

"On this island, I used to teach on the other side, where there are no roads. People were so poor after the war but still they wanted their children to learn. I would go to the school very early in the morning and I had a small stove to burn wood. I would heat water. Then when the children came I could bathe their feet and warm them. They had no shoes and it was cold."

I was deeply touched. When she left I sat down to write some friends in the States and asked them to buy the invisible man and woman toys used to teach anatomy in the states, and any maps or other visual teaching aids they could find. If they sent them to the school rather than us there would be no duty.

It took two months but when the things arrived the teacher came to our house again and cried in gratitude.

"We cannot even get these things in Greece."

We visited our friends whenever we were in town, or they climbed the mountain to visit us. Dimitri came regularly. Nikki, of course, was a regular fixture. Entertainment was limited and whenever a new movie arrived on the island, it was a big event although we could never persuade Nikki and Agapitos to attend. During the summer we had gathered in a courtyard outside a shop to watch the films, but now the entire village and much of the countryside crowded into the boat ticket office to see them projected on the whitewashed wall.

We saw Japanese films with French dubbed in, Italian films with German dubbed in, French films with Italian dubbed in as well as an occasional American western with Greek dubbed in. It was great fun trying to make sense of the polyglot mixture and even more fun watching the avidly participating audience. The movies were frequently shortened so there were improbable jumps such as when the hero was about to get stabbed and suddenly was seen kissing the girl. The crowd would cry out "Too many cuts! Too many cuts!" for all the good it did. During chase scenes everyone would cheer, and for love scenes there were sexy hisses and whistles. Whenever a bad guy said something, people would call out replies even if they didn't understand him. Everybody ate sunflower and pumpkin seeds instead of popcorn and the floor was a bed of shells afterwards.

We let Heather and Davidaki stay up late on movie nights as the Greek children did. Afterwards we'd stop to buy new flashlight batteries and race up the hill before they wore out. Greek batteries never lasted long and they often fizzled on us before we got home. Greek matches were the same and were the butt of many Greek jokes. If the first match from a new box of them lit without trouble, the Greeks would pretend to throw the box away. "Ah, we found the good one," they'd say.

An Alexandrian Greek moved to the village to open a new restaurant causing a stir because his Egyptian wife had blue tattoos on her face adding an exotic note to the local scene.

The Hong Kong flu passed through the island at the same time as a fierce storm and several old people died. The rest of us trekked to the town clinic for penicillin shots and nursed each other through.

The Elli bravely plowed through the waters on a regular basis bringing us mail and supplies, hardly ever missing a trip unlike the year before. All in all, it was proving to be a kind winter.

Chapter 58

Glendi (Party Time)

We decided to cheer everyone up by throwing a party, a *glendi*, on Christmas day and inviting everyone we knew. A week beforehand a messenger boy came to the house to summon us to Stellio, the postmaster. Three young men from New Zealand had put in an appearance and wanted to rent a house from him for a month or two. He knew a little English but their accent was beyond him, and almost beyond us at times. One, Leo, was writing his doctoral thesis and came prepared with a trunkful of books. Another, Brian, was writing a book of poems and the third, Trevor, was just exploring. We helped them negotiate rent with Stellio and invited them to our party. I queried them as to what they could teach the children as long as they were there.

Nikos and Tarsa provided us with some cypress prunings to serve as a Christmas tree which Heather and Davidaki helped decorate with things they had made like decorated thread spools, and we lit it up with beeswax candles. We strung paper chains around the house and set out bouquets of wildflowers and greenery we had gathered from the hillsides. It looked very festive.

I baked for days in the brick oven using all the skills I had learned from Tarsa, Nikki and our other neighbors. We created a banquet.

On Christmas morning after opening our gifts we quickly cleaned up our breakfast mess. I did some last minute cooking and gift wrapping.

Nikki and Agapitos were the first to arrive because Nikki wanted to help me with preparations. They were dressed in their best, Agapitos looking very dapper in his Sunday jacket.

Dimitri arrived on his donkey laden with food and drink as usual. He was especially jovial and entered singing.

Nikos and Tarsa came but did not stay long because they had relatives coming to their house. Spiro and Eleni hiked up the mountain, Eleni complaining because she had foolishly worn her high heels. I lent her a pair of sandals to see herself safely back down without breaking an ankle. All day long people came and went. I had made a large batch of wassail and another of mulled wine, both new to the Greeks who sampled it curiously. Even Cross-Eyed Nikos came dressed in his best, followed by Haralambos and his family. Our friend Yorgo and his wife came the five miles from his valley inland because he heard of the party and wanted to wish us well, saying it was like a name day. They left early for the long walk home. Sophia the weaver and Yorgo came and went.

She had delivered our *kouralou* the month before, thirty feet of beautiful striped rag rug. Most Greeks then cut up their *kourlous* to fit the house, tying off the ends in tassels. We loved ours just the way it was and the kids loved poring over it seeing if they could recognize old garments in it. They had discovered a tiny cloth covered button woven right in and were always eager to point it out to someone. We put away the *kouralou* for the party so the floor would be available for dancing.

Dimitri had brought the "peek op" as he called his battery record player, and the house filled with music. We began dancing. Nikki was doing a dance with me when she stopped short looking out of the window in gaping surprise. I turned and saw Heather and Davidaki's teacher and her husband, the island doctor, approaching. A hush fell over the other Greeks. They all sat down formally and became silent.

We welcomed them in. The teacher was dressed in bright polyester and they both carried ornate packages. They looked at our Christmas decorations with real interest and enjoyed sampling our peculiar refreshments.

We sat chatting about a half hour and they handed the packages to Heather and Davidaki. Heather's package held an expensive Italian doll and Davidaki received a large battery operated car. The couple must have sent to Athens for the toys. We were overwhelmed. They brushed away our thanks and the schoolteacher almost cried when I gave her a necklace the children had made for her. We had made the beads for necklaces for her and Nikki in the raku pottery firing we had attempted that fall. They left after extracting a promise from us that we would visit and "take a glass of Scotch" with them later that week.

Everyone relaxed after their departure and buzzed with excitement. Nikki looked at us with new respect and made the gesture equivalent to "Wow!", shaking her hand vigorously with all her fingers splayed. Dimitri made a monocle out of his fingers and showed us we were honored by being visited by gentry. Heather and Davidaki showed off their new toys and proceeded to play with them. I was not about to put them on the mantle as Nikki suggested.

The Kiwis arrived and so did Nancy, Brett and Stephanie. Our little house was packed to overflowing. David led us all in some dances and Dimitri began to do some wild leaping solos. We all made Nikki and Agapitos do the Balos together and Nikki blushed happily for an hour afterwards.

At one point we were talking with the Kiwis about a moon shot that had been made. Agapitos took part in the conversation and laughed at the whole idea.

"They are not sending rockets to the moon," he said flatly.

"They already have, Agapitos," I replied.

"Don't believe it because you read it in the newspaper, Andrianni," he said kindly. Then he scoffed, "Can I load my old woman on our donkey and take her to the moon? No. When I can do that I will believe it."

I laughed and gave it up but Brian earnestly tried to convince Agapitos, continuing the conversation with gestures and our dictionary as they went at it in the corner for an hour or so, much to Agapitos's amusement. Occasionally I'd hear Brian counting down or making a noise like a rocket ship while Agapitos ridiculed him.

Leo, another Kiwi, danced a wild impromptu dance with Dimitri who was so pleased he began to ply the young man mercilessly with raki. Having had experience with Dimitri's raki we tried to warn Leo that he had better go slowly. A while later he passed out on our bed. Nikki looked at him and shook her head sadly.

"*Ai, kaimeni,* the poor little one. He had *kako moira,* a bad fate. He came to your party and died."

Agapitos going along with the joke crossed himself and covered up the poor man, intoning a hymn as he did.

At midnight as things were still going full blast, Nikki grabbed me by the arm and whispered for me to come outside with her. Mystified I followed her into the field. The night had grown cold and starry. Nikki stood in front of me and began a prayer. She went on some time then made the sign of the cross over me, and kissing me on both cheeks said, "Now you are blessed, my daughter."

We stood silent a few moments. Then Nikki became jolly again and went to fetch me a bundle she had brought with her. I broke open the string and newspaper wrapping and gasped. Nikki was giving me her wedding blanket.

Each woman from the time she is a little girl sews for her eventual home, saving the things in a trunk. When she is a teenager she begins to work on her wedding blanket, spinning the whitest wool she can find by hand with her distaff and spindle. Then she either weaves it by herself or takes the yarn to a professional weaver to do it. Nikki had woven her own.

I held the coarse cream-colored blanket in my arms I didn't want to take it from her but one look at her told me I couldn't refuse it. I blinked away my tears and kissed her.

"Thank you, mother of my heart."

Chapter 59

To Kill A Chicken

"Come to my house on New Year's Day and we'll kill a chicken," Dimitri had said expansively to our Christmas party guests.

That wasn't to be taken literally. It was the Greek way of saying we'd celebrate in a big way, but the invitation was sincere.

On New Year's Eve we partied with our Greek friends, playing cards as was customary, and then ran into the Kiwis who had insisted on finding the whole foreign community and partying some more at their place. Dimitri had left Leo a gourd of raki at the Christmas party and he had made the most of it.

So New Year's morning found us in town, still slightly befuddled from the previous night's celebrations. I clutched an empty basket, determined to fill it with food before it was time to catch the bus for the valley. We found Nancy at a cafe.

"The stores are closed," she announced.

"How can that be?" The stores had never been closed on a holiday before.

"There's a new law. The government wants stores to close on Sundays and holidays."

We groaned; another stupid law that would be rescinded shortly. All the really dumb laws like no women wearing slacks or no men with beards or no singing after ten at night were always repealed a week or so later, but this one caught us at the wrong time. I thought about the country people. The rural Greeks often only came to town on Sundays or holidays and it was their only chance to purchase needed supplies. Right now I needed to be more concerned about our problem.

"What'll we do? We can't go to Dimitri's empty handed with this big a crowd," with the Kiwis and the children there would be eight of us.

"We'll have to," said David resigned.

"Oh no, we won't. Let's ask Dionysius if he'll sell us something," I refused to consider defeat

Dionysius was the cafe owner. He sympathized with our plight but needed all of his stock as it was his busiest day of the year. He finally consented to sell us some cookies, butter, and a tin of sardines.

Nancy and the Kiwis who had found us by this time, went one way taking the children and we went the other, walking the back streets and alleys of the village looking for food to buy.

"Look!" David pointed. On a clothesline outside a house hung a bunch of octopi drying.

We knocked at the door and a smiling housewife up to her elbows in flour, obviously preparing for company, greeted us. She laughed when we told her we wanted to buy her octopi. She took one from the line and gave it to us.

"Happy New Year," she said, waving aside our money. "This is the day for giving gifts."

Things were improving. My basket was slowly filling. Alert to possibilities I noticed a chicken tied to a bush by one leg. We asked some children playing in the street whose it was and they pointed out a door to us.

"Can we buy your chicken?" we asked the shrewd old lady who answered. She agreed but said she'd have to weigh it first.

She led us and the chicken through her house into a back room that was fitted out as a small grocery store. We asked if she would sell us other things as well and she said yes, if we would keep it a secret since it was now against the law. We filled the basket and she put the chicken on a scale. We thought the weighing went in her favor and she charged us a high price for the groceries but we were in no position to argue, and, indeed, were very grateful to her

I took the chicken in my arms and we went to the bus stop to meet the others. Heather and Davidaki wanted to hold the chicken. I let them carry her in turn and they stroked her as we walked.

"What are we going to name her, Mommy?" my son wanted to know.

"Chicken."

"That's not a name," protested my daughter.

"How about Cacciatore?"

"Okay."

They practiced saying it. I held the chicken a little gingerly out of concern for my dress, but she practiced admirable restraint. The others then gave us the news that the bus wasn't running that day either.

"Have the colonels gone nuts?" I asked.

"Let's hire a taxi," someone suggested.

We found Manolis the island taxi driver at a cafe. He did not want to take us to the valley because he intended to enjoy his holiday with his friends. We pleaded. We presented such an unusual spectacle, a straggly bunch of foreigners, hung over and clutching a chicken, we finally appealed to his sense of humor and he agreed to meet us shortly with two cars, his and a relative's because there were so many of us and because his friends would also want to witness this.

While we waited the group amused itself with the chicken, stroking it and clucking at it.

"Its name is Cacciatore," Heather announced.

"Will Dimitri really cook it?" asked Brian. I had been dreading that question.

"Of course he will," Nancy answered breezily.

Heather's jaw dropped and Davidaki let out a wail. "But Dimitri can't kill our chicken!"

"This isn't our chicken. It's Dimitri's chicken," I began explaining as the cars arrived.

After some bustling and a lot of squeezing, we were all settled and on our way. I held the chicken on my lap and tried to console the children. I wasn't feeling too happy about her fate myself since she was such a sweet, well-behaved chicken, but I tried giving Heather and Davidaki lectures on morality and eating animals. David explained to them that plants were alive too, giving rise to a new vision of horrors - carrots screaming in agony, and so it went all the way to the valley.

I thought Manolis would overcharge us and figured we deserved it having dragged him and his friends away from their celebration, but he hardly charged us enough to pay for the gas and drove off laughing and wishing us a happy new year.

We led the group up the rocky path through the valley to Dimitri's house. He saw us coming and ran across his fields to help us with our bundles and welcome us. He was happy and excited and kept thanking us all for coming. I thrust the chicken at him.

"Here, Dimitri. We brought you a chicken."

He laughed, "But I've already killed a chicken, Andrianni. You take her home with you."

"It's the day for giving gifts. You keep her. Happy New Year."

"Her name is Cacciatore," put in Davidaki.

Dimitri pronounced the awkward name several times, laughing.

He took the hen and put her in his poultry yard. She stood out as she was black and white speckled and all the rest of Dimitri's hens were red. The children and I sighed with relief.

We unpacked our treasure basket while Dimitri poured out raki for everyone insisting it was the best thing for hangovers. He exclaimed over all the food; we really had accumulated a lot by the time we were all done with our scrounging expedition in the village. He had prepared plenty for us all but Nancy and I began cooking. We shifted some tables together and soon had a feast spread out. Dimitri turned on the peek-op and the dancing and eating began.

My day began to dissolve into a rosy mist as my relief at not leaving Dimitri destitute and the chicken getting a new lease on life, and the wine all combined. Dimitri's neighbors, hearing the music and noise across the valley, came to join the party.

As the afternoon progressed, David took it into his head to lead the Kiwis down into the quarries. I was worried because I knew we all had been drinking, so I tried to talk him out of it. The quarries were dangerous if you didn't know them. David and I had been down them many times and he went down almost every time we went to Dimitri's. A deep tunnel led under the mountain, branched off into galleries, made a turn then led back up through another opening. The walls at the tunnel entrance were dark and weather stained but soon became pure white like sugar inside. Everyone was enthusiastic and David was confident despite my apprehensions. Nancy wasn't any keener than I to go into the damp tunnels, so we stayed behind chatting with Dimitri and his neighbors while the kids played with Cacciatore in the yard.

We laughed and joked, then Nancy, still feeling like Ariadne, deserted on the island by her lover, launched into a tale of her woes. Everyone sympathized then began telling us all the sad love stories of the island, going back into ancient days, even to the original Ariadne who was left on Naxos by Theseus, when they ran out of contemporary tragedies. I cried at one or two, Nancy cried at them all. Then we went back to telling jokes.

As the conversation wore on I began straining my ears for sounds from the direction of the quarries. It began getting dark and I just about made up my mind to go search for the men when we heard them returning to my enormous relief. They were all triumphant and exhilarated. Dimitri felt that called for another flask of raki.

Then the neighbors all insisted we go to their houses, so we walked the valley by lantern light, going from house to house, the whole rowdy lot of us. The Kiwis were staggering by this time and I guess Dimitri and his friends weren't too sober either.

At long last we ended up at Dimitri's again and decided to go home. Dimitri was having a wonderful time and didn't want the party to end. He begged us to stay the night. But I knew he'd give up his bed for the women and children. I had seen the bed earlier in the day. Living alone he dispensed with changing the sheets more than once a year. So I chided the group for being lazy. Nancy was on my side. She had seen the bed, too.

We left, Dimitri walking with us as far as the main road, singing all the way. There we bid him good night and happy new year and started on the long hike back.

We laughed and joked the whole way. Brian the liveliest of the lively crew, kept imitating a revival preacher leading us past temptation. Once we were all so tired we lay down in the road to rest. A motorcyclist came along and skirted us, the rider and his passenger laughing out a happy new year to us. I sat on a thorn bush once and had to be rescued.

We reached the path that led to our house. The rest of the gang went on to look for a cafe where they could get a nightcap.

As for the chicken, the next time we went to the valley the children immediately ran out back to check on Cacciatore and returned with her in their arms.

"Look, Mommy, here's Cacciatore," they said happily surprised as I had warned them Dimitri might have eaten her.

"Dimitri, haven't you killed that chicken yet?" I asked.

He looked at us, his leathery face grinning and his hand on his heart. "Andrianni, never in my life will I kill that chicken," he vowed.

He meant it, too. The last time I saw her I counted fourteen speckled chicks with her. Dimitri bragged she was his best hen.

Chapter 60

Archaia (Old Stuff)

We had taken advantage of this year's "swallow days" to hike in the hills in the vicinity of the ancient temple that had been dedicated to Aphrodite. It was a lovely place on a mountain spur with a sweeping view in several directions.

The temple no longer existed, nor did the one to Apollo, not far from it. The Franks sometime around 700 A.D. had demolished them both to create a great wall in the middle of the village. The Frankish Wall looked like a strange combination of modern collage art and ancient architecture with pieces of sculpture and sideways sections of columns all jammed together.

No one had seriously ever considered tearing the wall apart to reconstruct the temple because half the village had been living in, on and against the wall since it was built. Parts of it were rooms thick and had been turned into a warren of homes. The Frankish Wall had become an even more rare artifact of ancient days than the temples would be, albeit of a newer ancient world.

But both temple sites still drew visitors, including us. In addition to the beautiful views and broken remnants of the foundations, artifacts kept surfacing, and we never knew what we might find.

We trudged back tired from the long walk and ready to start cooking dinner. But to our surprise we found The Chipmunk, our police chief, on our doorstep in uniform.

"*Yia sou*, Panayotis. How's it going? Want some coffee?" David greeted him. Heather at my signal had scurried off to perform the duties of the household daughter and reappeared with a small tray holding a glass of water and dish of sweets.

The Chipmunk was impressed by her good manners and apologized for his visit. The new island customs officer had just been issued binoculars by the government and had alerted the police that we were walking around the temple site. He was afraid we were collecting "*archaia*", old stuff.

David immediately handed over our backpacks, opening them for inspection. We exchanged a wary look. Our packs contained only the remains of our picnic lunch, but we did have a small collection of archaia, loom weights and some shards of Aphrodite simulacra, tiny terra cotta statuettes ancient worshippers used to leave in temples for healing just as modern Greeks left the tin *tamata*, we also collected, buying them at festivals.

The Chipmunk was embarrassed and he refused to look in our packs. He agreed to coffee and we discussed the school while Heather proudly made it. Ever since we had enrolled the children in school our relationship with the town Greeks had become closer. We were entrusting our children's education to them and they loved us for it. As we sipped our thick, sweet brew, the children took out pictures they had drawn of what they thought the ancient temples looked like when they were in use. The poor Chipmunk was totally undone. This was a project he had never thought of. He asked to borrow the pictures to show his daughter, promising she would bring them to the children at the school the next day. I still gave his daughter illegal English lessons. She was shy and a slow learner, but a very sweet girl.

We waved good-bye to him and watched him go down the path relieved at having discharged his duty.

Then David turned to me. "I'm going to hide the loom weights and stuff."

They were on open display in our house. Even the little museum on Paros had so many crates of such things in even better shape than our meager collection they were simply stacked in orange crates unprotected in an unheated storeroom and in a yard in back of the museum open to the elements. But I didn't argue.

Brett and Stephanie came to visit and were alarmed at the news about the customs officer's zeal. Brett had found so many really valuable things around his house we had all become convinced his home was on the site of the ancient school of sculpture. His finds included a life-sized marble head of a Nubian woman and some Cycladic art shards. We had always envied him. Right now, if foreigners were coming under scrutiny by authorities, we were a lot less envious.

All of us had run into archaia. Tom had once told us some fishermen had approached him about being a broker with some yachtsmen for some artifacts they had pulled up in their nets. He had agreed until he saw what they had pulled up was museum quality pottery with intact vase paintings. He had panicked then and refused to have anything to do with the deal.

Every time David went spearfishing he found ancient barnacle-encrusted amphorae. Such items were displayed in all bank lobbies and in many offices in Athens. I always wanted one and David would have liked to bring one up but they were always inhabited by alert and vicious Moray eels. The eels made excellent sentries. We all immediately nicknamed the new customs man Moray much to his puzzlement.

Times spent in Athens museums as well as those at ancient sites had provided us all with a crash course in the distinctive periods of art, so we all knew what we were encountering when we ran into it.

Some things were timeless like the multitude of terra cotta cup handles that surfaced after every plowing. The loom weights were more easily dated as looms had changed design since the days of ancient doorway looms requiring the weights to hold the warp threads during weaving, but they also surfaced after each plowing. We had decided the ancients were as bad at littering as moderns.

Brett took his things down from the display shelves and hid them away. David glued our tiny collection into some wood forms that were part of his sculpture.

"I'll relaminate the wood so the sculpture will be fine," he promised me when I was concerned more about the modern art than the old.

We decided to be more careful when we visited the temple sites. From the mountainside we could spot the prison island of Yaros on the horizon. We had no intention of ever spending any time there.

Chapter 61

Nuptials

The swallow days fled and it was cold and rainy again, but not with the ice and snow the arctic winds had brought the previous winter. Nikki, Nancy and I were having coffee in our kitchen when David and the children came in from the studio in the front room to tell us they had just heard the Elli's horn.

"Mail!" Nancy perked up. She had begun getting letters from Hans through a friend in England.

"Nikki, do you need something from town?" I asked.

"Two drachmae of pepper, Andrianni."

She avoided trips to town in the winter as much as possible so I always offered to do errands for her.

She offered to wait with the children but they insisted on going with us so we parted at the path.

"*Na pate sto kalo,*" go with the good, she called as we gleefully rushed to the docks.

We made good speed and were there to see the gangway lowered. The first person stepping off the boat was Hans looking thin and drawn but handsome. Nancy staggered back and I thought she'd faint, but as Hans began to run towards her she recovered and rushed into his arms.

We stood happily by along with the villagers who actually began clapping and cheering as if watching a good love scene at the movies, while Hans covered Nancy's face with kisses and she wept in joy.

Then he came to hug us saying, "Thank you, thank you. Thank you for taking care of her for me."

He turned back to Nancy, "I am free now, poor but free. If you will have me I have asked at the British embassy and they will marry us. I bought us return tickets on the Elli. She leaves in a half hour."

Nancy was laughing and crying, "Of course I'll marry you, you crazy man. But how can I leave for Athens so fast. I'm not packed."

"I am not so poor that I can't buy you new clothes there."

"Oh, my God. My room is here in town. Let me at least get my toothbrush and comb."

We saw them off a short time later.

"We'll come back here to celebrate then leave on our honeymoon. We'll be on the next boat back," Hans promised.

We stopped to get our mail where Stellio was pleased to hand us a letter from Tina decorated with smiling faces and flowers she had drawn.

"Please tell the kind miss hello from me when next you write to her," he asked. Tina had become popular with all the Greeks.

I tore open the letter when we were at Dionysius's cafe. "She's engaged and will soon marry a Greek shipping agent. He has no sisters and doesn't care about a dowry."

We told Dionysius the news and he promptly poured us and himself an ouzo to celebrate. He had already poured everyone in the place free drinks to celebrate Hans and Nancy's nuptials.

"So much happiness after so much sadness. Viva!" he toasted.

We ran our errands and walked to Nikki's house to deliver the pepper and the news about Nancy. Nikki cried with so much with joy she threw her apron over her head.

Agapitos ceremoniously brought out a bottle of black wine. That put Nikki into hostess gear and she fetched out her fancy tablecloth and a liqueur set we had given her. A simple feast soon appeared and we celebrated all the lovely news.

"Nikki, you must come with Agapitos to their party when they return as husband and wife," I said.

She and Agapitos looked at each other in consternation. "Oh, no, Andrianni. He is a good man, but he is German. I cannot."

I thought she was carrying a grudge from the war. But the next day she came to explain.

"Andrianni, my daughter, you will understand."

She told me that the times during the war, when she a young woman raising three children another woman had birthed and under suspicion of having killed her with witchcraft, had been very hard.

"Agapitos was gone in the war and it had been so long since I had had word from him I thought he had been killed. I was alone, no one here from my home, Andrianni."

The occupation was hard everywhere in Greece and was only softened here on Paros because the Italians rather than the hated Germans were in charge at first. But everyone knew the Germans were running the show. The food supplies were swept away by the armies.

"I had picked all the greens from the hills for miles and still not enough to eat for those three little children. Ai, Andrianni, sores appeared on their legs and I knew they were starving. That was a sign the end was near. I had to do something to save them."

"What did you do?"

"I put on sack cloth, and poured ashes on my head. And I led the children through the village, keening for the dead orphans who were dying in front of me."

I sat back in horror. What desperation to drive quiet, shy Nikki to such an extreme. The story continued. The soft-hearted Italians took pity on them and issued Nikki extra rations of flour and sugar. It meant their survival.

"But the townspeople said it was because I collaborated with the enemy. Never, never would I do such a thing," she crossed herself fervently.

Nikki was pretty in her seventies, she must have been a beauty as a young woman, so some said she also slept with the enemy. That was equally preposterous for one as devout as Nikki.

The story explained a lot: her step-children's devotion to her, her reluctance to socialize with the villagers, and even her stepson's communism. He was adamant and argued politics with us non-stop whenever we saw him. He considered us spoiled children of a spoiled society but abided us good-naturedly because we loved Nikki and she us.

It certainly explained why she would not socialize in the village with a German. She had spent too much of her life outliving the cruel rumors.

"But you will bring my blessings to them, Andrianni. They deserve happiness."

The newlyweds were on the next boat as promised and the party was a great success. Nancy came to see Nikki bringing her a lace shawl from Athens. Nikki would look prettier than ever at church gatherings.

We saw Hans and Nancy off at the dock when they left on their honeymoon.

"I was a beaten man," Hans said. "Now I am a broke one, but she is truly gone. It was all worth it."

"Indeed, it is all worth it," beamed Nancy and Hans turned to embrace her happily.

"You better take good care of Nancy," cautioned David, still leery of the whole situation and distrustful that Hans had left Nancy waiting so long.

"That is my privilege!" declared Hans.

As we left the docks I saw an elderly Greek man look at them. "Germanos," he said, spitting to ward off the evil eye.

"He is a good person," I said sharply. "That is not necessary."

"Worse than the devil is the Turk. Worse than the Turk is the Bulgarian, and worst of all is the German," the man replied bitterly. David tugged at me.

"*Then perasi*, no matter," David said in Greek and the old man shrugged.

"The English girl deserves better," he said

Poor Nikki, I thought, that memories last so long here.

Chapter 62

Clean Monday

Unlike Catholic countries, Greece did not make a big deal of Carnival with parades or processions at least in the rural areas, but they did celebrate it. Some people dressed in costumes and parties sprang to life everywhere.

One night towards the end of the Carnival period, I heard a knock at our door and screamed when I opened it. A troop of creatures stood there totally shrouded in black except for plastic doll faces in place of heads eerily underlit by flashlights. The effect was not only startling but really frightening.

Then the one in the lead whisked off the shroud laughing. It was Yiannis the Fisherman. My heartbeat slowed again.

David was behind me laughing so loud I realized he'd been startled, too.

The other revelers disrobed and carried in a record player and bottles of wine. The children made them put on the costumes again and tried them on in front of our small mirror.

I began ransacking our kitchen for food. Fortunately I had just baked in our brick oven and could impress the town dwellers with my country bread.

"You must come to see my family on Clean Monday," Yiannis invited.

Clean Monday was one of our favorite holidays. It marked the end of Carnival's excesses and the beginning of austere Lent. The Greeks celebrated by going out in the countryside, picnicking and flying kites. No eggs or meat were served but everything else was there in abundance.

I prepared *taramasalata*, a wonderful fish roe mayonnaise dip, eggplant, and artichokes. We bought *lakertha*, a tuna preserved in oil that was a great delicacy. David and the children made a kite out of bright red paper I had found in the village and hoarded for the occasion. The kite was made in the Greek design of a many-pointed star surrounded by a paper fringe. This one was massive, a twelve-pointer and sturdy as was everything that David made. He and the kids were justly proud of it.

We packed up everything along with some of our good bread and set off for the sea cove where Yiannis said his family traditionally gathered. He saw us in the distance and ran to meet us with several children at his heels.

We were welcomed with great hospitality and given a place of honor on their picnic blanket. His mother, father, aunts, uncles, cousins, sisters and brothers unpacked dish after dish of fish and vegetables and even desserts from their baskets. My bread was praised to the skies and I was thrilled at its reception. I was wishing Nikki could see how impressed these townsfolk were but as usual she and Agapitos were celebrating quietly at home. We had promised to visit them on the way back.

The inevitable peek-op was produced and set in motion but before long it was retired because real musicians, Yiannis's friends, arrived to make live music.

Getting the kites up was the first order of the day. Everyone oohed and aahed over David's great red masterpiece. I had some linen cord we used for kite string. The kite soared up immediately in the strong sea breeze. It shone like a great red sun with its flaring fringe.

Then Yiannis wanted it to go higher and produced a spool of cotton to tie to my linen. He and David tied it on and began unreeling it. The wind picked up and the cotton line snapped sending the kite up the side of the mountain.

"Oh, it wants to be free," I said philosophically. David and the children had worked too hard on it to be philosophical. They, Yiannis, and a swarm of his young relatives ran off in pursuit.

The rest of us ate, drank wine, danced and waited. Much to our surprise the whole gang returned in a couple hours bearing the kite triumphantly.

"It just hovered there at the top of the mountain, the string hanging down at eye level. One of the boys just reached up and grabbed it," David told me grinning. "Yiannis and I gave him a few drachmas. He's happy."

Everyone celebrated with a glass of wine and a dance to a wild song from the musicians.

We partied all afternoon and everyone was happy about the kite except me. I had mixed feelings. I was happy for David and the children but I missed my inner vision of the great red kite soaring off free on its own high over the mountain.

Chapter 63

Departure

David had finished an entire show's worth of work. We hauled all the pieces out in the field to photograph them. It was impressive.

Yorgo Kano, our friend from inland, had come to do some work in a relative's field nearby and stopped by to visit.

David's sculpture was laminated wood and metal worked together in intricate forms. My favorite piece out of this collection was a harp-like fan of wood shapes held constrained by soldered brass straps. I had named it the Aeolian Harp because it seemed like it sent unheard music off in the wind, or as I called it "music for the mind."

"What does this mean?" Yorgo demanded. He had been accompanied by one of his cousins who was equally curious.

David was perplexed to answer. he always found it hard to talk about his work, which he termed simply "problem solving".

"It is not people. It is not something to use. It means something. It says something," Yorgo insisted, simplifying his Greek for us to extract an answer. I made a stab at it.

"There is wood. There is metal. They make war with each other and also David makes peace between them." I told him my thoughts about the "harp".

A look of comprehension came over Yorgo's face although his cousin was still puzzled. Yorgo circled each piece looking at it closely, sometimes touching one. He looked at David with admiration then turned to his cousin.

"This is deep, very deep," he pointed to David. "His mind is very deep."

We visited a while but they refused refreshments, saying, like Cross-Eyed Nikos believed, that hard work and food were incompatible. I had noticed no workers ever said that to Tarsa when she employed them. But, then, they didn't work so hard for her as they did for themselves.

With the sculpture show complete, it was time to think of leaving Greece, but it was painful to do.

The shopkeepers always saved any English newspapers or magazines the ferry crew discarded to wrap our purchases. It was our best source of news from the States. As belated as it was getting to us, we realized it was not good news. The Vietnam War was tearing our country apart, and people in public life we cared about were being assassinated. I began to feel I was reneging on my responsibilities as an American.

The letters from our parents who hadn't seen Heather and Davidaki in two years were getting frantic despite our and the children's frequent letters home. The children had adapted to Greek life, especially since they were attending school, They were more Greek than American. That was fine with us but was alarming our family.

And our money was running low. Our efforts to eke it out could only go so far. Unlike our Greek friends, we had no land to support us. We had nothing left to sell in the States.

We finally set a time after Easter as our departure date. We just couldn't leave before Easter. We'd spend a few days in Athens to say good-bye to Mother Acropolis and take care of final business before boarding a freighter.

David made wooden crates to hold the sculpture. As he hammered I wept.

"This is our real home," I said. "It's so hard to leave."

Greece had brought us so close to the core of real life. We had learned the real cycle of feeding ourselves from watching Cross-Eyed Nikos plow and savor the earth, the harvest and threshing, baking bread with Nikki. The simplicity dear Louis had described was very real to me.

So was the surrender to the intensity of life -- dancing wildly with my jiggling women friends, swimming in the warm blue sea, walking off in the hills outside of Vourvoura like legendary Zen monks with no thought of return, suffering the sorrow of Christ's death every year, then rejoicing at his rebirth, the exuberance of New Year's at Dimitri's.

The profound appreciation the Greeks taught us of such things as good water, good bread, sweet cherries had sensitized us better than any culinary school could.

The way the old mingled with the new without a break had given rise to that precious sense of "time out of mind" we had both discovered here.

The open love of such wonderful people as Nikki and Dimitri had turned them into family for us. And we were leaving them and taking the children. We had to remind ourselves we had done the same to our families in the States.

"They are our family. We have to come back," I sobbed.

"We will," David said.

The time grew closer. We went to the valley of Marathi for one last Sunday with Dimitri. As we left he thrust an ancient marble mortar, from the classical period, in my arms. It had been in his family since it was carved although all he used it for now was to hold chicken feed. I had always admired it.

I was overwhelmed. It was a tremendous gift. It also presented a packing problem. This was true archaia from the classical period, but there was no way I'd leave it behind Moray or The Chipmunk notwithstanding. With no way to disguise it I finally thrust it into a crate holding sculpture.

Family after family held parties for us in town. Rounds of cheese, bottles of homemade capers, baskets of dried figs, all sorts of treasures were thrust upon us at the last minute producing even more packing problems.

I, in turn, distributed our belongings. Nikki got any cooking conveniences, including my camp oven and gas burners to make her life easier. We handed tools over to Dimitri. We gave Cross-Eyed Nikos our high powered spirit lamp. The school got educational supplies. I gave personal things like clothes, scarves, jewelry to our town friends except for those I knew Nikki would wear. I wished we had more to give away.

We arranged for Manolis, the taxi driver, to bring a donkey train to our house to haul our things down to town and store them for a few days until we left on the Elli.

We were back to living out of backpacks until we boarded the freighter. Heather and Davidaki enjoyed all the extra attention and sweets being showered upon them but David and I wandered around in a fit of distracted mourning.

How could we be leaving our beloved home? I woke once in the night crying and David comforted me.

"My grandmother must have felt like this when she left Sweden," he said and I realized how true that was. It was a new thought to ponder.

Like Grandma Jenny, it was scary for us because we really didn't know what we would do when we got to America. We'd be arriving flat broke like her, but we had the show lined up and family waiting, so we were one up on Grandma in that regard. But leaving behind a way of life that had taken on such meaning for us, that had made life more vivid, where our basic qualities as people mattered so much more than what we did or had or who we knew, was wrenching.

Finally there was a massive party at Vasili's where the glassware bill must have impoverished the island for years to come.

Nikki refused to see us leave. We had said good-bye tearfully at her house.

At the docks even Stellio had come to see us off. The crowd bore the children and all our things on board and clustered around us jamming the aisles, already packed with Easter vacationers returning to Athens.

Suddenly Moray, the customs officer, appeared demanding we uncrate everything before we left so he could inspect it. I was sobbing and threw up my hands helplessly. The Chipmunk, our beloved, brave Chipmunk, stepped forward to defy him telling him the whole island knew we were leaving and if he wanted an inspection he should have done it days before, and Stellio backed him up.

Confronted with both other authorities on the island he backed off. Dimitri's mortar was safe.

The Elli sounded her last boarding whistle and the crew chased the townspeople off the boat. We darted to the stern to look at Paros one last time.

The hills were still green from the spring rains. Our little house on the mountainside stood out white against them.

I heard someone calling, "Andrianni, Andrianni."

I looked down at Brett who looked up at me with his eyes full of love.

"Good-bye. Paros will miss you."

Tears blinded me as David lovingly led me back to our seats.

CPSIA information can be obtained
at www.ICGtesting.com
Printed in the USA
FSOW02n1323150915
11024FS